SCATTERED BELONGINGS

This is a book about ordinary lives faced with the dilemmas of belonging and not belonging and of people who find themselves to be strangers in two cultures. It is a book about how the often painful experiences of being of "mixed race" in a world perceived in terms of "Black" and "White" can instead be something to name and celebrate.

Scattered Belongings presents personal and political testimonies and analyzes "mixed race" theories. The book takes a rigorous critique of "race" and "mixed race" as its starting point. The following section includes the moving narratives of six women of both continental African/African Caribbean and European parentage. Collectively, their testimonies illustrate the ways in which identities are shaped not only by "race," but also by ethnicity, gender, class, and locality. Finally, Jayne O. Ifekwunigwe demonstrates how the lived experiences of "mixed race" individuals can help us to understand the dynamic construction of identities in a globalizing world.

Jayne O. Ifekwunigwe is Lecturer in Sociology and Anthropology at the University of East London.

SCATTERED
BELONGINGS

Cultural Paradoxes of "Race," Nation and Gender

Jayne O. Ifekwunigwe

London and New York

First published 1999
by Routledge
11 New Fetter Lane, London EC4P 4EE

Simultaneously published in the USA and Canada
by Routledge
29 West 35th Street, New York, NY 10001

© 1999 Jayne O. Ifekwunigwe

Typeset in Garamond by Routledge
Printed and bound in Great Britain by
TJ International Ltd, Padstow, Cornwall

British Library Cataloguing in Publication Data
A catalogue record for this book is available from the British
Library

Library of Congress Cataloging in Publication Data
Ifekwunigwe, Jayne O.
Scattered belongings: cultural paradoxes of "race," nation and gender/Jayne O.
Ifekwunigwe
p.   cm.
Includes bibliographical references (p.) and index.
1. Racially mixed people. 2. Ethnicity. 3. Pluralism (Social sciences) 4. Race
relations. 5. Identity. I. Title.
HT1523.I36   1999
305.8–dc21   98–20493
CIP

ISBN 0–415–17095–8 (hbk)
ISBN 0–415–17096–6 (pbk)

Scattered Belongings

I am the descended daughter of both and neither
My forefathers are the so-called intrepid explorers of the
dark continent who stole kisses and cultures
The rusty and the dusty dealers in the Triangular Trade
The hyper-zealots who hopped the fence during the
Missionary Crusades – adding a bit of cream to the coffee
And of course – the chocolate brown Africans who were there

At the same time, the distant drones of my fertile
foremothers in Africa, Europe and the Caribbean lull me
to sleep, but never unconscious

For my Geordie gran (1904–1997)
and my LeGuan grandad (1893–1983)

They will stay together and play together now that they both have legs strong enough to run

Plate 1   Author's maternal grandparents, Lionel Freeman and Mary Freeman, South Shields, England. Date and photographer unknown.

CONTENTS

List of plates   xi
Prologue   xii
Acknowledgements   xv

1 Cracking the coconut: resisting popular folk discourses on
  "race," "mixed race" and social hierarchies   1

2 Returning(s): relocating the critical feminist auto-
  ethnographer   29

3 Setting the stage: invoking the *griot(te)* traditions as textual
  strategies   50

  Preamble: could I be a part of your family?
  Preliminary/contextualizing thoughts on psychocultural
  politics of transracial placements and adoption   62

4 Ruby   71

5 Similola   88

6 Akousa   102

7 Sarah   116

8 Bisi   132

9 Yemi   152

CONTENTS

10 Let Blackness and Whiteness wash through: competing
    discourses on bi-racialization and the compulsion of
    genealogical erasures   170

    Epilogue   194

    Select Bibliographies   197
    Index   215

PLATES

Plate 1 They will stay together and play together now that they
         both have legs strong enough to run   vii
Plate 2 The Hope of the Race   25
Plate 3 As I See, So I am Seen   26
Plate 4 Strength in Unity, United We are Strong   27
Plate 5 People in a Multitude Stand Together   28

PROLOGUE

We must remember so that others will not forget

> If race lives on today, it does not live on because we have inherited it from our forebears of the seventeenth century or the eighteenth or nineteenth, but because we continue to create it today.[1]

> The recent bag of re-poetics (recuperate, rewrite, transport, transform and so forth) proffers the opportunity to confront many of the assumptions and confusions of identity I feel compelled to "reconfigure." The site of this poetics for me, and many other multi-racial and multi-cultural writers, is the hyphen, that marked (or unmarked) space that both binds and divides...a crucial location for working out the ambivalences of hybridity....In order to actualize this hybridity...the hybrid writer must necessarily develop instruments of disturbance, dislocation and displacement.[2]

In the past six years or so, Wah's literary summons has been answered by a virtual flourishing of North American (Canada and the United States) texts in the forms of websites, fiction, poetry, autobiographies, biographies, and academic texts by "mixed race" writers who are often of "Black and White" parentage, middle class and/or academics and students.[3] On the other hand, in England, during that same time period, there have been relatively few books written by "mixed race" authors about "mixed race" identity politics.[4] These countries' different historical legacies *vis-à-vis* immigrant and indigenous communities might explain this discrepancy:

> While the United States (and Canada) is a country of immigrants where ethnic diversity is constitutive of the society, British society has aspired and continues to aspire to monoculturalism: the people of the empire have no claim on British territory.[5]

In a more profound way than in the United States and Canada, the rigidity of the class structure in Britain also limits the extent to which "hybrid" writers are recognized, published, marketed and received. However, Friedman would argue that on both sides of the Atlantic, a "hybrid" identity is not accessible to the poor:

The urban poor, ethnically mixed ghetto is an arena that does not immediately cater to the construction of explicitly new hybrid identities. In periods of global stability and/or expansion, the problems of survival are more closely related to territory and to creating secure life spaces.[6]

Scattered Belongings is a book with two major objectives. First, this text begins to redress the imbalance in British literature on "mixed race" theories and identities. Second, this book centralizes the everyday words of working-class and middle-class "mixed race" people in England. As sociocultural and political critiques of "race," gender, class and belonging, fluid contemporary "mixed race" narratives of identities engage with, challenge and yet have been muffled by two competing racialized, essentialized and oppositional dominant discourses in England. The first is the territorialized discourse of "English" nationalism, which is based on indigeneity and mythical purity. That is, "Englishness" is synonymous with "Whiteness." The second is the deterritorialized discourse of the English–African Diaspora, which is predicated on (mis)placement and the one drop rule. That is, all Africans have been dispersed and one known African ancestor designates a person as "Black." Through the personal testimonies of ordinary people, I will illustrate the ways in which, as we hobble toward the new millennium, "mixed race" de/territorialized declarations delimit and transgress bi-racialized discourses and point the way toward a profound re-alignment of thinking about belonging. As such, this book critically engages with the notions of biological and cultural hybridities as they are articulated in nineteenth- and twentieth-century theories of "race," "mixed race" and social identities.

This book is structured as a critical dialogue between cultural theories and personal/political testimonies. The main theory chapter traces the origins of the term "hybridity" back to its problematic beginnings in nineteenth-century "race" science and especially evolutionary anthropology and critiques contemporary cultural theorizing on "hybridities" which reframes "race" as difference(s). Drawing on personal narratives as both testimonies and performances of resistance, I also show how, as storytellers, six contemporary "mixed race" women tangle with the twin torments of "Englishness" being exclusively associated with "Whiteness" as well as the presumption that one's designated "Blackness" automatically inflicts one with a (mis)placed African diasporic condition. Never does "White English" birth parentage nor full-time English residence enable these women to carve out territorialized spaces that reflect both the realities of cultural upbringing and the complexities of de-territorialized ancestries. Their critiques also confront racialized obstructions whereby "Whiteness" is deemed the normative and naturalized signifier by which deviations of "Blackness" are determined as well as the presumption that "Englishness" is synonymous with "Whiteness." In the de/territorialized places, which "mixed race" cartographers map, the idea of "home" has, by definition, multilayered, multitextual and contradictory meanings. By virtue of both "White" English maternal *and* "Black" paternal continental African or African Caribbean parentage, "home" represents an ambivalent "Black and White" sense of both place (England) *and* misplaced longings (continental Africa, the Caribbean, and what Paul Gilroy would refer to as the Black Atlantic). Their family histories are braided from the gendered, bi-racialized and sexualized residues of imperial domination and colonized submission.

Notes

1 Barbara Fields (1990) "Slavery, race and ideology in the United States of America," *New Left Review*, p. 181, as cited in Rose Brewer (1993) "Theorizing race, class and gender: the new scholarship of Black feminist intellectuals and Black women's labor," in S. James and A. Busia (eds.) *Theorizing Black Feminisms*, London: Routledge, pp. 13–30.

2 Fred Wah (1996) "Half-bred poetics," *Absinthe*, Hyphenation: A Mixed Race Issue, 9 (2): 60–5.

3 For examples, see Maria Root (ed.) (1992) *Racially Mixed People in America*, London: Sage.; No Press Collective (1992) *Voices of Identity, Rage and Deliverance: An Anthology of Writings by People of Mixed Descent*, Berkeley: No Press.; Naomi Zack (1993) *Race and Mixed Race*, Philadelphia: Temple University Press.; Lisa Jones (1994) *Bulletproof Diva: Tales of Race, Sex and Hair*, New York: Doubleday; Lise Funderburg (1994) *Black, White, Other: Biracial Americans Talk About Race and Identity*, New York: William and Morrow; Shirlee Taylor Haizlip (1994) *The Sweeter the Juice: A Family Memoir in Black and White*, London: Simon and Schuster; Carol Camper (ed.) (1994) *Miscegenation Blues: Voices of Mixed Race Women*, Toronto: Sister Vision; Maria Root (ed.) (1996) *The Multiracial Experience*, London: Sage; Naomi Zack (ed.) (1995) *American Mixed Race*, London: Rowman and Littlefield; Judy Scales-Trent, (1995) *Notes of a White Black Woman*, University Park, Pennsylvania: Pennsylvania State University; James McBride (1996) *The Color of Water: A Black Man's Tribute to His White Mother*, New York: Riverhead Books; Marsha Hunt (1996) *Repossessing Ernestine*, London: Flamingo; Toi Derricotte (1997) *The Black Notebooks*, London: W. W. Norton. Also see *Inter-racial Voice*, the largest website edited by and about "mixed race" people, founded by Charles Byrd: http: //www.webcom.com/intvoice/

4 See *New Mixed Culture*, a website founded and maintained by Sabu, the first artist in Britain to put his work on the web: http://www.1love.com

5 Marie Hélène LaForest (1996) "Black cultures in difference," in I. Chambers and L. Curti (eds.) *The Postcolonial Question*, London: Routledge, pp. 115–22.

6 Jonathan Friedman (1997) "Global crises, the struggle for cultural identity and intellectual porkbarrelling: cosmopolitans versus locals, ethnics and nationals in an era of de-hegemonisation," in P. Werbner and T. Moddod (eds.) *Debating Cultural Hybridity*, London: Zed, pp. 70–89.

ACKNOWLEDGEMENTS

I would like to thank everyone I have ever met in my life.

Upon acceptance of the Academy Award for Best Supporting Actress in the film *L. A. Confidential*, Kim Basinger uttered such words.[1] The understood rituals associated with book acknowledgements are quite similar. In fact, Ben-Ari has written a provocative analysis entitled, "On acknowledgements in ethnography," which problematizes, deconstructs, and demystifies this time-honored tradition of paying homage to those who have directly or indirectly helped one to "get over":

> Acknowledgements are part of the processes of "management of meaning" within anthropology. They may, in other words be devised to do a whole range of things like show, report, camouflage, hide, command, beg, maintain, reason, qualify, or inform about a certain order or state.[2]

Reading this piece forced me to question the taken-for-granted form, function and personal/professional/political motivations underlying the expressions of gratitude that accompany most publications. Hence, may Basinger's all-encompassing "thank you" function as a collective thank you to all of the individuals who have helped me, supported me and challenged me across time and disparate spaces.

Having said that, I would like to extend special and boundless gratitude to particular individuals who have played pivotal roles in my life these past eight years:

To Drs Muriel and Aaron Ifekwunigwe who gave me life, love, instilled the importance of learning and as the Ifekwunigwe Foundation have provided me with emotional and financial support. To Ann Ifekwunigwe, my younger sister and my best friend, who has always been a long-distance phone call or an e-mail away. To the rest of the various branches of my family tree including my brothers Christopher and David and their families, Uncle Cecil and Auntie Doreen, Auntie Mary and Uncle Ron and my cousins Kevin and Heather and their families. To Thea Shaw who is an important honorary member of my family. To my godfather Dr Anezi Okoro, who has always marked my birthday and celebrated my accomplishments, and his family. In loving memory of my maternal and paternal grandparents and my namesake, my Guyanese great-grandmother, Jane.

In Bristol, to the twenty-five women and men who retrieved painful and joyful memories so that this eight-year enterprise could begin a new life in book form. Also, to my "Bristol Posse": Caroline and Catherine Naysmith, Bunge and Oscar Adedeji, Lorraine Ayensu, Folake Shoga, Tasha Rees, Melroy Grosvenor, Rachel Degarang, Kathy Waithe, Yeshiba and Akua Gabriel, Trevor Brown, Eddie Chambers and many others who have touched my life over the years. To Tunde Jegede for his tireless intellectual engagement with my work and for providing love, support and inspiration throughout this entire project. In London, to my second family: Jo Ann and Ashanti Ramsey and Company as well as to Bisi Silva, Onyekachi Wambu and to Maggie Inniss for friendship and for taking care of my hair. In Birmingham, to Jon Girling and Simon Jones. To Liza Asner, my oldest Stateside friend, to sister–friends, Portia Cobb, Patricia and Eraka Bath, Carle Gordon-Wakamatsu and Tonya Cannon, and to brother–friends, James Moseley, David Moragne, and Michael Cippola. To Sabu, whose important role as cyber adviser, portrait photographer and friend has been unfolding in tandem with the birth of this book, as well as to Charles Byrd of *Inter-Racial Voice*. In memory of Gein Eyoum Dedo, David Dornstein and Muli – "gone too soon." Finally, to H. B., as they say, "time will tell."

To Naomi Zack, Maria Root, J. A. Rogers, James F. Davis and Robert Young, among other scholars, for paving the "mixed-race" studies way. Thanks again to Naomi Zack for important critical feedback on the final manuscript. To Samba Diop, who is the linguistic donor of the terms *métis(se)* and *griot(te)* and who has been an invaluable critic as I have been reformulating these concepts. To Henri-Pierre Koubaka, cultural critic, ethnomusicologist and *métissage* adviser. To Heidi Mirza who is both a mentor and a friend. To Minelle Mahtani and April Moreno, supportive fellow "critical mixed-race studies" pioneers and excellent resources for "hot-off-the-press" references. To colleagues and students at the University of East London, especially Fred Brown who converted my Macintosh disks containing the PhD version of the thesis as well as Phil Cohen of the Centre for New Ethnicities Research, Barbara Harrison, Head of the Department of Sociology and Anthropology, Mike Rustin, Dean of the Faculty of Social Sciences and the students in the first run of Anthropology 234: Rules of *Métissage*: Anthropological Perspectives on "Race," Status and Color. To my mentors/PhD committee at the University of California, Berkeley/San Francisco: Nancy Scheper-Hughes, Carol Stack, Joan Ablon, Vè Vè Clark, as well as George De Vos and Richard Buxbaum. To Ben Okri, whose beautiful poetry and prose were a source of inspiration while I was writing up the thesis version of the book. To sociologists Stephen Small and Colin Samson, two other roving bi-continental academics and friends as well as other fellow PhD students at UC Berkeley, such as Claudia May, Sara Brose, Deborah Pruitt, Dan Perlman, Valerie Johnson and Caridad Souza. At the University of Bristol, to Michael Banton who was also extremely helpful during the first incarnation of the book in thesis form, to Rohit Barot who has always been supportive and encouraging, and to Steve Fenton who coined the phrase "Young Black Intelligentsia." In Cardiff, to Glenn Jordan and Chris Weedon for friendship and academic support. To Iman Hashim and to Ben Carrington, two recent and special friends/colleagues. To anyone else I may have inadvertently omitted in the United States, the United Kingdom, Nigeria, Guyana, South Africa or anywhere else I may have roamed. (Anyway, you already know how much I appreciate and value you.)

To the dynamic Routledge publishing team without whose faith in this project I would not have acknowledgements to write: including Mari Shullaw, senior editor in Sociology, for her patience and assistance as well as editorial assistant, Geraldine Williams, senior desk editor, Geraldine Lyons, and copy editor, Eve Daintith.

Last, to both present and future generations of *métis(se)* individuals and their families as well as emerging "critical mixed-race" scholars, may your personal and intellectual journeys be less arduous than mine and those with whom I have worked.

Notes

1 March 24 1998, *Barry Norman's Highlights of the Seventieth Annual Academy Awards Presentation*, BBC1.
2 Ben-Ari, Eyal (1995) "On acknowledgements in ethnography," in J. Van Maanen (ed.) *Representation in Ethnography*, London: Sage, pp. 130–64.

1

CRACKING THE COCONUT

Resisting popular folk discourses on "race,"
"mixed race" and social hierarchies[1]

It is Tuesday evening in Thatchapee.[2] I have walked the few short
blocks from my flat on the main road to the Mandela Community
Center, where I am a voluntary youth worker.[3] Although lately, the
youth are scarce and it's usually Irie, the local Jamaican *griot*,[4] with
natty dread,[5] whom many in Thatchapee have dismissed as "mad,"
who is holding court. We are all assembled in the community hall
where one has to shout to be heard over the pulse of the ragamuffin
reggae coming from the sound system. Irie and his disciples – all
White English women and men – are having a reasoning session. I
gather that part of Irie's lure is his "mad" mystique. I remember going
over to the table around which they were all sitting. Irie was
completely engrossed in his role as *griot* – rolling his eyes, frothing a
little at the mouth. His disciples were loving it. At one stage, he looked
over at me and winked, as if to say, "I and I know."[6]

On another occasion, I was talking with Irie about my involvement
in the field of anthropology, and in particular about the concept of
culture. Sitting upright in his chair, legs crossed, leaning forward
slightly, right index finger pointed, he exclaimed: "Culture – there's no
culture left in this world. They are all dirty."

"Race" as science fiction

In Irie's estimation, once "pure" cultures have now been sullied. Similarly, in
eighteenth- and nineteenth-century Britain and North America, the false
presumption held by evolutionary theorists that "races" existed as discrete,
bounded, biological and ultimately "pure" entities was the dominant

imperial White European/American mythology, which attempted to sanction any interbreeding across "racial" borders:

> If races are conceptualized as pure (with concomitant qualities of character, including the capacity to hold sway over other races), then miscegenation threatens that purity. Given the actual history of interbreeding in the imperial history of the past centuries, it is not surprising that various means have been found to deal with this threat to whiteness....These measures focused on blackness as a means of limiting access to the white category, which only the utterly white could inhabit.
>
> (Dyer 1997: 25)

The focus of my research enquiry has been stringent parameters for "White" group membership as they exclude and impinge on the lived English realities of socially designated Black individuals who are in fact (first generation) of continental African or African Caribbean (fathers) *and* (White) continental European or British (mothers) parentage.

> the critical focus of investigation...becomes the (ethnic) boundary that defines the group, not the cultural stuff it encloses...a dichotomization of others as strangers, as members of another (ethnic) group, implies a recognition of limitations on shared understandings, differences in criteria for judgement of value and performance, and a restriction of interaction to sectors of assumed common understanding and mutual interest.
>
> (Barth 1969: 7)

Hence, across time and imperial spaces, I am particularly concerned with the transatlantic science fictionalization of Blackness and Whiteness in the United States and Britain for the purposes of the maintenance of social boundaries which have always been permeable and inherently paradoxical in nature (Gist and Dworkin 1972).

This chapter is organized into four sections. The first section offers a critique of "race" as a scientific concept. The second section problematizes the idea of cultural "hybridities" and creates a critical join between this contemporary idea and earlier conceptions of "racial" "hybridities." The third section addresses the ways in which the science fiction of "race" is kept alive by popular folk conceptions of "race" and social hierarchies. The final section engages with unresolved terminology debates about how to name "mixed race" people. For the purposes of analyses, I also offer my original formulations of *métis(se)* and *métissage* as stand-in responses to the limitations and ambiguities of existing terms.

This science fiction of "race" and social hierarchies fueled eighteenth- and nineteenth-century anthropological conceptions of human diversity in general and intergroup mating in particular (Young 1995; Stocking 1982). Nineteenth-century "race" science in general and evolutionary anthropology in particular maintained that discrete "races" existed, which could be differentially ranked on the basis of heredity, physical characteristics and intelligence (Rich 1986; Rogers 1952). The biological distinction between varieties and species was the intellectual precursor to the major scientific debate of the nineteenth century over whether human "races" were of one species, monogenesis, or separate species, polygenesis:

> In eighteenth century anthropology a distinction was made between species on the one hand and varieties on the other. Species were regarded as immutable prototypes, perfectly designed for their role in the divine economy of nature. Varieties, by contrast, were merely those members of a single species who – because of such conditioning factors as climate and geography – had changed their appearance in one way or another.
>
> (Gossett 1965: 35)

Influenced by evolutionist Herbert Spencer, Darwin silenced advocates of polygenesis (Hannaford 1996; Goodwin 1994). However, as human history has proven time and time again, designated same species status does not guarantee access to the fruits of citizenship: humanity, equality and justice (Malik 1996; Goldberg 1993).

Prior to Darwin's important intervention, American and European scientists such as Prichard, Lawrence, White, Cuvier and Saint-Hilaire waged warfare over the unity versus the diversity of the human species (Hannaford 1996; Stocking 1982). In particular, Linnaeus suggested that successful reproduction of fertile offspring was proof positive in support of monogenesis (Gould 1994). Interestingly enough, however, for my purposes, it was the American physician and natural historian, Samuel Morton, who introduced the concept of biological "hybridity" to the separate origins position:

> Among human races, he admitted that mulattoes were fertile, but his own research into crosses between Whites and Negroes indicated that mulatto women bear children only with great difficulty. If these women mated only with other mulattoes, Morton argued, the descendents of this union would be even less fertile and the progeny would eventually die out. From his conviction that half-breeds cannot propagate themselves indefinitely, Morton was led to the conclusion that Whites and Negroes are not varieties of a single race but entirely different species.
>
> (Gossett 1965: 59)

One of Morton's most vocal opponents was Bachman, who maintained that it was virtually impossible for "hybrids" to be "relatively sterile" as Morton claimed. Moreover, Bachman (1850) insisted that not only were "mulattoes" as fertile as so called "pure races," but that he could provide evidence of successful intermarriage and procreation among "mulattoes" across five generations. Finally, he adamantly opposed the idea put forward by Morton and his colleague Agassiz that there was a "natural/moral repugnance" between so-called "races," which functions as a social prophylactic (Stanton, 1960). Whether classified as "pure" or "hybrid," according Black African people the same species status was not equivalent to allowing them equal status and Bachman still justified ownership of slaves on the grounds that: "We have been irresistibly brought to the conviction that in intellectual power the African is an inferior variety of our species" (Bachman 1850: 291–2).

Two additional key players in the game of origins were Nott and Gliddon (1854) who were also students of Morton. In their 800-page volume, *Types of Mankind*, they asserted that individuals without at least one White ancestor were "uncivilized" and lacked the alleged superior mental capacity of their "pure" White European/American counterparts. Similarly, French anthropologist Paul Broca asserted:

> The union of the Negro with a white woman is frequently sterile while that of a white man with a Negress is perfectly fecund. This might tend to establish between the two races a species of hybridity analogous to that existing between goats and sheep which we termed unilateral hybridity.
>
> (Broca 1864: 28)

Accomplished by the insemination of the Black female by the allegedly potent White male, this act of "racial enhancement" justified sexual violence against enslaved Black African women in the antebellum American South, premancipation Latin America, i.e. Brazil, and the Caribbean (De-costa-Willis and Martin Bell 1992; Hill-Collins 1990). In *Sex and Racism in America*, African American sociologist Hernton refers to this (ir)rationalized sexual act as "the sexualization of racism:"

> The sexualization of racism in the United States is a unique phenomenon in the history of mankind; it is an anomaly of the first order. In fact, there is a sexual involvement, at once real and vicarious, connecting white and black people in America that spans the history of this country from the era of slavery to the present, an involvement so immaculate and yet so perverse, so ethereal and yet so concrete, that all race relations tend to be, however subtle, *sex* relations.
>
> (Hernton 1965: 7)

The inextricable link between sex and racism was never stronger than in the plantation Southern United States, wherein "the one drop rule" was instituted in order to keep the offspring of White male plantation owners born to enslaved Black African women under their control for sexual and economic exploitation (Davis 1991; Omi and Winant 1986). "The one drop rule" of social hypodescent dictates that one known African ancestor made a person "Black" (Rogers 1944; Spickard 1989; Spencer 1997). Hence, the (il)logic of this system ensured that "mixed race" children of White male slave owners became Black slave laborers:

> A slave was a slave because he was black. Slaves by definition could not be white. The fact that slavery was getting whiter, that in reality many slaves were more white than black, was a fact with which the proslavery argument could not cope. Either it could ignore the problem, which it did explicitly, or it could brusquely dismiss it by applying the one drop rule to persons in slavery, which it did implicitly.
>
> (Williamson 1995: 73)

Across the United States, by 1915, the one drop rule had become firmly entrenched in the collective American conscience (Zack 1993; Colker 1996). Legal repercussions of this structural mechanism for the maintenance of the White/Black power imbalance manifest themselves in virtually every social institution: marriage, housing, property ownership, inheritance, voting rights and privileges, education and health (Paredes 1997; Degler 1971; Jordan 1974). My contention is that the Black essentialism of the one drop rule is as integral to our understandings of both colonial and contemporary Black/White social stratification in the former British Empire and the future United Kingdom, respectively. Furthermore, I would argue that across historical time and global spaces different structural principles based on popular folk conceptions of "race" and hierarchy have been generated and justified that illustrate the ways in which ideologies of sexualities and "racial" differences are always intertwined. As Young asserts:

> The history of meanings of the word "commerce" includes the exchange both of merchandise and of bodies in sexual intercourse. It was therefore wholly appropriate that sexual exchange, and its miscegenated product, which captures the violent, antagonistic power relations of sexual and cultural diffusion, should become the dominant paradigm through which the passionate and economic and political trafficking of colonialism was conceived. Perhaps this begins to explain why our own forms of racism remain so intimately bound up with sexuality and desire.
>
> (Young 1995: 182)

As I have already mentioned, popular folk concepts of "race" and hierarchy began their ascendancy in Victorian anthropological discourses (Hannaford 1996; Goldberg 1993). If we take 1859, the publication date of *The Origin of Species: The Preservation of Favoured Races in the Struggle for Life* by Charles Darwin as our analytical starting point and 1900 the rediscovery of Mendelian genetics as the pivotal end point, it becomes clear that there were historical events in both the United States and Europe that galvanized the production of so-called scientific knowledge for the purposes of legitimating White European and American racial supremacy as well as the subjugation of non-White people in the Americas, the Caribbean and the newly formed imperial dominions in Africa and Asia (Malik 1996). From the seventeenth to the eighteenth century, the Enlightenment was characterized by the rise of secular knowledge, in the form of rationality, reason and scientific enquiry (positivism) and was spearheaded by social revolutions. However, it became self-evident that the Enlightenment philosophies of universal humanism and liberal democracy pertained to certain citizens and excluded others (Goldberg 1993). In *Race, Culture and Evolution*, Stocking describes the specific focus of these supremacist scientific enquiries:

> Darwinian evolution, evolutionary ethnology, and polygenist race thus interacted to support raciocultural hierarchy in terms of which civilized men, the highest products of social evolution, were large brained white men, and only large-brained men, the highest products of organic evolution, were fully civilized. The assumption of white superiority was certainly not original with Victorian evolutionists; yet the interrelation of the theories of cultural and organic evolution, with their implicit hierarchy of race, gave it a new rationale.
>
> (Stocking 1982: 122)

In the early twentieth century, these dangerous ideas formed the basis of the Eugenics movements (Gossett 1965). It was Darwin's cousin, Francis Galton, who coined both the phrases "Eugenics" and "nature and nurture." The scientific mission of the Eugenics Movement was the eradication of "inferior races" and the elevation of "superior races" based on the idea that intelligence, criminality and other social "traits" were in and of themselves determined exclusively by heredity:

> I have never found an inter-mixed or inter-married white–negro couple where the stamp of social inferiority was not plainly traceable as the result....Intermarriages between whites and blacks, just as much as wrongful sexual relations without marriage, are essentially anti-social tendencies and therefore opposed to the teachings of sound eugenics in the light of the best knowledge available to

both races at the present time...the conclusion would seem warranted that the crossing of the Negro race with the white has been detrimental to its progress.

(Rogers 1944: 32)

In 1869, Francis Galton looked at the distribution of intelligence within and between so-called different "races." Through quantitative measurements, he deduced that the intelligence of "Negroes" was, on average, two grades below that of Englishmen, while the intelligence of the "Athenian race" of the fifth century was two grades above the Englishman (Galton 1870). It would follow from Galton's analysis that he would not advocate the mating of supposedly mentally inferior Black Africans with supposedly mentally superior White Europeans. While diminished intelligence of the next generation was the excuse propagated by Galton for not condoning so-called mixing of the "races," other scientists pointed to the "weaker constitution" of "racial hybrids." Provine surmised that "if these scientific proponents of racial supremacy argued that races of man differed in hereditary physical and mental characteristics then they would view crossing between distant races with suspicion or outright antagonism" (Provine 1973: 790).

In the inter-war period, this spurious campaign of selective breeding to ensure "racial hygiene" and "purity" culminated, of course, in the Nazi Experiment and Hitler's Final Solution:

> Any crossings of two beings not at exactly the same level produces a medium between the level of the two parents. This means: the offspring will probably stand higher than the racially lower parent, but not as high as the higher one. Consequently, it will later succumb in the struggle against the higher level. Such mating is contrary to the will of Nature for a higher breeding of all life. The precondition for this does not lie in associating superior and inferior, but in the total victory of the former. The stronger must dominate and not blend with the weaker, thus sacrificing his greatness. Only the born weakling can view this as cruel, but he after all is only a weak and limited man; for if this law did not prevail, any conceivable higher development of organic living beings would be unthinkable.

(Hitler 1925 [1992]: 258–9)

In *Showing Our Colors: Afro-German Women Speak Out*, Opitz (1986) describes forced sterilizations and abortions for German women who gave birth to "non-Aryan" children including Afro-Germans, who were themselves also involuntarily sterilized. In *Race and Empire in British Politics*, Paul Rich reveals "the [presumed] moral problem" and the threat to "racial hygiene" of "half-caste" children in Britain in general and the port cities of Liverpool and Cardiff in particular (Rich 1986: 130–5). The same discourses of persecution and pathologization characterize Akousa's (Irish and Bajan (Barbadian) parentage) reflection on the status of "mixed race" people in England:

I think at the end of the day, White society has never accepted me. They've seen me as a contamination to their stock. Diseased person, and even worse than havin' two Black parents, worse than even that. If you come to extermination, we would probably go first. Nazi Germany that's the sort of vibe I get off White people.

In apartheid South Africa of the 1950s, the 1927 Immorality Act which was "to prohibit illicit carnal intercourse between Europeans and non-Europeans" as well as the Groups Areas Act and the Population Registration Act were all socially engineered to enforce particular beliefs about "racial hygiene" (Banton 1967). The prevailing view was that White South Africans were "pure" and Black South Africans were "polluted" (Comaroff and Comaroff 1991; Kuper 1974). The intention of such legislation was to protect the "public health and safety" of the "pure White Volk" who were not like their Black counterparts, Biblical descendants of Ham.[7] Finally, in England, from the "Rivers of Blood" speech of Enoch Powell in the 1960s to the "political pornography" of the National Front in the 1990s, in part, campaigns of racial hatred have encouraged acts of social exclusion and violence against anyone even mildy tinted with "a touch of the tar brush." The British "race" relations guru, Michael Banton, succinctly states: "The metaphors of 'blood' and 'stock' have bitten deep into the English vocabulary and are unthinkingly but daily recapitulated by teachers, dramatists, journalists and politicians" (Banton 1967: 373).

Certain contemporary texts produced by Black African American and White American/British academics seem to revert to a controversial "race" science which reinforces the distorted principles of the Eugenics Movement of the turn of the century (Kohn 1996). Some of the texts include: Charles Murray's and Richard Herrnstein's (1994) *The Bell Curve* and Christopher Brand's (1996) *The g Factor*. Murray and Brand are prospective heirs to the contentious throne held by Arthur Jensen since 1969. All three theorize about alleged links between "race" and intelligence (Kohn 1996; Fraser 1995). African-centered counterdiscourses are equally as contentious. For example, Francis Cress Welsing's (1991) *The Isis Papers*, advocates Black supremacy based on the "super-properties" of melanin (the pigment which lends color to the skin and protects it from the harmful rays of the sun), which "Blacks" are said to possess in greater abundance than "Whites." When will scholars learn that according to Audre Lorde, "The master's tools will never dismantle the master's house" (Lorde 1996: 158).

Old whine, new vassals: persistent problematics of biological and cultural "hybridities"

The events and situations that have produced racial blending reach far back into the misty and unrecorded annals of history. Whenever and wherever peoples move about coming into contact with others different in race and culture, amalgamation and acculturation are possible.

(Gist and Dworkin 1972: 1)

In other words, intergroup mating and marriages were and have always been commonplace. "Hybridity" named these acts of social transgresssion (Young 1995). "Hybrid" meaning "impure," "racially contaminated," a genetic "deviation" was the zoological term deployed to describe the offspring of "mixed race crossings." In the twentieth century, "hybrid" and "hybridity" have been reappropriated to signal cultural synthesis (Canclini 1989). Indirectly, Malik speaks to the dialectical tension between biological and cultural notions of "hybridities:" "The biological discourse of race and the cultural discourse of difference both arise from the inability to reconcile the two" (Malik 1996: 265). The major difficulty with the concept of cultural "hybridity" is the way in which it has been appropriated by mainstream academic discourse without recognition of its problematic origins in nineteenth-century "race" science fiction (Fisher 1995; Papastergiadis 1995).

The presumption is that since the nineteenth century, discourses on "hybridities" have shifted their intellectual focus from the homogeneous pseudoscientific grafting of "races" to the fragmented heterogeneous multivalent fusion of cultures. For example, Minh-ha points to the universality of the contemporary culturally "hybrid" condition: "In the complex reality of post-coloniality it is therefore vital to assume one's radical 'impurity' and to recognize the necessity of speaking from a hybrid place, hence of saying at least two, three things at a time" (Minh-ha, 1992: 140).

In Welcome to the Jungle: New Positions in Black Cultural Studies, Mercer celebrates the advent of cultural "hybridity" as a (postmodernist) survival strategy: "In a world in which everyone's identity has been thrown into question, the mixing and fusion of disparate elements to create new, hybridized identities point to ways of surviving, and thriving, in conditions of crisis and transition" (Mercer 1994: 5). In *Colonial Desire: Hybridity in Theory, Culture and Race*, Young substantiates:

> Today the notion is often proposed of a new cultural hybridity in Britain, a transmutation of British culture into a compounded, composite mode. The condition of that transformation is held out to be the preservation of a degree of cultural and ethnic difference. While hybridity denotes a fusion, it also describes a dialectical articulation, as in Rushdie's "mongrelization".
>
> (Young 1995: 23)

Werbner and Modood (1997) have edited an anthology entirely dedicated to and entitled *Debating Cultural Hybridity*. In the introductory chapter, "Dialectics of cultural hybridity," Werbner's closing remarks pinpoint the major problematic of discourses that celebrate cultural "hybridities" independent of their epistemological origins in scientific racism. She states: "Hybridity as a loaded discourse of dangerous racial contaminations has been transformed into one of cultural creativity: 'insults' have been turned into 'strengths'" (Werbner and Modood 1997: 21). In essence, in England, there has not been a culturally "hybrid" rupture, which is transforming the meanings of place and belonging for all her constituents. Rather, instead, in an attempt to delude late twentieth-century "rainbow" members of "the global village" into believing that opportunities, resources, commodities, icons and even individuals are located on an imaginary "gender-neutral" level playing field where everyone has equal access, cultural "hybridities" with their purported disconnection from "race" science fiction have replaced biological "hybridities."[8]

"Race" as social, cultural and historical artefact

> Scientific scholars generally agree that there is actually no such thing as race, that mixing has been universal and perpetual and that human traits so overlap that it is impossible to describe the characteristics of one "race" to the exclusion of all others. These scholars prefer to think in terms of a "gene pool" that produces certain traits among an inbred people more frequently than among others. What seem to be races, one might say, are actually clusters of traits.
>
> (Williamson 1995: xiii)

The anthropological fact about what Naomi Zack (1993) refers to as "the ordinary concept of race" and what I have named a popular folk idea is that it has absolutely no biological foundation (Hannaford 1996). Of one species, human populations are also ambiguous, unbounded heterogeneous groups capable of interbreeding across generations (Root 1996). Bestowing the concept of "race" with biological properties ignores a fundamental scientific fact, which is that human individuals and populations vary enormously in terms of phenotypic (visible) traits – skin color, hair texture and color, eye shape and color, general facial features, body structure, as well as in the frequency of occurrence of particular blood types (A, B, AB and O) (American Anthropological Association (AAA) 1997). What is also significant is that the frequency in expression of these physical markers and the prevalence of particular blood groups "each vary independently of one another, knowing the frequency of one trait does not predict the presence or frequencies of others" (AAA 1997: 2).

Mendelian genetics developed in order to determine the statistical probability of the occurrence of *a single trait*. Gregor Mendel was a biologist who studied the reproductive life of garden peas. Although conducting research at the same time as Darwin, until the rediscovery of his heredity findings in 1900, Mendel's influence on modern genetics was not recognized:

> The facts which Mendel observed contradicted in several ways the expectations of Darwinian evolutionists. These earlier evolutionists had expected to find that heredity operated to produce a uniform blend, as if the heritable traits of the mother and those of the father were respectively a trickle of ink and a trickle of water which mingled in their offspring to form a uniform watered ink. But this is an oversimplification. The role of bisexual reproduction proves, as the result of Mendelian observation, to be much more complex than this. Inheritance is passed along to the offspring as a long series of characteristics contributed by the father and the mother, and these have to be conceived not as ink and water mingling but as a pile of beads sorted anew for every individual. For many traits these sortings follow certain statistical rules.
>
> (Benedict 1940: 56)

In other words, particular physical traits which have been bestowed with popular "race" meaning are not inherited in a uniform fashion. Rather, at the point of conception, genes are dispersed and particular characteristics are passed on randomly and separately. Furthermore, all human beings are members of a single species, *Homo sapiens*. We all can and do interbreed and reproduce progeny who can in turn interbreed. A "race" should be renamed "a self-contained breeding population that has a higher percentage of individuals with certain physical characteristics than some other population" (Zack 1993: 14). However, *there are no discrete genetically homogeneous races*, which means there are no "pure" "races" (Gist and Dworkin 1972; Linton 1936). In fact, there is more genetic variation within a group socially designated as a "race" than between so-called groups socially identified as different "races":

What is clear is that the genetic differences between the so-called races is minute. On average there's .2 percent difference in genetic material between any two randomly chosen people on Earth. Of that diversity, eighty five percent will be found within any local group of people. More than half (nine percent) of the remaining fifteen percent will be represented by differences between ethnic and linguistic groups within a given race. Only six percent represents differences between races. That's six percent of .2 percent. In other words, race accounts for only a miniscule .012 percent difference in our genetic material.

(Hoffman 1994: 4)

Yet, despite this statistically insignificant genetic variance, *it is the popular folk concept of "race" which persists in the collective British and American imagination* (Miles 1989; Omi and Winant 1986; Small 1994). Over time, this symbolic attachment to perceived physical differences has wielded immense social and political power (Goldberg 1993; Malik 1996). The naturalization of the folk popular conception of "race" means that the symbolic meanings attached to real or manufactured physical differences are used to create, explain and justify social inequalities and injustices as well as to determine differential access to power, privilege and prestige (Stolcke 1993; Jordan and Weedon 1995).

The popular folk conception of "race" is a powerful social imaginary, which when operationalized as institutionalized racism and racialization is imbued with immense meaning and power (Miles 1989; Omi and Winant 1986). Anthias and Yuval-Davis, among other scholars, would advocate differentiating between racism and racialization on the grounds that the former legitimates the concept of "race" as "a valid scientific typology" (Anthias and Yuval-Davis 1992: 11) Racialization is: "a dialectical process by which meaning is attributed to particular biological features of human beings as a result of which individuals may be assigned to a general category of persons which reproduces itself biologically" (Miles 1989: 76). As a perspective, racialization demonstrates the ways in which "race" is actually a mutable non-biological concept with specific historical, culture-bound, symbolic and structural meanings (Small 1994). This variability in turn determines status, position and power relations for individuals in any geographical and historical contexts.

By extension, in both the United States and Britain, as I have defined it, bi-racialization is a substructure of racialization in that it speaks to the specific structural, symbolic and oppositional relationship forged between people socially designated as Black[9] and those deemed White (Dyer 1997; Fine *et al*. 1997; Frankenburg 1997). Bi-racialization purports that in the United Kingdom and the United States this dialectical process both converges with and eclipses other modes of social stratification based on social class and most importantly gender and ethnicity. [10] Anthias and Yuval-Davis add: "Gender and racialized ethnic divisions are both under-pinned by a supposedly 'natural' 'relation'" (Anthias and Yuval-Davis 1992: 18). Biology and culture are inaccurately conflated and specific social mean-ings attached to physical characteristics create politically charged, manufactured hierarchically ranked conceptions of Blackness and Whiteness, which in turn govern inter-group relationships. [11] Lawrence refers to these constructs of Blackness and Whiteness as "optical perceptions" (Lawrence 1995: 26). The process of bi-racialization dictates that separate inferior Black and superior White social and symbolic designations determine subjectivities and define specific and exclusive group memberships. Moreover, these interdependent cohorts co-exist in symbolic opposition:

> there is a direct and abiding connection between the maintenance of white supremacist patriarchy in this society and the institutional-ization via mass media of specific images, representations of race, of blackness that support and maintain the oppression, exploitation, and overall domination of all black people.
>
> (hooks 1992: 2)

In simple terms, the one drop rule determines Black status, bi-racialization guarantees that Black people maintain a subordinate position.

The popular folk concepts of "race," which give shape and form to bi-racialization, place a high premium on perceived phenotypic (physical) differences between groups (Delaney 1879; Dominguez 1986). In "ordinary" terms, access to structures of opportunity can be denied or extended to indi-viduals on the basis of the social meaning attached to perceived phenotypes (physical characteristics) – skin pigmentation, hair texture, hair and eye color. Senegalese anthropologist Cheik Anta Diop would argue that pheno-type is the major determinant of the qualitative nature of inter-group relations: "In the historical and social relations among people, the only intervening factor at the outset is the phenotype, i.e. the physical appear-ance, and consequently, differences that may exist at this level" (Diop 1991: 124).

Yet, because popular folk concepts of "race" have no grounding in biolog-ical science, their social manifestations are at best paradoxical (Mills 1997). Popular folk concepts of "race" cannot easily accommodate phenotypic ambi-guities, which manifest themselves in *individuals* as a result of "racial" interbreeding across generations. For example, Ruby is of Black Nigerian and White English parentage. She is married to a White Englishman and has three children whom she describes as "not straightforwardly White:"

When we had children, I fully expected my children to be Black. At least to be dark apparently non-White. My first daughter Pauline she's about the darkest of them. She has Afro features in as much as she has dark curly hair. It's not curly like this though, it's much more like the perms Europeans go to have done – pretty little curls....When the second one was born, she was outrageously fair. She had very blonde hair and looked very much like John – not a bit like me. When the third one was born, Jake, what I first thought when he came out, when I saw him, was "Oh, it's me dad." Because he just had that face....He's as White as the rest, but he had a very Negroid face....I suppose it's only as they have been growing up, that it came to me. That I was the only Black member in a totally White household.

Bisi, who is also Black Nigerian and White English and married to a White Englishman adds:

The question of what race are my children? What do they think? How do they feel? It's difficult as well. I think Elizabeth said, "I'm one-quarter Nigerian" (very specific, very precise), but I'm three-quarters English, Mummy." Which is true? I ask my son sometimes, "Do you think you are White?" I don't know whether he says it to please me or not but he says, "Well no, not really."

As these extracts illustrate, different even contradictory social, cultural and generational meanings are attached to popular folk concepts of "mixed race," color, and status:

The status and role of a particular mixed-blood group can be taken as an index of the larger race problem; and in turn the development of the mixed-blood class reacts back upon the general racial situation modifying it to a significant, sometimes determining, extent.

(Stonequist 1937: 50)

Furthermore, there are social, cultural and political variations in the global classificatory rules that determine the social status of different local so-called "mixed race" communities (Stonequist 1937; Davis 1991). Conventionally, across space and time, although *scientifically impossible to predict*, microambi-guities of phenotype and genotype have been socially managed, regulated, legislated and reconciled based on a series of socioculturally specific rules, which in turn determine not only who can mate and/or marry whom, but also the differential status designations of the subsequent offspring (Root 1996; Williamson 1995; Young 1995). Historically, these different regula-tory strategies frequently highlight gendered and bi-racialized power relationships. For example, in the United States, the Caribbean and South Africa, the most common bi-racialized liaisons during and after slavery were between White European/American men and Black African women (Degler 1971; Freyre 1956). On the other hand, in Britain, before the 1950s, bi-racialized sexual unions principally involved Black continental African/African Caribbean men and White British women (Richmond 1955). Yet, in keeping with the contradictions of patriarchy, while the sexual exploits of the majority White male in the Americas, the Caribbean and other imperial locales were neither policed nor disparaged, White English women who consorted with Black African Caribbean and conti-nental African men were ostracized as being licentious (Rich 1986; Fryer 1984).

In *Who is Black?*, Davis (1991) claims that there are at least seven rules, which he refers to as "statuses," which determine the social position of "mixed race" individuals in specific cultural contexts. In the first status posi-tion, the individual occupies a lower status than either of her or his parents, i.e. *mulattoes* of the Ganda of Uganda, Anglo-Indians in India and Amerasians in Korea and Vietnam. In the second status position, the indi-vidual achieves a higher status than either parent, i.e. the *mulattoes* of Haiti and the *mestizos* of Mexico. In the third status position, the individual is a member of an intermediate buffer group with marginalized status, i.e. Coloreds in South Africa. The fourth status position is negotiated on the basis of social class and color, i.e. in the Caribbean including Puerto Rico and Guyana as well as Brazil and Colombia. The fifth status position is a variable one, which is supposedly independent of socially designated "racial" traits, i.e. in Hawaii. The sixth status position also known as "the one drop rule" or "social hypodescent" dictates that the individual occupies the same position as the lower status parent, i.e. in the United States and, I would argue, in the United Kingdom. The seventh status group entitles the indi-vidual to a position of an assimilated minority, i.e. individuals in the United States with "partial" Native American, Filipino, Japanese or other "*racially distinctive minority ancestry other than Black*" (my emphasis). The specific requirements for membership in the seventh status group articulate loudly and clearly what is almost always silenced in any discourses on the so-called "mixing of races." That is, according to social engineers, in the popular imagination, (Black) African ancestry still represents the ultimate in genealogical degeneration.

The tangle of terminology[12]

Two little 6-year-old girls have been separated from their peers for disrupting the Nando afterschool project on the outskirts of Thatchapee. Sandra has a White English mother and a Black Jamaican father. She has blonde curly hair, hazel eyes and a complexion the color of milky English tea. Her comrade Aneya has a White English mother and a Black Libyan father. She has black curly hair, dark brown eyes and coloring reminiscent of roasted almonds.

I am sitting at the table with them as they talk about their friends, various members of their family, as well as what they are going to do over the weekend, since today is Friday. Aneya says to Sandra, who has been talking about her father who lives just outside Bristol, "He's White isn't he?" She knows Sandra's mum is White English like her's since the two families often play together. Sandra says, "No, he's Bl...," she begins to say "Black" and then says, "I mean dark brown."

Rather than representing a portrait of "mixed race" girls as unruly, at the age of six, Sandra and Aneya have exposed the major problematic of "race" (Ahmed 1997; Weekes 1997). Their discussion highlights the cultural paradoxes of "race" and color, which multiple generations of "mixed race" women, men and children in England silently negotiate in their everyday lives (Phoenix and Owen 1996; Russell *et al.* 1992). These individuals descend from lineages that cut across so-called differently configured and gendered Black/White "races," ethnicities, cultures and classes. Their roots are both endogenous and exogenous (Ang-Lygate 1997; Maja-Pearce 1990).

In varied cultural and historical contexts,[13] countless terms are employed to name such individuals − "mixed race," mixed heritage, mixed parentage, *mestizo*, *mestiza*, *mulatto*, *mulatta*, creole, colored, "mixed racial descent," mixed origins, dual heritage, dual parentage, "multiracial," "bi-racial," multiethnic to the more derogatory half-caste, zebra, half-breed, mongrel, *oreo*, Heinz Fifty Seven. In the Spring of 1997, Tiger Woods, the youngest winner of the US (golf) Open created a storm in the United States' Black communities when, on *The Oprah Winfrey Show*, he denied his "one-drop

Blackness" (his father is African American and his mother is Thai) and instead claimed "Caublinasian," which is his own linguistic amalgam of his "Caucasian, Black, Native American and Asian" ancestries.

Similar to Maria Root's (1996) assertion in her "Bill of Rights for Racially Mixed People," my official existential position *vis-à-vis* categorization and identification is that individuals should have the freedom to name themselves however they see fit and to change that designation whenever the spirit and life circumstances moves them:

> The human approach to experience is categorical…what we don't label others will, leaving us at their mercy. We are better off to supply labels of our own and to be up front about the identifications we seek.
>
> (Wolcott 1995: 81)

However, my politicized stance is that I am mindful of the heavy hand of bureaucratization as well as the inadequate ways in which government bodies, such as the Census,[14] have "classified" generations of individuals who by virtue of birth and lineage do not fit neatly into preordained sociological and anthropological categories (Aspinall 1997; Owen 1996). Hence, the primary purpose of my (re)formulation of the multilayered conceptual terms *métis(se)* (and *métissage*) is twofold. First, as Trinh Minh-ha states, I am "re-naming to un-name" (Minh-ha 1992: 14). Second, and more importantly, for the purposes of analyses, I offer *métis(se)* in part as *a shorthand stand-in* in response to what I believe are the inadequacies of previous terms, which either reify "race," are too ambiguous to be useful or do not adequately address the complexities of bi-racialized transnational belongings. Installing *métis(se)* as a lexical intervention is to momentarily free me from the tangle of terminology so that I may address more pressing and in fact derivative concerns, such as racism and bi-racialization. Perhaps from this we may imagine a future entirely free of the reinscribing badges of bi-racialized differences.

In Britain, my own research as well as others (Phoenix and Tizard 1993; Aspinall 1997; Alibhai-Brown and Montague 1992) reflect the fact that "mixed race" people themselves as well as parents, carers, practitioners, educators, policy makers, academics and curious lay people are all hungry for a uniform but not essentialist term that creates a space for the naming of their specific experiences without necessarily reinscribing and reifying "race." Informal and formal conversations with myriad "mixed race" people have also demonstrated that to date we have not found a way to formulate discourses that do not reinscribe a dominant binary Black/White "mixed race" paradigm. Yet, the complex specific transnational histories, and social, cultural, and political dynamics, which give rise to the many and varied "mixed race" communities in Britain, defy compression into one grand narrative. Nevertheless, I am now convinced of the importance of trying to formulate an analytical scheme that can address multiracialized, bi-racialized, and generational hierachies of differences within the marginalized spaces of "mixed race."

In anthropological and literary terms, *métis(se)* and *métissage* are generally associated with France, French-speaking Canada and certain Francophone countries such as Senegal (Lionnet 1989; Marquet 1983; Burley *et al.* 1992). In the French–African (Senegalese) context, in its conventional masculine (*métis*) and feminine (*métisse*) forms, *métis(se)* refers to someone who by virtue of parentage embodies two or more world views, i.e. White French mother and Black Senegalese father or what Senghor would refer to as a "EuroAfrican" (Marquet 1983). However, in this version, *métis(se)* is not exclusively a racial term used to differentiate individuals with one Black parent and one White parent from those with two Black parents or two White parents. *Métis(se)* also pertains to people with parents from different ethnic/cultural groups within a country, i.e. in Nigeria, Ibo and Yoruba or in Britain, Scottish and English. As Diop explains:

> in the Senegalese context, an essential element is that there is a spectrum of shades going from the lightest (almost "White") to the darkest and everything in between. Thus, as far as I know, people are not identified by color but rather by participation in and identi-fication with the CULTURE. I underline culture for it is important (i.e. language and customs)
>
> …when someone is a *métis(se)* say a Wolof and a Mandinka, it is not obvious because the skin color, bodily features and hair remain the same; basically, this is *intra-métissage* just like when White French and White English mix…the moment a Black and a White mix, the picture radically changes for, in addition to language and culture, skin color becomes more obvious…my suggestion is that Black and White *métissage* in Senegal and many parts of Africa can be referred to as "colonial *métissage*" for lack of a better term.
>
> (Samba Diop 1998, personal communication)

That is, the term recognizes the specificities of ethnicities as they are main-tained and redefined within national borders. In a globalizing world, one can increasingly claim that there are transnational/multiple migrants who, by virtue of their cumulative experiences of travel, education and labor, represent cultural *métis(se)*:

> The mixed blood is therefore also of mixed culture – a cultural hybrid as well as a racial hybrid. Persons having a mixed culture may and do emerge aside from the process of race mixture. In other

words, an individual may be a cultural hybrid but not a racial hybrid.

(Stonequist 1937: 54)

Similarly stated: "The place of my hybridity is also the place of my identity" (Minh-ha 1992: 14).

In the English milieux where this work is situated, *métis(se)* becomes a twice-pilfered "French–African," in particular, "Senegalese" appropriation of the continental French *métis(se)*. In translated continental French, *métis(se)* is synonymous with the derogatory English "half-caste" and "half-breed" (Henri-Cousin 1994). (Re)deploying this term demonstrates the portability and mutability of language as well as its potential reinterpretation across borders. My linguistic informants are "Senegalese" – that is Black continental African. As mentioned, what they suggest is that alternative translations of *métis(se)* can extend beyond "racial" that is "Black"/"White" discourses to encompass convergences across ethnicities, cultures, religions and nationalities (Samba Diop 1993, personal communication; Koubaka 1993, personal communication). The Senegalese interpretation of *métis(se)* clears space for "the consideration or recognition of individuals as bearers of multiple subject positions; that is how 'racialized' identity intersects with other aspects of identity such as gender" (Hashim 1996: 8).

In England, at the moment, there are a multitude of labels in circulation that allegedly describe individuals who straddle "racial" borders. More often than not, received terminology either privileges presumed "racial" differences ("mixed race") or obscures the complex ways in which being *métis(se)* involves *both* the negotiation of constructed Black/White "racial" categories as well as the celebration of converging cultures, continuities of generations and overlapping historical traditions. The lack of consensus as to which term to use, the limitations of this discursive privileging of "race" at the expense of generational, ethnic and cultural concerns as well as the blatant avoidance of inherent hierarchical power dynamics within, between and among multiracialized and bi-racialized formations led me to *métis(se)* and *métissage*.

My analysis of *métis(se)* takes place on three levels. First, as a primary *general* analytical term *métis(se)* accounts for individuals who according to popular folk concepts of "race" and by known birth parentage embody two or more world views or in genealogical terms, descent groups. These individuals may have physical characteristics that reflect some sort of "intermediate" status *vis-à-vis* their birth parents. More than likely, at some stage, they will have to reconcile multiple cultural influences. The degree of agency afforded a *métis(se)* individual is contingent in part upon local popular folk "readings of their phenotypes", *vis-à-vis* systems of categorization and classification that may reinforce eighteenth-/nineteenth-century "race" science fiction. Social class, gender, generation and locality are also important variables.

At the secondary level *proximate métis(se)* and *mediate métis(se)* forms recognize the importance of *generation* in attempting to understand family formations whatever their multiple configurations. *Proximate métis(se)* individuals have *immediate* known birth parentage, which, according to popular folk concepts of "race," embodies two or more world views or in genealogical terms, descent groups. For example, someone with a Chinese mother and an English father or an Indian father and a Jamaican mother (first generation). This would also include individuals such as Ruby's and Bisi's children (second generation) (mother is Nigerian and English; father is English). *Mediate métis(se)* identifies individuals who have *immediate* known parentage, which according to popular folk concepts of "race" are "presumed" to embody the same world views or in genealogical terms, descent groups. However, their known grandparentage or known great grandparentage does not reflect this pattern. For examples, I would consider myself to be *mediate métisse*. My mother is Guyanese (my maternal grandfather), Irish and English (my maternal grandmother) and my father is Igbo (Nigerian). Another example would be my cousin Kevin's son and daughter. Kevin's mother (my mother's sister, Mary) is Guyanese, Irish and English. Kevin's father (Mary's husband) is Northern Irish. Kevin's wife Sharon is White Canadian.

Relying on popular folk concepts of "race," the third level of analysis, *multiracialized métis(se)* addresses *the specificity and multiplicity of individual* circumstances in general. *Multiracialized métis(se)* refers to individuals whose known parentage cannot be subsumed under the popular folk binary "race" categories of Black and White, i.e. Chinese and Mexican or Iranian and Indian.[15] *Bi-racialized métis(se) is a subset of multiracialized métis(se)* and speaks to the historically created, oppositional relationship that has been forged between popular folk concepts of Blackness and Whiteness and their attendant symbolic "phenotypic markers." For future reference, the individual participants in my research project are all *bi-racialized métis(se)*.

Métissage is a mind set or a shorthand way to interrogate theorizing generally associated with *bi-racialized and multiracialized métis(se)* subjectivities: ruptures, diaspora(s), globalization, polyvocalities, heteroglossia, oscillations, contradictions, paradoxes, "hybridities," "polyethnicities," "belonging nowhere and everywhere," creolization, *mestizaje*, "blending and mixing," polyglot, transnationalities, transgressions, multiculturalism, endogenous and exogenous roots and multiple reference points.

Bhaba's "Black" (?) Sheep

By signaling the *process* of opening up hybrid spaces and looking at the sociocultural dynamics – as performances – of "race," gender, ethnicity, nation, class, sexuality and generation and their relationship to the mechanisms of power, my conceptualization of *métissage* is similar to Homi Bhaba's notion of a "third space:"

20

What is at issue is the performative nature of differential identities: the regulation and negotiation of those spaces that are continually, *contingently*, "opening out," remaking the boundaries, exposing the limits of any claim to a singular or autonomous sign of difference – be it class, gender or race. Such assignations of social differences – where difference is neither One nor the Other but something else besides, in between – find their agency in a form of the 'future' where the past is not originary, where the present is not simply transitory. It is, if I may stretch a point, an interstitial future, that emerges in-between the claims of the past and the needs of the present.

(Bhaba 1994: 219)

With specific reference to the "political hazards" of so-called "race" mixing, in *The PanAfricanist Worldview* Opoku Ageyman takes a more polemical stance *vis-à-vis* the alleged interstitial positioning of what he refers to as "mulattoes:"

There is no question that a certain calculation went into the making and grooming of mulattoes. To have only a black and white dichotomy was to have an uncomfortably sharp polarization. A black–brown–white situation, on the other hand complicated the equation of forces to the advantage of the color group which had created the brown, as well as an existential crisis by imposing itself on the top of the human ladder.

(Ageyman 1985: 87)

Although my configuration of *métissage* attempts to rupture particular bi-polar/bi-racialized notions of Blackness and Whiteness, unlike Bhaba I do not situate this reformulation at the interstices, nor do I endorse Agyeman's tripartite ideological system. Instead, I argue that the situational positioning of global *bi-racialized and multiracialized métis(se)* subjectivities, of which *métissage* is derivative, are circumscribed and delimited within particular ever-changing *local* geopolitical and sociohistorical milieux within which hierarchical and frequently gendered power relations are centralized. That is, narrated across time and space, the testimonies of *bi-racialized métis(se)* identities featured in *Scattered Belongings*, lucidly illustrate the ways in which, acting *métis(se)* subjects can and do negotiate, challenge and subvert *all* of the subject positions – "One" (White) the "Other" (Black) or "Neither" (*métis(se)*). In the words of Gloria Anzaldua: "I, a mestiza, continually walk out of one culture and into another, because I am in all cultures at the same time" (Anzaldua 1987: 76).

In general, I intend to demonstrate the portability and mutability of the terms *métis(se)* and *métissage* as explanatory devices that contain unifying but not essentialist possibilities for the spatial and temporal dimensions of identities politics in a multiracialized and a bi-racialized world. At its best, with multiracialized and bi-racialized dynamics of power as the pivotal point, *métissage* functions as a prescriptive antidote to diaspora(s) angst. Aijaz Ahmad adds:

> It is also the case, however, that the entire logic of the kind of cultural 'hybridity' that Bhaba celebrates presumes the intermingling of Europe and non-Europe in a context already determined by advanced capital, in the aftermath of colonialism. In this account, non-Europeans hardly ever encounter each other and never without a prior European modulation of the very field of that encounter. Nor do these celebrations of hybridity foreground the unequal relations of cultural power today. Rather, intercultural hybridity is presented as a transaction of displaced equals which somehow transcends the profound inequalities engendered by colonialism itself.
>
> (Ahmad 1995: 17)

The story is old. Our testimonies are new.

Notes

1 In order to "reestablish race in anthropological discourse", the American Anthropological Association has designated "Is it 'Race'? Anthropology on Human Diversity" as the 1997–1998 theme. Current running commentaries on the anthropological reclamation of "race" published in the *Anthropology Newsletter* have facilitated my rethinking on "race." The American Anthropological Association (1997) Draft Official Statement on "Race" has been an invaluable guide as I continue to navigate the murky waters where studies of "race" lurk. This chapter has also been greatly enhanced by Naomi Zack's rigorous critical feedback.
2 Thatchapee is the fictional name of the inner city community in Bristol where I lived and worked from 1990–1992. Unless otherwise stated, to protect the privacy of project participants, in the text, I have also fictionalized all of their names and any identifying place names.
3 I had originally returned to England in general and Bristol in particular to engage in comparative anthropological research on social and cultural constructions of adolescence for continental African and African Caribbean youth. I wanted to build on prior ethnographic research conducted in Northern California wherein I was interested in the emergence of political consciousness for young African American women and men. In other words, I was interested in the different and similar ways in which these young people, many of them teen parents, defined youth and adulthood as well as if they had an understanding of the relationship between structures of inequality and their own life

choices and chances. However, Bristolian Black youth's collective lack of interest in formal long-term participation in my research project eventually resulted in my shifting focus to the transformative and transgressive possibilities of identities politics.

4 A West African term that describes someone who functions as a tribal poet, storyteller, historian or genealogist and whose role is to recount culturally specific and provocative parables of daily life.

5 Dreadlocks that are left to flourish on their own.

6 A Rastafarian term that describes when Rastafarians convene to "reason" about life. Rastafarian spiritual philosophy presumes the oneness of the human spirit. Hence, "I and I" as opposed to "You and I."

7   The sons of Noah were three in number: Shem, Ham and Japheth....That Shem was of the same complexion as Noah his father and mother – the Adamic complexion – there is no doubt in our mind. And that Ham the second son was swarthy in complexion, we have little doubt. Indeed, we believe it is generally conceded by scholars, though disputed by some, that the word Ham means "dark," "swarthy," "sable." And has always been conceded, and never as we know of seriously disputed, that Japheth was white.
                    Delany, Martin (1879) *The Origins of Races and Color*,
                              Philadelphia: Harper and Brother, p. 18

8 In a footnote to the introduction to Smadar Lavie and Ted Swedenburg (eds.) (1996) *Displacement, Diaspora, and Geographies of Identity*, Chapel Hill: Duke University Press, p. 24, Lavie reminds us that "much of the work on 'hybridities' is gender-neutral (for instance Paul Gilroy's)." As a possible intervention, she advocates Donna Haraway's notion of a "cyborg" wherein gender is necessarily marked: "A cyborg is a cybernetic organism, a hybrid of machine and organism, a creature of social reality as well as a creature of fiction" Donna Haraway (1991) "A Cyborg Manifesto: science, technology and socialist feminism in the late twentieth century," *Simians, Cyborgs and Women in the Reinvention of Women*, London: Free Association Books, p. 149.

9 For the purposes of analysis, I am not working with the term "Black" as a political category which in Britain would include South Asians, Chinese and perhaps Irish. Instead, I am leaning on the "one drop rule" notion of Black, which presumes one known African ancestor.

10 In the final section of this chapter, I will introduce the concept of multiracialization, of which bi-racialization is a part. The main difference between bi-racialization and multiracialization is that the former specifically addresses the oppositional Black/White binary, while the latter casts a wider net that includes other structural configurations that are not necessarily "Black"/"White."

11 In Chapter 10 I will provide a critique of the dialectics of Blackness and Whiteness.

12 On February 7 1998, at South Bank University in London, Tracey Reynolds, of the Black Women's Subcommitee/British Sociological Association, invited me to organize a day-long workshop and seminar based on some of the ideas that I have developed in this book. Both the lively debates and discussions that took place on the day as well as the ongoing e-mail exchanges and telephone conversations that followed have precipitated the refinement of initial theorizing on the conceptual category *métis(se)* as it meets what I refer to as the limits of the personal, the political and the categorical. I am particularly grateful to Peter Aspinall, Sabu, Heidi Mirza, Jo Ann Ramsey, Minelle Mahtani, April Moreno,

Peter Bond, Cheryl Gore, Shazia Ali and Aishah Simmons for their insightful and informed constructive criticisms. Samba Diop was the original donor of the analytical concept *métis(se)*. During the process of reformulation, both he and Tunde Jegede have been important intellectual catalysts and sparring partners.

13 In correspondence, Aspinall (1998) (personal communication), has reminded me of the importance of differentiating between the terms used by agencies/practitioners/academics, by people who are themselves "mixed race," by official agencies such as the Census, by the scientific community, and by the media and the press. In addition, his research reflects the fact that "mixed race" individuals use "collective" terms such as "mixed" or "mixed race," while also in free text fields describing the specificities of their particular "mixture." In other instances, he found that they "declared only part of their mix, i.e. 'half-' or 'quarter-'."

14 In Chapter 10, I discuss the problematics of "ethnic" categorization in both the 1991 and the approaching 2001 Censuses.

15 These are the respective ancestries of April Moreno (1998, personal communication) and Minelle Mahtani (1998, personal communication), two postgraduate students of "critical mixed race" theory with whom I have worked. Their work strives to construct a more inclusive "critical mixed race discourse," which transcends the current, dominant, Black/White discourse.

Plate 2   Author's maternal great-grandmother and namesake, Jane Freeman, Le Guan, Guyana, date unknown. Photograph by Gordon Parks. Frank Loris Peterson *The Hope of the Race* (1934) Nashville, Tennessee: Southern Publishing Company.

Plate 3 Portrait of the author, Lincoln, England, April 1998. Photograph by Sabu, "New Mixed Culture," http: //www.1love.com

"Strength in Unity, United We are Strong"

Plate 4   (Anglicized translation of author's Igbo surname). Author's paternal grandparents, Chief Aaron Nsiegbuna Ifekwunigwe and Florence Ifekwunigwe, Onitisha, Nigeria, Summer1976.

"People in a Multitude Stand Together"

Plate 5 (Literal translation of author's Igbo surname.) Author's nuclear family, Egypt, Summer 1976.

2

RETURNING(S): RELOCATING THE CRITICAL FEMINIST AUTO-ETHNOGRAPHER[1]

In this world through which I travel. I am endlessly creating myself.

Frantz Fanon

It is out of chaos that new worlds are born.

Audre Lorde

This chapter unfolds as a kaleidoscopic series of narratives, which I place under the subheadings of "Turning(s)." Some of the narratives will be photopoetic chronicles of my childhood. Others will be my re-telling of pivotal moments that have shaped my complex subjectivity. The rest will be frozen snapshots of experiences reconfigured as anecdotes. Although by no means definitive, collectively these texts capture my particular complex evolving everyday lived realities as a *métisse* woman. However, as cumulative text these individual evocations also pinpoint problematic anthrohistorical and psychosocial issues that I will tackle and critique throughout the book. Ultimately, these narratives of self contextualize my specific feminist "standpoint" as auto-ethnographer:

> The notion of traveling through space is integral to the unfolding of history and the development of the individual's consciousness with regard to the past. The voyage over geographic space is an expanded metaphor for the process of one person's coming to know who she is.
>
> (Willis 1985: 220)

Turning(s)

Sparkling grape juice, jacket potato baked to perfection – crunchy on
the outside, soft on the inside, courgettes (zucchini) with tomato and
onion sauce, green salad with lettuce, tomatoes, cucumbers, apples,
avocados, and tossed with a honey mustard dressing, corn on the
cob, hot relish, chutney, melon, strawberries and cream.

It is late 1991, I am sitting in the sunny front room of Bisi's home in central
Bristol. We have just finished eating one of Bisi's famous eclectic lunches.
Bisi is my sister–friend as well as one of the six newfangled *métisse griottes*
featured in this text. She has the uncanny and consistent ability to prepare
the most creative and the most sumptuous meals from bits and pieces found
in her kitchen. These are the fruits of labor of a mother of four and an
accomplished visual artist.

This gathering is one of the last times I will spend with Bisi and the
other regulars – her sister Yemi, Sarah, Angustia, Aduah – before returning
to the United States to write my Ph.D. dissertation. Bisi is working on
another animation piece and asks us if we will share some of our experiences
on camera. The challenge is to recall a turning point in our lives, or rather a
choice/decision we made (or that was made for us), which changed our lives.
Bisi said it was going to Greece, where she met her husband. That question
was easy for me: The countless times I have been uprooted, transported and
transplanted intially as part of my parents' belongings and then subsequently as an adult in pursuit of education and (self-)knowledge. As I write,
I am still returning.

Turning(s)

There is a naming tradition in Igbo families wherein one names children on
the basis of the events that are transpiring at the time the mother is pregnant or at the moment the child is born. Through my Igbo name as well as
those of my siblings, one can chronicle our early family history spent in
England and Nigeria:

For my lineages

> *What is in a Name? or What is in a Name. or We Need to Re-Member so That
> Others Will not Forget*

30

Number One
24 December, 1959
Muriel St. Clair Freeman
Daughter of Mary Freeman of South Shields, England and Lionel
Freeman of Le Guan, Guyana
and Aaron Ezebuilo (a king will have many enemies) Ifekwunigwe, son
of
Chief Aaron Nsiegbuna (may poison not kill) Ifekwunigwe and Florence
Ugoye (pride of the Oye Market) Ifekwunigwe of Nando, Onitsha
Nigeria
are married by Archbishop Patterson in Onitsha Cathedral, Nigeria

They return to England
Daddy finishes medical school and starts rotations
Money is scarce
Life is uncertain
Mum is carrying her first child

28 February, 1961
My older brother Christopher is born
in Sorrento Hospital in Birmingham, England
Chukwuma
Only that greater force knows what the future will bring

Number Two
Daddy finishes rotations
Our family moves back to London
Mum is carrying her second child

12 July, 1963
Jayne is born in Hammersmith Hospital, London, England
Daddy is offered and accepts a position heading the teaching hospital at
the University of Ibadan in Nigeria
Obiageli
Someone who came into the world to enjoy life – the privileged one

Number Three
Our family settles in to life in Nigeria
Daddy goes off to Uganda on business
Mum is carrying her third child
Daddy and a Swedish doctor are in an automobile accident
Swedish doctor is killed instantly
National news confuses facts
Daddy is presumed dead

Friends flock to family home to console Mum
To offer assistance with funeral arrangements

Daddy has already phoned Mum from emergency room in Uganda
He is very much alive
5 June 1965
David is born in Ibadan Hospital, Nigeria
Chukwumeka
That greater force has done a very good thing

Number Four
1960 – Nigeria gains independence from Britain
The country is carved up into three regions
North/East/West
Hausa/Igbo/Yoruba
January, 1966
Igbos, Easterners, our people, kill Prime Minister Sir Abubakar Tafawa
and the Premiers of the Northern and Western Regions
Our family is living in Ibadan – the West – Yoruba Land
Northern and Western soldiers are going door to door
Killing any and all Igbos
Mum is carrying her last child

Our family flees in the middle of the night to the East to Igbo Land to
Nando, Onitsha, to my Grandparents Papa and Mama
Papa is the Chief there

Mum requires a Caesarean section
She has us all that way

14 December, 1966
She gives birth to her last child
A girl – Ann Mary in Enugu, Nigeria
In a civilian hospital converted into army barracks
There are wounded soldiers on either side of her
Nkiruka
Hope for the future
The future will be brighter

Ifekwunigwe
The meaning of my Igbo surname?
It means
People in a multitude stand together
Strength in unity
United we are strong

18 February, 1991
Bristol, England

Turning(s)

I was about four. We were living in Nigeria during the Biafran War.[2] For obvious reasons, it was no longer safe for our family to be living there. So it was agreed that my mum, my siblings and I would return to England. However, my father, a Biafran physician, decided to stay behind to provide medical relief.[3]

At Port Harcourt, we boarded a mercenary plane without seats and were strapped to the floor, wherein we began a days-long journey ending with a crash landing in Lisbon, Portugal. My only memory of that journey is stepping out onto the steps of the aircraft to depart and just vomiting.[4] Mum contacted the British Embassy and my maternal grandparents, who were by then divorced. We eventually made our way to semi-rural Nelson, Lancashire, the post-industrial North,[5] where my Guyanese grandad was living with his second wife, whom we would later refer to as Auntie Dan.

Turning(s)

My father, a stranger of sorts, returned from Biafra.[6] As a result of his wartime research on pediatric malnutrition, for a year, he was granted a fellowship at Harvard University's School of Public Health in Cambridge, Massachusetts, United States of America. During that time, we all lived in Harvard's International House, which was a safe, exciting, multicultural haven from the seeming brutality that can characterize East Coast living. Our first New England educational moments coincided with the period of forced desegregation of the city of Boston's public schools.

Turning(s)

We survived Cambridge, Massachusetts, returned to England, only to learn that we were moving again – to California, back to the United States. Daddy had been offered an academic medicine position at the University of California, Los Angeles. In preparation for our departure, my English gran would sing "California here I come, right back where I started from, open up those golden gates, California here I come…"

I was about 10 years old when we left rural Nelson, Lancashire, England, where I was obliviously happy. Oblivious in the sense that I do not recall any overt experiences of racism. Retrospectively, however, I do recall my first years at the Anglican school, which my older brother and I attended, wherein as the youngest member of the school, I was treated like a little fuzzy haired, sun-kissed, school mascot of sorts. Older pupils took turns giving me piggy back rides around the tarmac playground.

Under quite stressful circumstances, Mum tried to give me and my three siblings as normal an upbringing as was materially possible. For my older brother Christopher and me, this included horse riding lessons and old-time dancing. In fact, at the time that our family was to emigrate to the United States, having just secured a silver medal, my brother Christopher and I were among the old-time dancing stars of Nelson. I am convinced we were on our way to garnering the gold medal, had the move not interrupted our practice sessions. Needless to say, I was not enthusiastic about yet another migration. At that time, England was my home.

I was then dropped into the middle of pulsating urban West Los Angeles where American school children of many hues deemed me and my siblings simply inappropriate in every way. Wrong hairstyle, funny clothes, and "Why do you talk like that?" I distinctly remember one cheeky classmate of mine named Peter, who derived great pleasure from hearing me say his name – with my "hybrid" English accent, of course! I was a chubby school girl and I used to wear plaits in my hair and silky ribbons to match my unfashionable (by urban Westside LA standards) English ensembles – cardigans, plaid pinafore dresses, knee-high white socks, and sandals – with the toes left in. At recess, Peter's assignment was to yank one of my silky ribbons from my head, dangle it in front of my face and then begin running around the playground. Not to be outdone, I ran after him all the while shouting, "Peetah, Peetah, give me back my ribbon." As per usual, a small crowd of our peers assembled at the edge of the playground quite amused by the spectacle. Years later, I realized Peter fancied me more than the attention he received from his classmates.

There is something to be said for Labov's theories on code-switching (Trudgill 1974). My siblings and I had it down to a fine art. I had learned that the only way I was going to survive on the playgrounds of West Los Angeles was by mutating my vowels and consonants to more approximate an American accent. I learned that my brothers and my sister had taken the linguistic plunge as well. It became our secret, we would speak "American" at school and resort to the "Queen's English" at home under the watchful eye of our quasi-ex-colonial Nigerian father. The worst crime was to be caught "speaking American" at home. We all knew it and we would monitor each other's speech, eavesdrop on telephone conversations, anxious for a slip-up, and the opportunity to turn the culprit into the man who revered *The Oxford English Dictionary* as much if not more than the Bible. Mum was a bit more relaxed. In fact, I noticed her speech patterns slowly shifting under the weight of American assimilation.

Turning(s)

As I have already mentioned, at the age of 10, I terminated full-time childhood residency in England. Although, while gradually becoming Americanized, almost every summer, my family and I still returned to England, where we divided our time equally between my gran in

Birmingham and my grandad in Nelson. However, in 1989, I embarked on an exploratory anthropological journey that would lead to my two-year ethnographic and autobiographical sojourn in Bristol. In 1995, I returned again to Bristol. In 1996, I found my way back to London, the city of my birth, which is where I live at the moment. Being Nigerian–Irish/English–Guyanese and having lived in England, Nigeria and the United States, I am the quintessential product of the "Triangular Trade." I view the world through a kaleidoscope of cultures. Like so many daughters (and sons) of the diaspora(s), I have a historical sense of myself that is rooted in Africa, Europe, the Caribbean and, most recently, North America.

My mother was raised by a White English Geordie mother and a Black Guyanese anglicized father. My Igbo Nigerian father was born and raised an African, which by definition also means partial psychic infiltration by both Mother England during colonialism and Christianity during the reign of the missionaries. Hence, in no particular order, my upbringing was an interesting *mélange* of Victorian English, South Shields Geordie, Onitsha Igbo, Le Guan Guyanese, Anglican Christian, and assimilating Southern California (upper middle-class Jewish West Los Angeles) cultural traditions. Moreover, despite the lure of acculturation and/or assimilation in Los Angeles, I can recall many examples of the ways in which Britannia ruled our roost. For one, the aforementioned codeswitching. Another was the strictly enforced eating with knife and fork at the dinner table.

Turning(s)

Our family had lost all our belongings in the Biafran War. We began the slow recoupment process in England. Through the resilience of my parents, we eventually found our feet again in Southern California. At the moment, my parents live in a verdant, upper-middle-class community in the hills of West Los Angeles, which was predominantly Jewish when I lived there during my formative pre-adolescent and adolescent years. Today, in part, due to the exorbitant real estate prices and unstable economy, there are fewer families with children and more couples without children living in this area. Both my parents are professionals, so one could say that in this country and perhaps in Nigeria, I grew up in an upper middle-class background. However, with the class system or rather the caste system in England, we would probably be considered middle class. Unlike the Horatio Alger myth of economic mobility and success which operates in the United States, in England if one is born into a working-class family, moving out of those ranks is extremely difficult. Being what British society would classify as "Black," compounds the problem. Moreover, in England, despite the existence of the post-Thatcherite *nouveaux riches* and current newfound Blair/Labour-induced economic optimism, rank, particularly in the upper echelons, is still determined by pedigree. On the other hand, in the United

States, the class system is supposedly structured exclusively on the basis of color-blind accumulated capital.

In Bristol, by virtue of my schooling and the way I spoke, most continental African, African Caribbean, South Asian and *métis(se)* people I encountered referred to me as middle class. I was differentially received in White English communities. In middle- and upper-class White English circles, my acceptance was contingent upon my being introduced via mutual White English buffer-friends or acquaintances. Unless I spoke and depending on my manner of dress, at times, working-class White English individuals presumed bi-racialized same-class status. In general, I am conscious of the ways in which my multicultural, transnational upbringings have provided me with access to education, travel and other forms of privilege. While living and working in Bristol, these attributes were an invaluable form of "cultural capital" and facilitated daily travel and negotiations within geographically close but socially and economically segregated communities (Bourdieu 1984).

Turning(s)

While growing up in a predominantly White upper-middle-class Jewish suburban Los Angeles environment, how easy it was for me (and my siblings) to privilege and celebrate my (our) "White English bits" at the expense of my (our) Brown Guyanese and Black Nigerian identities. I regret that until my adult years, save cuisine and the occasional wedding or christening, much of my Nigerian heritage had been submerged or maybe subverted. While Bisi's and Yemi's (two of the women whose stories are featured in Chapters 8 and 9) father's code telephone language was Yoruba, my father's was Igbo. Like the two of them and the rest of my family, I too was able to decipher the gist of the conversation by stringing together the English words that did not have Yoruba, or in our case Igbo, equivalents. Unfortunately, my Father's schedule did not permit Igbo instruction, so until very recently, I have remained mute in my native tongue.

Turning(s)

In 1978, I made a momentous journey with Mum to Guyana to meet the Caribbean branch of our polychromatic family tree. Because my Guyanese grandfather had internalized "the British" in British Guyanese, my close relationship with him ensured that I had much to learn about what it means to be Guyanese in the African Caribbean sense of the term. Hence, the plight, or rather the challenge – some may say the advantage – of being *métisse* and a child of so many diaspora(s).

Turning(s)

I was born in 1963, in Hammersmith, London, England the first daughter of an Irish–English–Guyanese mother and a Nigerian (Igbo/Biafran) father. As I have been researching, ideologies and ambiguities associated with British/English social, cultural and pseudoscientific constructions of "race" and their impact on the lived realities of multiple generations of *métis(se)* people, I have learned a great deal about my own multigenerational, transnational, and multiethnic family. I have an older brother, Christopher, a younger brother David and a younger sister Ann. Each one of us has different emotional and experiential ties to England, not to mention Nigeria, Guyana and the United States. By virtue of genotypic inheritances, each of us also has a different relationship to the phenotypic skins we inhabit. My younger brother David and I are relatively speaking the "darker" members of our family and we have our mum's facial features. On the other hand, my older brother Christopher and my younger sister Ann are "fairer" than we are and have our father's African features.

I am painfully aware of the legacy of pseudoscientific and bi-racialized nineteenth-century rhetoric and the ways in which these hierarchical and oppositional discourses of perceived differences permeate the everyday binary language of Black and *métis(se)* families. We are constantly discussing so and so's "good" and "bad" hair textures, "fair" and "dark" skin complexions, "thin" and "thick" lips, "broad" or "pointy" noses, "African" or "European" bums – the list of qualitative descriptions is endless. This book strives to unravel firmly entrenched filaments of the archaic yet still omnipresent constructs of "race" and color, which are socially reproduced as Black African (self-) hatred and White European (self-) supremacy.

I grew up in two bi-racialized "one drop" societies – the United Kingdom and the United States – as well as in Nigeria. In all three social millieux, Black women (and men) still purchase skin bleach to lighten their skin and women (and men) still chemically relax or weave synthetic or human hair into their beautiful African locks in order to create that "pseudo-European look." I am aware of how easily these insidious concepts seep into people's consciousness and destroy a fundamental love of self.

"What am I going to do with my hair?" I would say. "What have you done to your hair?" my mum would exclaim. Up until this past year when I decided to reclaim my naturally "kinky" hair, I, too, was enslaved by my locks. In Europe, North America, the Caribbean and even South Africa, I have spent many hours in numerous Black hair salons attempting to tame what I was conditioned to believe were "nappy" and unattractive tresses. In fact, those who have known me over the years can trace the emergence, the lapses and the resurgence of my political consciousness by the particular hairstyles I have sported: relaxed, curly perm, short and natural, braids with extensions and the ultimate – almost bald. Today, under the loving and gentle care of Ms Margaret Inniss, hair stylist/braider and *confidante extraordinaire*, I have been slowly coaxing my locks back into either tight Senegalese twists or tiny braids.

Turning(s)

Genealogical and folkloric information about the maternal side of my family I acquired over many cups of tea with my Geordie gran in Birmingham, while she was still alive. However, even before my discussions with Gran, that 1978 trip to LeGuan, Guyana with my mum, the year after the Jonestown massacre, convinced me that "racial" and ethnic intermingling had taken place for multiple generations on my grandad's side. I met aunts, uncles, cousins and other relations who ranged in appearance from cinnamon-colored Amerindian to pink-skinned, blonde-haired blue-eyed Dutch. As it happens, my Guyanese grandad who married my English gran was allegedly himself *métis*. Although I never met him, according to my gran, my great-grandfather was Scottish. On that journey, I did meet my great-grandmother and my namesake, who, although I did not know it at the time, was supposedly Amerindian, transplanted LeGuan African and East Indian.

Turning(s)

Piecing together the paternal Nigerian side is less straightforward, since it is partially based on conjecture – phenotypic evidence and informal family historical sleuthing. My paternal Papa was an Igbo chief; my paternal Mama was also Igbo. I continue to investigate my father's side of the family in an attempt to discern whether his very fair *oyingbo* complexion,[7] red hair and brown eyes, and that of three out of four of his siblings are a result of what some people would refer to as natural variation. Contrary to what many people may believe, he is not an albino. Whenever European men and continental African women, as one example of many, come into contact with each other there are likely to be voluntary or involuntary sexual interactions. In the case of my father and his siblings, I have reason to believe that two generations or more before my father's birth, a missionary encounter on either Papa's or Mama's side added a bit of cream to the coffee, and resulted in my father's pink skin, reddish hair and light-brown eyes. Or, as my brother Chris says, "Somebody hopped the fence." The fact that Papa was a chief means that his family would have had more contact with British missionaries. As already mentioned, enhanced by the Scottish, Irish and the English on my mum's side, both my brother Chris and my sister Ann have also reproduced Daddy's coloring.

Turning(s)

While still living in Bristol, I remember a conversation I had with some of what Bristol-based sociologist Steve Fenton refers to as the "YBI" (Young Black Intelligentsia). I had just seen John Akomfrah's 1992 film *A Touch of the Tar Brush*, which interrogates taken-for-granted notions of Englishness and presumptions that being English is synonymous with being White. My sister-in-law Shauna was pregnant with my nephew, David Aaron, Jr. I described the baby's pedigree for the group – Tanzanian, German, African American, Cherokee, Nigerian, Irish, English and Guyanese. Beyond the designated conventional one drop category Black, we speculated about how to name and locate this prospective multinational and multiethnic child. Without missing a beat, Devon said, "Why, he/she will be English of course!"

Turning(s)

When I reflect on my studies at the University of California, Berkeley, one aspect of my postgraduate student life I thoroughly enjoyed was attending talks by various visiting professors. Not long after returning from Bristol, at the School of Education, I attended a lecture by English sociologist Paul Willis. Afterwards, using a mutual friend as an entree, I introduced myself. While I was talking with him, I noticed that there was a rather puzzled expression on his face. I suddenly realized that, like so many other transatlantic linguistic monitors, he was trying "to place my accent" – by now among other influences an odd mixture of Bristolian English and Berkeley Californian. Eventually he exclaimed, "I cannot figure out if you are American or English!" "Well," I replied, "to be precise I am Americanized Nigerian–Irish–English–Guyanese." At which point, he said, "Today, that means English."

Turning(s)

In Berkeley, California, while writing up my Ph.D. dissertation, I made my usual nocturnal run to the local 7–11 convenience shop for a fix of a vice I had acquired while writing – 44 ounces of a healthy cocktail of aspartame-laced diet sodas – caffeine-free Diet Coke, Diet Coke and Diet Pepsi – also known as "the Big Gulp" and at the time it cost precisely 96 cents. Anyway, before leaving the shop, I completed my second ritual, which entailed perusing the newstand for any relevant headlines. Staring back at me was a special issue of *Time* magazine.[8] It had a red cover with a picture of a very attractive woman on it. By the woman's face, the copy read: "Take a good look at this woman. She was created by a computer from a mix of several races. What you see is a remarkable preview of..." And underneath her face

39

and the title of the special issue were the words: "The New Face of America: How Immigrants are Shaping the World's First Multicultural Society."

This special edition of *Time* is yet another example of the dangerous ways in which confused media such as the active imaginations of Madison Avenue advertising executives induce fantasies about a future replete with inter-racial cyborgs. Yet, as discussed in Chapter 1, the notion of biological "hybridity" is itself problematic. The presumption here is that the "races" that are being mixed are themselves discrete and pure. Moreover, as to be expected, there is a conflation of constructs of "race," nationality, ethnicity and culture and, of course, the image of immigrant as interloper is propagated. One need only stroll down the streets of Berkeley, California or Bristol, England to be reminded of the obvious: these heralded acts of so-called transracial transgression actually transpired long before they were re-invented by the American (and British) media.[9] And this "old story" continues...

Locating the critical feminist auto-ethnographer

> We cannot escape our origins however hard we try, those origins which contain the key – could we but find it – to all that we later become.
>
> (Baldwin 1955: 27)

"Where are you from?"

On an empowered day, I describe myself as a diaspora(s) daughter with multiple migratory and ancestral reference points in Nigeria, Ireland, England, Guyana and the United States. On a disempowered day, I am a nationless nomad who wanders from destination to destination in search of a singular site to name as home.

Writing home/no fixed address/reconfiguring the English–African Diaspora

An important and ongoing discussion among historians provides the theoretical backdrop for the second half of this chapter. That is, certain scholars refute the notion that it was the dispersal of continental Africans during the transatlantic slave trade that created the first and only significant African diasporic rupture. Although arguably the most socially and culturally disruptive, the forced migration of continental Africans for the purposes of labor exploitation was not the first African Diaspora. Cheik Anta Diop (1991), Ivan Van Sertima (1976) and Runoko Rashidi (1992), among other revisionist scholars, have provided ample historical and archeological evidence that continental Africans circumnavigated the globe – the New World in general and the Americas in particular – many centuries before the celebrated journey of Christopher Columbus among other explorers. These scholarly interventions pave the way for re-conceptualizations of contemporary (pre- and post-Columbus) African diasporas. In turn, these periodized reformulations of African diaspora(s) carve out cogent spaces for contemporary discourses on the English–African diaspora. In particular, as I have defined it, the English–African Diaspora conventionally comprises African post-colonial constituents from the Caribbean, North and Latin America, and continental Africa who find themselves in England for labor, schooling, political asylum, and frequently, by birth.

In the English–African Diaspora, the idea of "home" has particular layered, textured and contradictory meanings for *métis(se)* individuals. In a travel essay chronicaling his re-discovery of Britain, Black Nigerian and White English writer Adewale Maja-Pearce wages existential war with the meaning of "home" as it is experienced as competing and conflicting bi-racialized nationalisms:

> I had to learn as best I could to be at home, but even the word "home" had complex connotations. Where was home? Was it Nigeria, my father's country? Or was it Britain, my mother's country? And how far did allegiance to the one involve a betrayal of the other? My inability to see was inseparable from the sense of betrayal.
>
> If I didn't look, if I didn't admit the reality of the particular corner of the world in which I happened to be in this case Britain – "The blessed plot, this earth, this realm, this England" – then I couldn't properly live here. This in turn meant that I was released from the necessity of confronting the nature of my allegiance because to admit Britain, to say that I was British was to deny Nigeria. I was like a man married to one woman but trying to remain faithful to another. If I wasn't careful I would lose both, and in the end I would be the one to suffer for it: to live like this is to condemn oneself to a half-life, which is the predicament of the outsider.
>
> (Maja-Pearce 1990: 12–13)

In his personal exploration, Maja-Pearce (1990) laments "the half-life of the outsider" and in so doing he articulates the complex nature of belonging for other transnational *(métis(se))* subjects. In addition, he conveys a broader collective African diasporic consciousness forged from the lived realities and the legacies of interwoven (post-)colonial histories characterized by racism, sexism, class discrimination, ethnocentrism and other forms of oppression (Gilroy 1993). Somers and Gibson would refer to these individual/collective testimonials as "public narratives...those narratives attached to cultural and institutional formations larger than the single individual, to intersubjective networks or institutions, however local or grand, micro or macro" (Somers and Gibson 1994: 62). Locating *métis(se)* declarations in spatial, temporal, and indeed multiple African diasporic contexts, Boyce-Davies's conception of migratory subjectivity is also relevant: "as elsewhere denotes movement...asserts agency as it crosses the borders, journeys, migrates and so re-claims as it re-asserts" (Boyce-Davies 1994: 37).

These transnational alliances are predicated on the profound paradoxes of citizenship (Gilroy 1996; Cohen 1994). Though daughters and sons of Africa's various diasporas are living in England, they must acknowledge the actual and significant impact of White English exclusionary practices on reconstructions of cultural and transnational local identities (Mercer 1994). Stuart Hall refers to this ongoing psychopolitical project as "Identity Politics One":

> the first form of identity politics. It had to do with the constitution of some defensive collective identity against the practices of racist society. It had to do with the fact that people were being blocked out of and refused an identity and identification within the majority nation, having to find some other roots on which to stand.
>
> (Hall 1991: 41–68)

The outcome of the prescribed specificity of White Englishness is that Black sons and daughters of the English–African Diaspora are denied full citizenship (Hall 1996). The one drop rule also means that *métis(se)* children with White English mothers or fathers are also denied access to an English identity that they can rightfully claim on the basis of parentage.

As we approach the twenty-first century, there are at least several ongoing and unresolved political debates. First, should English-born Black people, *métis(se)* or with both parents from either continental Africa or the Caribbean, demand to be included under the pre-existing English umbrella? Alternatively, as children of a global African diaspora, should they carve out a separate space wherein they acknowledge links and foster social, cultural and political allegiances with other diasporic constituents in the United States, Canada, Brazil, the Caribbean, among other points on the globe? From the vantage point of agency and not victimization, is there some way of reconciling their subjugated connections with former Empire, which will then enable them, whether *métis(se)* or not, to proudly wear the badge of belonging to/in England? Most importantly, are indigenous White English residents prepared to re-define what it means to be English in order to include on equal footing both *métis(se)* as well as English-born children of so-called immigrant parents, whose natal origins are South Asian, Caribbean or continental African? As the year 2000 approaches, as a nation, England has yet to crack these conundrums.

As cultural critiques, the testimonies of the six *métisse* women tackle these transnationalist complex concerns. The women's stories also chart what Ang-Lygate refers to as "the spaces of (un)location where the shifting and contextual meanings of diaspora reside – caught somewhere between, and inclusive of the more familiar experiences of (re)location and (dis)location" (Ang-Lygate 1997: 170). However, as cumulative text, their individual evocations also illustrate the collective psychosocial problematics of a wider African diaspora(s)' angst in its specific geopolitical manifestations (Hesse 1993). In the conclusion to their edited collection, *Place and the Politics of Identity*, Pile and Keith indirectly legitimate the (English–African Diaspora) as a shifting political space where senses of place are (re)negotiated and identities are (re)constructed:

> spatiality needs to be seen as the modality through which contradictions are normalized, naturalized and neutralized. Politics is necessarily territorial but these territories are simultaneously real, imaginary and symbolic...spatiality should simultaneously express people's experiences of, for example, displacement (feeling out of place), dislocation (relating to alienation) and fragmentation (the jarring multiple identities). Spatialities represent both the spaces between multiple identities and the contradictions within identities.
>
> (Pile and Keith 1993: 224–5)

Despite, or perhaps because of, my own itinerant *métis(se)* African diasporic family background prior to 1989, my cultural perception of my birthplace and former home was, if not predominantly White, most definitely English.[10] However, in the Summer of 1989, I flew to England. This time, I returned on my own and on my own terms. At the point of my arrival, I did not realize that I would depart three years later with the beginnings of a critical autoethnography:

> critical ethnographies provide another genre wherein the represented culture is located within a larger historical, political, economic, social and symbolic context than is said to be recognized by cultural members...autoethnographies have emerged in which the culture of the writer's own group is textualized. Such writings often offer a passionate, emotional voice of a positioned and explicitly judgemental fieldworker and thus obliterate the

customary and ordinarily, rather mannerly distinction between the researcher and the researched.

(Van Maanen 1995: 9–10)

Nor could I anticipate the profound ways in which I would be forced "to step in and step out" (Powdermaker 1966: 15–16) of roles while simultaneously resisting the insider/outsider label of "inappropriate Other":

> The moment the insider steps out from the inside she's no longer a mere insider. She necessarily looks in from the outside while also looking out from the inside. Not quite the same, not quite the other, she stands in that undetermined threshold place where she constantly drifts in and out. Undercutting the inside/outside opposition, her intervention is necessarily that of both not quite an insider and quite an outsider. She is, in other words, this inappropriate other or same who moves about with always at least two gestures: that of affirming "I am like you" while persisting in her difference and that of reminding "I am different" while unsettling every definition of otherness arrived at.
>
> (Minh-ha 1990: 374–5)

For the first time my plan was not to visit family, but rather to do exploratory research for my impending Ph.D. thesis, which, at that stage, would be examining the emergence of political consciousness among Black youth in England. This critical feminist ethnographic work would take me out of the primarily "lily-White" English working-class and middle-class communities, which reflected my early childhood, and into the more ethnically and so-called racially mixed but not necessarily more harmonious communities in Manchester, Birmingham, London and Bristol:

> It is, however, clear that in specific contexts some forms of difference may be more important than others. It follows from this that the interrelations between the various forms of difference will always require specifications in given historical contexts. We cannot assume we know the significance of any particular set of intersections between class, race and gender prior to our analysis of these intersections. The task for feminist anthropologists, as for scholars in other disciplines, is to find ways of theorizing these highly variable intersections between the various forms of difference.
>
> (Moore 1988: 197)

In short, according to Marcus and Fischer, what I was attempting was an anthropological "repatriation" with cultural critique as my motivation

(Marcus and Fischer 1986: 111). It was then that I first experienced the English–African Diaspora.

Points of entry/sites of convergences

In the United States, I had conducted extensive ethnographic research on cultural constructions of adulthood for African American young men and women. In their homes in the context of extended families, in schools, in community centers, or just "hangin' out," they told me what it was like to be a young African American man or woman living in a legislated social context wherein the criteria for adult status differed remarkably from their own conceptions. I had worked most extensively with young African American women, many of whom were young mothers. I also discovered that popular culture, in the form of then burgeoning rap music, was another important way to understand African American youth cultures. I was particularly interested in young women rappers' roles in this sociopolitical movement, and was already convinced that their songs offered both political commentary and cultural critique.

With the African Diaspora as the framework, I planned to look comparatively at the lived experiences of African American youth in the Bay Area in California, USA, which I had already done, and the lives of African Caribbean young people in Bristol, England my proposed research project. In Spring 1990, I arrived in Bristol and began acquainting myself with the young people in Thatchapee, the community I had chosen to plant myself in. Most of the youth I encountered in these various contexts were very friendly and seemed interested in talking with someone who would leave America to come to this "Debi Debi" (naff, awful) place. However, over time, these same young people expressed no interest in officially participating in my project. In fact, in so many words they said, "Jayne, we enjoy talking with you, but we have no interest in your project." I could not hide my disappointment nor my frustration. Though, I was somewhat relieved since, despite the comradeship created by both my personality as well as my direct connection to the heralded "States," I still detected a certain amount of social distance between us – one that I sensed time would not bridge. This was brought on by the age difference, at times gender, culture, perceived power differential with my role as voluntary youth worker and social class:

> "Cultures" do not hold still for their portraits. Attempts to make them do so always involve simplification and exclusion, selection of a temporal focus, the construction of a particular self–other relationship, and the imposition or negotiation of a power relationship.
>
> (Clifford 1986: 10)

My favorite expression while living there and one that I still use today is: "As you see, so are you seen." I think this revelation is the most fascinating aspect of doing ethnographic fieldwork. For me, it became the turning point of my research. When I returned to England, I did not have a clear sense as to how I would refer to myself, whether I would identify as American or British. Until I got to know people, they decided for me. I was "that American gyal." Having said that, the injuries of race and color were omnipresent in Thatchapee. I was also referred to as "that red-skinned American gyal" or less frequently "that half-caste American gyal." These last two expressions were meant to mark my light skin and my presumed *métisse* status. Because of the bi-racialized politics of colonialism, residents of Thatchapee assumed, and usually rightly so, that any light-skinned person was *métis(se)*. Although this assumption was complicated by the fact that in a genealogical sense, most of the residents from the African Caribbean were themselves *métis(se)*.

Who is on the ethnographic fringes depends on who is defining the center:

> Ethnography is actively situated *between* powerful systems of meaning. It poses its questions at the boundaries of civilizations, cultures, classes, races and gender. Ethnography decodes and recodes, telling the grounds of collective order and diversity, inclusion and exclusion. It describes processes of innovation and structuration, and is itself part of these processes.
>
> (Clifford 1986: 2–3)

On my daily travels, in addition to the young people, I found myself meeting people from every segment of both Bristolian and Thatchapee societies. However, I found that I made the most profound connections with individuals who lived life at what Anzaldua (1987) would refer to as "the borderlands." Deemed "marginal" people, those presumed to be on the edge, seemingly unbelonging, these men, women and children were generally *métis(se)*. Some of them I never even actually spoke with. We communicated in our silences. I eventually decided to go with the proverbial flow and focus on the poetics and politics of what I was then calling "mixed race" identities thereby producing a microethnography:

> Also known as focused or specific ethnography, microethnography zeroes in on particular settings (cultural events or "scenes") drawing on the ways that a cultural ethos is reflected in microcosm in selected aspects of everyday life but giving emphasis to particular behaviors in particular settings rather than attempting to portray a whole cultural system.
>
> (Wolcott 1995: 102)

After some thought, more than twenty-five *métis(se) griot(tes)* wanted to testify. However, demands of daily life affected each person's ability to commit to the project.

The primary twenty-five testimonies of redemption came from (a) *métis(se)* people from diverse social worlds whom I had met along the first year of my journey; (b) others from people I knew such as social workers, teachers, youth workers, artists who were not necessarily *métis(se)* but who knew people who might want to participate; and (c) others still from other *métis(se)* friends of participants. For at least two reasons, those I did speak with convinced me of the importance of this undertaking. First, embarking on such an endeavor would force a creative tension between the process of doing "insider/outsider" anthropology and the product, an ethnography that perpetuates the cultural anthropological remit: "interest in other peoples and their ways of life and concern to explain them within a frame of reference that includes ourselves" (Hymes 1974: 11). Second, "getting the news out" (Wolf 1992: 1) would bring to life the words of novelist Michelle Cliff: "We are not exotic – or aromatic – or poignant. We are not aberrations. We are ordinary. All this has happened before" (Cliff 1980: 7).

Project participants' local synthesized individual and collective voices represent the significant part of a greater multigenerational whole comprising people in England with Black continental African or African Caribbean fathers *and* White British or continental European mothers. More pointedly, in general, they map the specificities of the local, yet they also problematize the parameters and boundaries delimiting the local and the global:

the local exists nowhere in a pure state...the local is only a fragmented set of possibilities that can be articulated into a momentary politics of time and place...this is to take the local not as the end point but as the start. This is not to idealize the local as the real, but to look at the ways in which injustices are naturalized in the name of the immediate. In conceiving of the local as a nodal point, we can begin to deconstruct its movements and its meanings.

(Probyn 1990: 187)

In particular, the six *métisse* women's living stories meld the macrostructural bi-racialized and gendered processes of diasporic and indigenous English histories with the microstructural concerns of identity politics as they are manifest, negotiated and reinvented through the simultaneous prisms of gender, generation, "race," class and ethnicity.

Notes

1 Mindful of the ongoing debates as to what constitute feminism(s), I have chosen Barbara Smith's definition of feminism as my working definition: "The political theory and practice that struggles to free all women: women of color, working class women, poor women, disabled women, lesbians, old women as well as white economically privileged heterosexual women" (Smith 1990 "Racism and women's studies" in G. Anzaldua (ed.) *Making Face, Making Soul*, San Francisco, CA: Aunt Lute Press, p. 25).

2 See Flora Nwapa (1980) *Wives at War*, Enugu: Tana Press; Sonia Bleeker (1969) *The Ibo of Biafra*, New York: William and Morrow; Chinua Achebe (1983) *The Trouble with Nigeria*, Oxford: Heinemann; C. Ojukwu (1969) *Biafra*, New York: Perennial; Arthur Nwankwo (1972) *Nigeria: The Challenge of Biafra*, London: Rex Collings; Elechi Amadi (1973) *Sunset in Biafra*, London: Heinemann; Rex Niven (1970) *The War of Nigerian Unity*, London: Evans Brothers; Dan Jacobs (1987) *The Brutality of Nations*, New York: Paragon; Chukwumeka Ike (1976) *Sunset at Dawn*, London: Fontana; Frederick Forsyth (1969) *The Making of an African Legend: The Biafra Story*, Harmondsworth: Penguin; Buchi Emecheta (1986) *Head Above Water: An Autobiography*, London: Fontana. For a compelling fictionalized account of the impact of the war on two families, see Anne Giwa-Amu (1996) *Sade*, London: Ace.

3 Dan Jacobs, author of *The Brutality of Nations* (see note 2) visited my father in Biafra and reported the results of a survey my father had conducted on famine-induced starvation:

> Ifekwunigwe found in March 1968 that, during this early period of starvation, 89 percent of those affected were children under five years of age, while the remaining eleven percent were children five to fifteen. This resulted from a shortage of protein foods, as small children need proportionately more protein for their growing bodies than do adults. Later, however, the elderly would be affected, and the following year, when carbohydrates would be in short supply as well, all age groups would suffer malnutrition and starvation.
>
> (Jacobs 1987: 313)

4 While reading an earlier version of this manuscript, my mum insisted that it was my older brother Christopher and not I who vomited on the steps. However, there are several versions to every story, and I did not let my mother deter me. The fact that I remembered and believed my retelling of the story to be the truth seemed most important.

5 In 1992, not long after leaving Bristol to return to Berkeley, I met someone from England and he informed me that Nelson, one of my many former home towns, has one of the highest suicide rates in Britain. This information nearly spoiled my sugar-coated memories of life there.

6 The precise date of his return is fuzzy to me. However, on my last visit to Los Angeles I acquired an old local (Nelson, Lancashire) newspaper clipping from my mother. Dated January 30 1970, it discloses the contents of a letter from Lord Hunt, leader of the official British Government fact-finding party in Biafra: "This is just to say that Aaron is well and doing a magnificent job caring for some 1,500 children in the hospital. He has faced grave danger and has remained at his post when other doctors fled."

7 (also *oyigbo*) An Igbo colloquial expression which means "White person" or "European person." When we traveled back to Nigeria with our father, we were implicated as *oyingbos* as well.

8 Fall, 1993 *Time* Special Issue, "The New Face of America: How Immigrants Are Shaping the World's First Multicultural Society."

9 Gary Younge "Beige Britain," the *Guardian*, May 22 1997.

10 Two of the major assumptions I intend to challenge in this book is that Whiteness is the normative and naturalized signifier by which deviations of Blackness are determined as well as the presumption that Englishness is synonymous with Whiteness. See Chapter 10 for an extensive discussion of these problematics.

3

SETTING THE STAGE: INVOKING THE *GRIOT(TE)* TRADITIONS AS TEXTUAL STRATEGIES

Nkolika
It is better to recount what happened than to have perished.

(Igbo proverb)[1]

Setting

Cultural identity...is a matter of "becoming" as well as "being." It belongs to the future as much as to the past. It is not something which already exists, transcending place, time, history and culture. Cultural identities come from somewhere, have histories. But, like everything which is historical, they undergo constant transformation. Far from being eternally fixed in some essentialized past, they are subject to the continuous "play" of history, culture and power. Far from being grounded in a mere "recovery" of the past, which is waiting to be found, and which when found, will secure our sense of ourselves into eternity, identities are the names we give to the different ways we are positioned by and position ourselves within the narratives of the past.

(Hall 1990: 225)

Until recently, demographic statistics point to the fact that the majority of English born *métis(se)* children have White birth mothers (Owen 1997). The group of individuals I spoke with reflect this trend. There are serious policy implications that stem from this seemingly innocent statistical fact. Although it was not the focus of my particular research, I am mindful that as a matter of urgency, researchers need to address the psychosocial implications of the fact that many *métis* men, including those with whom I spoke, have not been fathered by their continental African, African Caribbean or

50

African American birth fathers. There is a gaping hole in the literature on "Black" masculinities, which could be filled by a critical exploration of the lived experiences of *métis* men who were raised by White English women. In Chapter 10, I begin a woman-centered discussion of the bi-racialized mothering paradox that the dictates of the one drop rule create. That is, if they raise them, White birth mothers of *métisse* daughters are said to be in fact caring for "Black" daughters. More feminist and psychoanalytical research needs to explore the implications of this mothering project for the pyschosocial wellbeing of *métisse* women. Social and historical research also needs to unearth the stories of continental African male students (Nigerian and Ghanaian men in particular) who fathered *métis(se)* children in England and then returned to their countries of origin. Some of these individuals already had continental African wives and children "back home."

The birth fathers of the twenty-five project participants represent continental African, Caribbean African and American (African) diaspora(s). The birth mothers of the sixteen women and nine men with whom I spoke come from England, Scotland, Ireland, Germany, Trinidad and Jamaica. The age of the primary participants ranged from 13 to 45. To maintain their anonymity, with the exception of Andrew and Yemi, all respondents chose to fictionalize their names. Within the narrative Chapters 4 to 9 that follow, unless otherwise stated, I have also fictionalized all identifying place names and individuals.

The sixteen women

Sharon's birth mother is English and her birth father is Ghanaian. She grew up in long-term foster care with a White English family in a racially isolated working-class community in the north of England.

Claudia's birth mother is Scottish and her birth father is Nigerian. She was adopted by a White English middle-class family and was raised "White" in the north of England.

Zaynab's birth mother is English and her birth father is Nigerian. She was born in Bristol and was adopted by a White English middle-class family.

Janice was adopted by a White middle-class English family in Croydon. Her birth mother is English and her birth father is from Dominica.

Ruby's birth mother is English and her birth father is Nigerian. She was raised in a children's home in suburban London.

Similola's birth mother is German and her birth father is Tanzanian. She was also raised in a children's home outside Cardiff, Wales.

51

Delia's birth mother is English and her birth father is Nigerian she was raised in a children's home in the north of England.

Elise grew up middle class in South London with both her Scottish birth mother and her Jamaican birth father.

Harmony grew up middle class in Bristol with her birth mother who is English and without her birth father who is from Ghana.

Lena grew up working class in Birmingham with her English birth mother and without her Nigerian birth father.

Akousa and **Sarah** are sisters. They grew up in a working-class African Caribbean community in Liverpool with their Irish birth mother and without their Bajan (from Barbados) father.

Bambi grew up middle class outside London with her Trinidadian mother and without her White American father.

Yemi and **Bisi** are sisters. They grew up middle class in Ibadan, Nigeria with their English birth mother and their Nigerian (Yoruba) birth father.

Twilight was born in Jamaica to middle-class multigenerational *métis(se)* parents. She spent her formative years in Jamaica and England.

The nine men

Andrew's birth mother is English and his birth father is Ghanaian. He spent his childhood in middle-class Ghana with his father and in working-class Bristol, England with his mother and at times, in foster care.

Charles grew up middle class in the north of England and in Ghana at times without his Ghanaian birth father and with his English birth mother.

Red is Bambi's husband. He grew up middle class in various cities in both England and the United States, at times without his African American birth father and with his English birth mother.

Cyrus grew up middle class in North London without his Nigerian father and with his English birth mother.

Clive also grew up middle class in North London with both his Jamaican father and his English mother.

Ossie grew up working class in South London with both his Guyanese birth father and his English birth mother.

Louie grew up in working-class Manchester without his Nigerian birth father and with his English birth mother.

Leo grew up in working-class Liverpool without his Jamaican birth father and with his English birth mother.

Oliver's birth father is from Barbados and his birth mother is English. He was brought up in racial isolation by a middle-class adoptive White English family.

With the exception of Bristol-born Zaynab, Harmony and Andrew, everyone I spoke with was born and had come of age elsewhere (i.e. in the UK: London, Birmingham, Liverpool, Manchester, Newcastle, Glasgow, Cardiff; as well as the United States, Nigeria, Ghana, and Jamaica). However, during that two-year-long pregnant postmodern moment, we were all living in Bristol, England, which was the point of convergence for us all and the site for many collaborative exchanges and debates on the existential and dialectical nature of bi-racialized and gendered *métis(se)* be-longings in the English–African Diaspora. As Boyce-Davies asserts: "An intersection may be encountered as a site of conflict, confusion, anger or may be seen as a nexus of engagement, a growth of specific identity and creativity" (Boyce-Davies 1994: 57).

Together we crafted narratives of belongings for future generations of *métis(se)* children and adults in England:

> The margins, our sites of survival, become our fighting grounds and their site for pilgrimage. Thus, while we turn around and reclaim them as our exclusive territory, they happily approve, for the divisions between the margin and center should be preserved, and as clearly demarcated as possible, if the two positions are to remain intact in their power relations...the work space and the space of creation is where she [or he] confronts and leaves off at the same time a world of named nooks and corners, of street signs and traffic regulations, of beaten paths and multiple masks, of constant intermeshing with other bodies – that are also her own – needs, assumptions, prejudices and limits.
>
> (Minh-ha 1991: 17/26)

Participants found their way to Bristol either for work, education or for personal reasons. Their current geopolitical subject positions can only be articulated in light of the city of Bristol's previous involvement with the slave trade. This unspoken association mirrors the uneasy historical relationship other English–African Diaspora constituents have with the former British Empire: "They see their place in the metropolis as the inevitable consequence of an earlier act of trespass and transgression" (Oguibe 1994: xx). Similarly, Gilroy adds:

> It starts from recognition of the African Diaspora's peculiar position as "step-children" of the West and of the extent to which our imaginations are conditioned by an enduring proximity to regimes of racial terror...it seeks deliberately to exploit the distinctive qualities of perception that DuBois identified long ago as "double consciousness".
>
> (Gilroy 1993a: 14)

I collected the original narratives in Bristol via open-ended tape-recorded interviews, between 1990 and 1992: "Much of human communication takes place in the realm of the non-verbal...in the space between the lines" (Jones 1994: 5). Participation in this project consisted of respondents providing me with a series of tape-recorded testimonies about their childhood, gender politics, racial and ethnic identity, class background, nationalism, family, sexuality, creativity, parenting and racism, among a variety of topics. The *métisse* women's and *métis* men's contributions consisted of a series of open-ended audiotaped testimonies. I acquired separate *cahiers* (notebooks) for each *griotte/griot* and I used them to record my responses to each of their storytelling sessions as well as to keep track of all of the questions generated from each session of listening.

By the time the edited testimonies appeared as text, I had listened to them in full four times. The first time was immediately after each session. While their voices were still singing in my head, I formulated questions that were in direct response to their testimonies. These questions would serve as a guide, not as the basis, for the next storytellying session. I repeated this approach until the participants had finished testifying, at which point we had sucessfully reached the core or the marrow – what was/is significant to each one of them in their everyday lives. I refer to this interview technique as the "artichoke method." The ethnographer has to peel off several layers of skin before the heart of the matter is revealed. Upon finishing the sessions, I listened to every single testimony again for insights and patterns. The third listening entailed labor-intensive transcription, which was at times encumbered by regionally specific accents. The final listening was for clarification and verification of specific segments of testimonies.

From the first to the fourth listening, so much was undoubtedly lost in committing oral performance to tape, and then translating the tapes to text: the cadence and rhythm of the *griottes/griots* regionally specific accents, the visual beauty carved out in detail on their "EuroAfrican" faces, and the cultural *métissage*, which manifests itself in both their living spaces and sociocultural worlds. However, it was at the final stage, that I realized that I had far too much rich and evocative material to work with and that I would have to wittle down my original focus to one or more key themes. When I began the process of writing, I confirmed for myself what I had suspected earlier – there was no way that I could adequately do justice to all twenty-five life stories. Including them all in the final "polythesis," which ethnographic film-maker David MacDougall (1993) refers to as "an inter-play of voices" – and I add ideas – would have been a lengthy process and one that would ultimately have resulted in my truncating their experiences. I tried working with fifteen, then nine and then finally six.

The task of selecting the final six was not an easy one. All twenty-five were eloquent and engaging storytellers. In order to produce a coherent final product that neither fragmented nor trivialized the lived experiences of the individuals I had worked with, I needed to narrow the focus. The pivotal issue that reappeared in all of my exchanges with participants was the ways in which over time and across disparate spaces individuals devised strategies to reconcile the psychic split between their genealogical holistic transna-tional sense of themselves and bi-racialized fragmented socially mediated ideas of self. I was particularly interested in the centrality of their White mothers in the retelling of their life stories.

In order to highlight the problematic bi-racialized relationship between White mothers and one drop rule "Black" daughters in particular, first the polythesis and now this text feature the narratives of six women – two sets of sisters and two women who had grown up in care with what I refer to as mother surrogates. Speaking with two sets of biological sisters enabled me to illustrate the similar and different pathways to womanhood forged by two *métisse* daughters growing up with the same White mother. In the midst of the then burgeoning Black Power Movement, Akousa and Sarah were raised in Liverpool by a working-class White Irish mother and without their Black Bajan father. Yemi and Bisi were brought up in Nigeria during the turbu-lent post-colonial 1960s and neocolonial 1970s by middle-class parents – in particular, a Northumberland White English mother and a Yoruba Black father. Ruby, Nigerian and English and Similola, Tanzanian and German, spent their formative years in care in middle-class, all-White English or Welsh children's homes outside London and Cardiff, respectively. They were each socialized by "mother surrogates" prior to the explosive debates about welfare policy as it pertains to transracial fosterage, placement and adoption.

As a Nigerian–Irish/English–Guyanese anthropologist, my own auto-ethnographic narrative, which unfolds in Nigeria, Lancashire, England and Los Angeles, California, is also interwoven with their stories to create a Bakhtinian "dialogic" patchwork: "Each story is re-created in the interaction between teller and listener. It is their relationship which causes a particular tale to come to life" (Gersie and King 1990: 32). Ethnographic fieldwork then becomes a series of conversations wherein according to Bakhtin, "language lies on the borderline between oneself and the other...the word in language is half someone else's" (Bakhtin 1953/1981: 293). In so doing, I purposely challenge conventional ethnography and tackle phenomenological and epistemological concerns associated with prior conceptualizations of diaspora(s), race, nation, gender, generation, identity and, most notably, family. Consequently, as insider and outsider, I blur the boundaries between subjective experience and objective social scientific inquiry: "Boundary-drawing around colonial space(s), then, is less an exercise in taxonomy than a politics of representation. Boundary-marking effects on races, subjects, narratives, and the academy" (Tiffen and Lawson 1994: 234).

The stage

> Ritual theatre, let it be recalled, establishes the spatial medium not merely as a physical area for simulated events but as a manageable contraction of the cosmic envelope within which man (and woman) – no matter how deeply buried such a consciousness has lately become – fearfully exists. And this attempt to manage the immensity of his (her) spatial awareness makes every manifestation in ritual theatre a paradigm for the cosmic human condition.
>
> (Soyinka 1978: 41)

In *Presentation of Self in Everyday Life*, sociologist Erving Goffman's (1959) seminal work on self formation and presentation as performance, he uses the analogy of the theater to describe the ways in which individuals manage their identities in social milieux. Accordingly, there is "front stage" behavior and "back stage" behavior. In the equally important treatise *Black Skin, White Masks*, psychiatrist Frantz Fanon (1967), exposes the psychic blurring of self and other as Black ("Negro") identities are distorted by the lenses of the White imperialist gaze. *Beyond the Masks* by feminist theorist Amina Mama (1995) explores the historical and pyschosocial processes of gendered and racialized subjectivities. In *Shadow and Act*, Ralph Ellison describes the ways in which African American entertainers "in order to enact a symbolic role basic to the underlying drama of American society assume a ritual mask" (Ellison 1953: 47). Cultural historian Becky Hall reenacts a similar feminist psychodrama:

> Fascinated by the materiality of black skin and the discursive production of "race", it is through my own body that I investigate the fantasies of blackness and whiteness troubling the English cultural imagination that is also my own.
>
> (Hall 1996: 164)

I incorporate all of these voices and argue that as social actresses the six women I spoke with perform different dialectical dramas within the private domain among their immediate and extended multidimensional families and in the realm of the public amid the essentializing and homogenizing gazes of society writ large:

> If we analyze those people and actions by linear models, we will create dichotomies, ambiguities, cognitive dissonance, disorientation, and confusion in places where none exist. If, however, we follow the cultural guides which (African–American) women have left us, we can allow the way in which they saw and constructed their own lives to provide the analytical framework by which we attempt to understand their experiences and their world.
>
> (Barkley Brown 1989: 929)

Invoking the *griot(te)* traditions as textual strategies

Extending Barkley Brown's metaphor, the process of writing an ethnography is akin to quilt-making. I have all of these seemingly disparate bits and pieces in the form of participants' testimonies, my own cumulative scratchings, as well as different theoretical strands and I wish to stitch all of them together to form a coherent pattern. Hence, the primary objective of this chapter is to provide the rationale for my appropriation of the West African oral tradition of the *griot(te)*. *Griotte* as it appears in the feminine form is a West African, Senegalese – that is Wolof – term that describes a traditional storyteller. However, though they may not be specifically named *griots*, most African cultures have a specific term to describe someone who functions as tribal poet, storyteller, historian or genealogist and whose role is to recount culturally specific and provocative parables of daily life: "The griot was not only educated to be a professional performer, but through his philosophical and psychological skills he developed an insight into humanity" (Chester and Jegede 1987: 17). Moreover, these definitions will have different operationalized meanings in different cultural contexts and more importantly at different historical moments. For example, in traditional Senegalese society these individuals, usually men, were part of a caste, were generally attached to royal families and learned the craft of storytelling or "praise singing" on an apprenticeship basis: "In West African societies where there is a *griot*, however, genealogical descent is paramount. A *griot* learns from his father or ancestors. Thus, the person of a griot has more importance than the performance itself (Diop 1995: 246).

However, with the impact of social change the *griot's* traditional role has changed. Membership in this group no longer necessitates specific training handed down from one generation to the next. There are now what one could only call *faux griots*. That is, one can now call oneself a *griot* without having received specialized training from an elder *griot*. Upon hearing of a ceremony or public celebration taking place, which will honor the members of an elite family, an enterprising individual could simply approach the head of the family and for a certain amount of money offer to sing the praises of the family in much the same manner as a court jester or entertainer. Furthermore, scholars of African popular culture – most notably music – have also broadened the usage of *griot* to describe the performance styles of artists such as the Senegalese Baaba Maal, Malian Salif Keita or Alpha Blondie from Cote d'Ivoire. With the exception of a community of women musicians in Mali, women performers are generally not recognized in this genre. In the light of this gendered oversight, my research seeks to redress women's invisibility by placing women in the role of *griotte*.

I invoke the concept of the *griotte* as a feminist textual strategy that both destabilizes the conventional authority of the ethnographer and forces a tension between orality and literacy or rather the spoken and the written word.[2] I argue that the ways in which the women I worked with tell their stories are as newfangled *griottes*. Their memories preserve and reinterpret past senses of cultures and provide scathing sociopolitical commentaries and cultural critiques of contemporary English–African Diasporic life and its manifest bi-racialized problematics: "It is the *griotte's* (*sic*) retelling the story of those who have come before and reinvigorating the essential wisdoms for the life of the human community and its future" (Farrar 1995: 23). By virtue of contradictory bi-racialized classification in Britain, *métis(se)* individuals' narratives of self and identity both reflect the gender, generational, racial and ethnic tensions of English society and are located outside it in an imagined but not imaginary space. This narrative duality works in a similar fashion in Smadar Lavie's ethnography, *The Poetics of Military Occupation: Mzeina Allegories of Bedouin Identity Under Israeli and Egyptian Rule*: "Mzeina allegories, like all allegories, have a dialectical nature. They elevate, yet devalue, the immoral profane world of global politics by memorializing ordinary events as grotesque didactic tales emphasizing indigenous ethics and morality" (Lavie 1990: 318).

They simultaneously construct dual narratives, which embody individual and collective historical consciousness. They tell their own lived stories. At the same time, their memories preserve and reinterpret senses of past interwoven cultures. In his essay, "The choices of identity," Martin Denis-Consant talks about identity as narrative:

> The narrative borrows from history as well as from fiction and treats the person as a character in a plot. The person as a character is not separable from its life experiences, but the plot allows for the reorganization of the events which provide the ground for the experiences of the person/character....Narrative identity, being at the same time fictitious and real, leaves room for variations on the

past – a plot can always be revised – and also for initiatives in the future.

(Denis-Consant 1995: 5–20)

Through the narrativization of both their identities and the lived paradoxes of bi-racialization, these new millennial storytellers weave provocative tales of transgression and performances of the psyche: "Power is the ability to take one's place in whatever discourse is essential to action and the right to have one's part matter" (Heilbrun 1989: 18).

Navigating the texts: reader's guide to the griottes' *testimonies*

> Social thinkers must take other people's narrative analyses nearly as seriously as "we" take our own. This transformation of "our" objects of analysis into analyzing subjects most probably will produce impassioned, oblique challenges to the once-sovereign ethnographer. Both the content and the idioms of "their" moral and political assertions will be more subversive than supportive of business as usual. They will neither reinforce nor map onto the terrain of inquiry as "we" know it. Narrative analyses told or written from divergent perspectives, as I have said, will not fit together into a unified master summation.
>
> (Rosaldo 1989: 147)

As a "literary experiment" (Fine and Martin, 1995) the specific focus of Chapters 4 through 9 is the narration of differents ways in which cultural memories shape contradictory meanings of "race," self and identity for six women who, by virtue of birth, transgress boundaries and challenge essentialized constructions of self, identity, place and belonging:

> When a writer is not even covertly autobiographical, the web of memory and invention is still there, but not so subtly woven that we may never unravel it. And yet we want deeply never to stop trying, and not merely because we are curious but because each of us is caught in her own network of memory and invention. We do not always recall our inventions, and long before we age we cease to be certain of the extent to which we have invented our memories.
>
> (Bloom 1996: viii)

Their specific lived realities epitomize psychosocial struggles to make sense of explicit epistemological tensions between subjectivity and alterity: "Wherever oral traditions are extant they remain an indispensable source for reconstruction. They correct other perspectives just as much as other perspectives correct them" (Vansina 1985: 198).

In particular, the six individual chapters corresponding to six separate testimonies by each of the primary six *métisse* subjects, will address the different ways in which as *métisse* women they confront problematic tensions between and among cultural constructions of "race," nation, gender and ethnicity:

> Discourses of marginality such as race, gender, psychological "normalcy," geographical and social distance, political exclusion, intersect in a view of reality which supesedes the geometric distinction of center and margin and replaces it with a sense of the complex, interweaving, and syncretic accretion of experience.
>
> (Ashcroft *et al*. 1989: 104).

These reconciliations of the psychic split between subjectivity and objectivity by their very actions expose what is at the heart of interpretive social science. Through the staged textual interaction between me the ethnographer and the six *métis(se) griottes*, the reader is a witness to the death of the authoritative ethnographic voice and the rebirth of the collaborative dialogic exchange:

> the ethnographer should be decentered in terms of the authority of voice, but at the same time should be front and center in the text so that the reader is constantly aware of how biased, incomplete and selective are the materials being presented.
>
> (Wolf 1992: 130)

As their stories will reveal, the six women grapple with the everyday confusion associated with having to assume an essentialized Black identity when their lived experiences and family backgrounds are more complex and varied – despite the fact that by virtue of lineage, they can and do situate themselves within at least two specific and yet overlapping historical narratives.

> A form of mediation, the story and its tellings are always adaptive. A narration is never a passive reflection of a reality....The functions of both the tale and the mediator–storyteller are thus introduced at the outset....The mediator–storyteller, through whom truth is summoned to unwind itself to the audience, is at once a creator, a delighter, and a teacher.
>
> (Minh-ha 1991: 13)

In the age of experimental ethnographies, as anthropologists we must all rethink our designated role as those best suited to claim and assert the authorial voice:

> All history is thus: a radical selection from the immensely rich swirl of past human activity. The uniqueness of this book lies in its taking seriously the selection that is made by those people who gather together at this shrine.
>
> (Price 1983: 5)

Accordingly, invoking the *griotte* tradition as textual strategy challenges conventional views on ethnographic authority. In the following six chapters with the tones and rhythms of their particular classes and cultures, the six *griottes* each spin stories that demand cultural reconceptions of "race," nation, gender and generation: "Autobiography, at its very core, is a process of self-creation. When autobiographers are conscious of this process, they can use its power in the struggle for personal freedom" (Langness and Frank 1981: 93). Collectively, they weave a tapestry of daily life within the English–African Diaspora and beyond which until now has been misrepresented by many and understood by few: "The *griot(te)* (*sic*) tradition travelled into the diaspora, the word recording the experience, the song reviving the spirit....History was in the journey and memory was retained in the proverbs of storytelling" (Jegede 1994: 21). In so doing, their powerful voices break free of the heavy hand of ethnographic interpretation:

> it so often through verbal expression that as human beings we somehow get a handle on our experience of ourselves and of the world; and such experiences are themselves in turn formulated and struggled for and transcended by our collaborative deployment of words.
>
> (Finnegan 1992: 233)

Notes

1　As told to me by Ike Achebe, son of the masterful Igbo novelist Chinua Achebe.
2　　Of course, the part I like above others is the one on the *griottes* and I find enlightening the way in which you have formulated the concept, not within Africa, but in Britain. That is in a new environment; this gives a welcome flexibility, applicability and transposition of the concept to a milieu other than its original one. Very refreshing for someone like me who works on the griots for your reflection of the griotte concept serves as a reflecting mirror to the African traditional one.

> (Samba Diop 1997, personal correspondence)

COULD I BE A PART OF YOUR FAMILY?

Preliminary/contextualizing thoughts on psychocultural politics of transracial placements and adoption

Obu ghi onye tara ahu riri onweya
A skinny person did not necessarily eat part of himself [herself]
(Igbo proverb)

Irrespective of who his (or her) (*sic*) parents are, a child born into a family is part of that family, so he (or she) (*sic*) naturally belongs, and needs from them love, companionship, help, guidance, encouragement, advice, and example in positive living. He (or she) (*sic*) needs these things irrespective of his (or her) (*sic*) parents' racial origins. If he (or she) (*sic*) is born into a community where tolerance prevails, then there is no special problem. However, a coloured (*sic*) child born in Britain, for instance, not only needs the things I have mentioned, but is severely handicapped without them, because the community considers his (or her) (*sic*) colour a handicap and therefore imposes special pressure and proscriptions upon him (or her) (*sic*). He (or she) (*sic*) needs those things not as insulation against the pressures, but as sources from which to draw strength in order to meet and deal with them with wisdom, courage and resolution.

(Braithwaite 1962: 101).

Whatever the extenuating circumstances, children cannot be blamed for the situations in which they find themselves. As victims of circumstances, it is frequently *métis(se)* children in care who pay the highest social and psychological price. In fact, very young *métis(se)* children are "two and a half times more likely than others to spend part of their childhood in local authority care" (Boushel 1996: 2). Ruby and Similola are examples of two *métisse* women who as young *métisse* children grew up in (local authority) care. It is through the British Child Welfare State (or its precursor) that they both create home and family and forge class-specific, gendered and bi-racialized identities. In 1998, we still need to seek explanations for the over-representation of multiple generations of *métis(se)* children in care (Boushel 1996; Barn 1998). We also need to examine critically the private and public traffic in Black and *métis(se)* children which emerges from this epidemic.[1]

Ravinder Barn's (1998) research addresses the psychosocial reasons why it is primarily single, poor, White English mothers who must relinquish their *métis(se)* children to the care system. At the roots of this endemic social and moral crisis are the twinned evils of bi-racialization and patriarchy, which leave too many White, Black and *métis(se)* mothers without sufficient emotional (and if necessary material) support to raise balanced and healthy *métis(se)* daughters and sons. These same institutionalized structures of domination also do not publicly applaud White, Black and *métis(se)* fathers who are raising their children either in conjunction with their partners or alone.[2] However, the crux of the persistent *métis(se)* family "concern" is the fact that our individual and collective triumphs and struggles are neither legitimated, normalized nor celebrated (Benson 1981; Wallman 1984).

"From the auction block to the adoption block"[3]

In the preceding two chapters, my discusssions of methodology point to the fact that many more voices contributed to this ongoing conversation than the six women whose stories appear in this text. In fact, beyond the original twenty-five respondents, I spoke with countless people espousing varied social and political perspectives including those with and without immediate *métis(se)* kin or partners. Among the conversants was a particular middle-class married couple. Joan is Black Yoruba from Nigeria and Peter is White English. They have one son, to whom they are the birth parents, and another adopted son, who is of Jamaican and English parentage. Part of the conversation addressed the politics of adoption and the commodification of *métis(se)* children in this process. In the adoption market, as a so-called interracial middle-class married couple, Joan and Peter are considered prime candidates for the adoption of *métis(se)* children.

Joan told me about the countless messages she received on her answering machine from desperate social workers – some with thinly disguised financial "incentives." On one occasion, she had just finished her shopping at the local Sainsburys. Three aisles over was a social worker, working overtime, who caught Joan's attention and presumably that of the rest of the supermarket. She shouted over to Joan, "Have I got a beauty for you. She will be born in a few weeks. The father is... (she puts her fingers to her lips and kisses them) and the mother is..." (she repeats the gesture). At this point, Joan recalls wanting to disappear.

The supermarket – a place where objects are bought and sold – is an appropriate site for this particular transaction. It reinforces the notion of adoption agencies as newfangled slave markets: "First we had the auction block, now we have the adoption block."[4] The social worker has come to do her shopping, but she also has goods to offer in exchange for parental services. Based solely on the physical attributes of the child's Black Jamaican father and White English mother, she predicts the potential value of the unborn child. In fact, she describes the unborn offspring of this English and Jamaican union, in much the same way as she might request a tasty cut of Chateaubriand at the butcher's. The same way over two hundred years ago in Bristol, local newspapers advertised young enslaved Africans (boys, girls and young men and women) for sale, describing in detail their redeeming physical traits: "in 1768 there is offered 'a healthy Negro slave named Prince, 17 years of age; extremely well grown'" (Fryer 1984: 59). Many of them were later sold to the highest bidder at public auctions (Fryer 1984; Ramdin 1987; Gerzina 1995). In contemporary times, with the expressed intention of finding adoptive and long-term foster families, the British Agency for Adoption and Fostering's in-house newspaper and Black newspapers such as *The Voice* (in collaboration with local councils) feature photographic portraits of African Caribbean, continental African and *métis(se)* children. In so doing, these visual representations with accompanying narratives often embellish the physical qualities of the children, and are designed to visually entice and emotionally provoke prospective foster and adoptive parents with the available goods:

> Sheffield has a number of black and mixed race children who need adoptive homes. Leon, aged 5...is of black African Caribbean and white British heritage, with golden skin, blonde wavy hair, blue eyes and a lovely smile. He is clear about his racial identity...[5]

Bi-racialized "institutions of violence"

I introduce the concept of bi-racialized "institutions of violence" as an explanatory framework for the ways in which children, such as Ruby and Similola create family. Ruby and Similola construct personal narratives which address specific bi-racialized violence experienced in White English children's homes. However, the testimonies of Akousa, Sarah, Yemi and Bisi, as well as my own, also point to the lived psychosocial tyrannies of growing up *métisse* within one's birth families. The term – institutions of violence – stems directly from the work of the founding father of the anti-psychiatry movement in Italy, Franco Basaglia, as well as from the writings of sociologist Erving Goffman (1961) and anthropologist Nancy Scheper-Hughes

(Scheper-Hughes and Lovell 1987). The thrust of the idea is that social relationships within all institutions of violence – prisons, mental hospitals,
schools, children's homes and families – are based on the dynamics of power.
In other words, "the common thread in all these situations is the violence
exercised by those who hold the weapons against those who are hopelessly
dominated" (Scheper-Hughes and Lovell 1987: 60). Nancy Scheper-Hughes
(Scheper-Hughes and Lovell 1992) takes this idea one step further in her
ethnography on mother love and child death in a shantytown in
Northeastern Brazil; here she refers to the "everyday violence" of poverty,
racism and sexism, and persecution by the State. These sociohistorical
circumstances necessitate a kind of spiritually based triage wherein favela
mothers are confronted with difficult moral and ethical dilemmas regarding
their infants' and children's mortalities.

Bi-racialization is a concept that threads itself throughout the entire text
(Miles 1989; Small 1994; Anthias and Yuval-Davis 1992; Omi and Winant
1986). In this book, I refer to bi-racialization as a noun or in adjectival form
in order to describe the multiple and contradictory ways in which the
construct of "race" is operationalized – or rather, takes on dynamic qualities.
To be blunt, the bi-racialized mandate is that one one is either Black or
White and never the twain shall meet. In particular, the hallowed constructs
of nation, ethnicity and culture are collapsed and become bi-racialized. More
specifically for our purposes, English then becomes shorthand for White and
Black is synonymous with anyone who does not match the limited physical
profile of a White person, which includes *métis(se)* individuals with a White
birth parent.

As bi-racialized children, English and Nigerian Ruby and German and
Tanzanian Similola grew up "Black" in the White English contexts of children's homes. Their recollections reflect the significant ways in which
institutions of violence have become bi-racialized – or rather, the ways in
which the children's lives become bi-racialized. At the same time, other
aspects of their ethnic and cultural identities, such as their Nigerian or
Tanzanian heritages, are rendered invisible and obsolete.

Powerlessness and agencies

Ruby and Similola's recollected lived realities of transracial fosterage give
legitimacy to the silenced voices of multiple generations of *métis(se)* adults
who travelled through the system prior to the Children's Act of 1989.
Equally as important, in the shadows of the ongoing and often explosive
debates surrounding transracial adoption and in light of the overrepresenta-
tion of first and second generation *métis(se)* children in care, their testimonies
bear witness to the challenges facing contemporary *métis(se)* wards of the
current British Child Welfare State and their carers. Their implicit critiques
of contemporary 1990s institutions of violence – wherein legislation and the

real needs of the child still often diverge – do serve an important purpose. They are the gateways to the understanding of previous bi-racialized institutions of violence, post-World War II, if not earlier, to the late 1960s and early 1970s, within which *métis(se)* children's past, present and future realities were neither properly legislated nor recognized. Testimonies from Ruby and Similola, provide the primary evidence for and against pre-legislated children's care.

Over the years, there have been countless reforms and acts impacting the lives of children in Britain:

> The last 30 years have seen a variety of shifts in the social work policies and practices surrounding the adoption and fostering of children from ethnic minority groups. These variations cannot be ascribed to any one particular cause; they represent a nexus of changes in society, demographics, politics and social work theory and practice.
>
> (Gaber and Aldridge 1994: 12)

Because of (mis)perceptions of the ethnic and racial composition of Britain – such as, there was not a sizeable English–African Diaspora until the post-World War II migration wave – much of the legislation was not sensitive to the needs of children of the English–African Diaspora (Kareh 1970). For example, prior to the 1989 Children's Act, social service providers and adoption agency officials only had to pay attention to the religious needs of the child. Now, under Section 22 of the 1989 Children's Act, providers must acknowledge the religious, cultural, linguistic and racial heritage of the child:

> Before making any decision with respect to a child whom they are looking after, or proposing to look after...a local authority shall give due consideration...to the child's religious persuasion, racial origin and cultural and linguistic background.
>
> (Gaber and Aldridge 1994: 231)

Nevertheless, Barn's (1998) research findings indicate that although Asian and African Caribbean children are always matched with families of a similar background to their own, *métis(se)* children pose a "dilemma" for social services. Consequently, in a care situation, the diverse cultural needs of *métis(se)* children are not always met and they may be placed with a White foster carer. However, Olumide (1998) argues that since the majority of *métis(se)* children in care come from homes of origin wherein the birth mother is White that a White foster care arrangement more adequately reflects their circumstances than a placement with a Black foster carer.

The transnational, transracial debate

On both sides of the Atlantic there is continual debate over the repercussions of placing Black and *métis(se)* children with White families or family surrogates (Tizard and Phoenix 1994; Gilroy 1987). This issue is particularly controversial when addressing the placement of *métis(se)* children, who can claim at least two heritages – and technical membership in both Black and White communities. Some argue that a *métis(se)* child should be acknowledged as *métis(se)*, while others claim that since the child will be treated as Black by society, she/he should be referred to as Black (Cohen 1994; Richards 1994; Simon 1994; Bartholet 1994). However, under the new Children's Act, in theory, the social worker or the adoption agency must try to find a home that either reflects or is sensitive to the *métis(se)* child's heritage. As I have mentioned, in practice, appropriate matching is not always accomplished.

Like children of color in general, *métis(se)* children are overrepresented in the British foster care/adoption system, and with the exception of infants, are the hardest to place (Boushel 1996). If they are not adopted, this usually means they will spend their childhood in a home or in long-term foster care. If these children are placed, who takes them home? In Britain, in March 1983, there was an uproar among the Association of Black Social Workers and Allied Professionals (ABSWAP) over the placement, for adoption and fostering, of continental African, African Caribbean and Black and *métis(se)* children with White English families, who they felt could not provide Black continental African, Black African Caribbean and *métis(se)* children with the tools to formulate a "positive black identity" in a bi-racialized world. The ensuing debates led to the submission of ABSWAP's argument to the House of Commons Select Committee.

Subsequently, as previously mentioned and cited, there have been numerous analyses of this controversy, that have been both for and against transracial placement. The proponents argue against the narrow limits of a specific construction of social identity that imposes notions of a "positive black identity" – as if "race" were the only dimension to social identity. Opponents point to "cultural genocide" as the logical outcome if Black and *métis(se)* children are placed in White English homes.

One of the central themes of this book is the myriad ways in which constructions of the public, the official, the State, Blackness and Whiteness both converge and diverge with the lived realities of the private, the unofficial, and with being multigenerational *métis(se)*. For in-care survivors, discourses on the private and the public merge. The frequent conflation of "race," ethnicity and nationality in public policy and everyday practices complicates reclamations of place and belonging for multiple generations of *métis(se)* people. Ruby and Similola create family within the limited contexts of predominantly White English in-care situations. Their poignant stories

demonstrate the cumulative impact of growing up within bi-racialized institutions of violence. Residues of childhood pain and conflict provide
sedimentation for their at-times contradictory adult conceptions of personhood. These personal formulations in turn reflect the broader ambiguous
cultural meanings of "race" and differences in our society.

Cultural surrogates and mother surrogates

As their narratives will reveal, for Ruby and Similola, who each spent their
entire childhood in children's homes, older White English women played a
pivotal and extensive role in molding and shaping bi-racialized conceptions
of family in general and the maternal and the female in particular. Hence, it
is here that I introduce the concept of "cultural surrogates." These are individuals – male and female – who temporarily or permanently take over the
parenting role of the biological parent(s) for individuals in care – in children's homes, fosterage or adoption. It is through these cultural surrogates,
that *métis(se)* children and youth first learn about differences and alterities as
experienced as oppositional Blackness and elusive Whiteness. Cultural
surrogates inadvertently and intentionally also attach loaded and coded
meanings to imagined superior White English/British cultures and at the
same time, subvert Black continental African and/or African Caribbean
cultural variants, in all of their complexities. Birth parents of first- and
second-generation *métis(se)* children and youth also frequently commit the
same injustices.

"Mother surrogates" are a specific subset of the aforementioned "cultural
surrogates." They are specifically female and are generally the middle-aged,
middle-class, White English matrons who ran the all White children's
homes and supervised the "civilizing mission." A particular generation of
métis(se) children lived socially isolated and at times extremely emotionally
abusive childhoods in such environments. In fact, with all of the term's
loaded connotations, Nigerian–English Ruby refers to the matron of her
children's home as a "benevolent missionary."

The writer Thelma Perkins, of Jewish English/Trinidadian parentage, also
grew up in a children's home and co-authored *In Search of Mr. McKenzie* with
her sister Isha McKenzie-Mavinga about their attempts to locate their
Trinidadian father and extended family. Thelma Perkins sheds a different
light on the older White nurturers:

> Mount Zion, the house in Chislehurst which was the children's
> home, was staffed entirely by single white women, whom the chil-
> dren called aunties and, apart from the director of home, we rarely
> had contact with men....The aunties were quite young, although
> to the children they seemed old. They were all committed
> Christians, dedicated to saving our souls as well as being respon-

sible for our physical welfare. They came from all over the country to work at the home, having been recruited through the mission's work in other cities. They had no formal training; the only qualification appeared to be a desire to serve the Lord and a liking for children. Working in the home and looking after us was a kind of pre-vocational training before going on to missionary training college...

(McKenzie-Mavinga and Perkins 1991: 9)

The link between children's homes and missions and the concomitant construction of orphans and Africans by the aunties/future missionaries is emblematic of the civilizing intentions of both.

As the tainted seeds of a forbidden union, Ruby's and Similola's fates seemed sealed even before they emerged as the sun-kissed daughters of White English and German mothers. Social and cultural constructions of orphan, children's home resident, foster child, or adoptee by either the child, the carers or the general public is connected to perceptions of the permanence of the surrogacy arrangement. Young children in care learn different ways of negotiating both the uncertainties and the certainties in their lives. None the less, Ruby, and Similola's reconstructions of childhood illustrate the indelible impress of circumstance on their conceptions of selves, families and communities. In other words, filtered down bi-racialist state ideologies, perceived rejection and abandonment by their White English and German birth mothers, their socialization by predominantly White English women carers and their being cut off from their Black continental African fathers and cultures all contribute to residual feelings of longing, confusion and anger. For these two *métisse* women and others like them, this resentment translates into a search for identities and communities. Ruby's and Similola's figurative sojourns of introspection and their physical journeys to their father's homelands – Nigeria and Tanzania, respectively – result in empowering reclamations – of parentage, of heritage and of selves. In the epilogue, I will focus more specifically on the act of testifying as both transformative and redemptive.

Notes

1 For an important contextualizing discussion of the mythologization of the "black family" and associated debates concerning nationhood in general and transracial placement, fosterage and adoption debates in particular, see Paul Gilroy (1987) *There Ain't No Black in the Union Jack*, London: Hutchinson, pp. 59–71.
2 Many of my insights regarding bi-racialized gender politics emerge from extensive dialogue with Jo Adams, a social worker and the lone parent of a *métisse* daughter aged 11 (Jo Adams, 1997, personal communication). See also, C. T. Kannan (1972) *Inter-racial Marriages in London*, London: Kannan; Yasmin

Alibhai-Brown and Anne Montague (1992) *The Color of Love: Mixed Race Relationships*, London: Virago.
3 VèVè Clark 1993, personal communication.
4 VèVè Clark 1993, personal communication.
5 Sheffield City Council advertisement in Special Fostering and Adoption special, *Voice*, March 3 1997.

4

RUBY

"I was the one Black member in a totally White household"

Marie Garson, an African Caribbean social worker had introduced me to Ruby. Ruby is a 43-year-old Nigerian (paternal) and English (maternal) social worker who grew up in a children's home outside London. She is the only one of the original twenty-five participants whom I spoke with exclusively in my home. This deprived me of a contextualized sense of who she was. None the less, profound sadness laced with occasional happiness are the two words that best capture my sense of her. Like many *métis(se)* she is a survivor – a warrior on the frontlines by virtue of her bloodlines.

She was a roll-ups smoker and coffee drinker. These indulgences helped alleviate some of the tension during our initial talks. We sat at my kitchen table, which along with much of the rest of the furniture in my flat, was a gift from my Igbo friend, Chedi. His Oxfam shop – a second-hand shop – was closing down at the exact moment I was moving in to my place. Beyond its utilitarian functions, that table, covered with a tablecloth fashioned from a piece of African cloth I acquired at another second-hand shop, was the site for many late-night into early-morning reasoning sessions involving individual members of all segments of the Thatchapee community. However, the most provocative and stimulating were usually those involving *métis(se)* people as well as what a White English sociologist referred to as the "Young Black Intelligentsia" in Thatchapee.

As her testimonies will tell, Ruby's accounts of her childhood in a suburban London children's home resonate so deeply with the following description of Tod Perkins' and Isha McKenzie-Mavinga's time in separate English children's homes. Their Russian–Jewish mother placed them there in the 1940s. Their birth father was Trinidadian. As adults they both attempted to find him.[1]

We grew up as White-thinking children of mixed race, with the same missionary attitudes to Black people that most White people had. The hymns we sang in Sunday school and the illustrations in our story and school books told of uneducated savages with unkempt hair, grass skirts or, worse, no clothes at all, who carried spears, beat drums and utttered unintelligible noises. They did not believe in Jesus. We did not associate ourselves with these images.

We did not think beyond our immediate surroundings. Our world was far removed from that of our little brown brothers and sisters, whom we were taught about in the home and who were, like us, children of Christ, spiritual brothers and sisters: any more tangible, realistic comparisons between ourselves and the children of heathens went unimagined. We were totally ignorant of Black culture, language and food, although these should have been important aspects of our upbringing. In the home, children were not seen as individuals; we were an undifferentiated group. No matter that we had brown skin and black curly hair that required special treatment.[2]

Ruby: growing up Black and English in care

In terms of race, gender and all that sort of thing, the home that I went to was a girls-only home, so it was a total female environment: the staff were female the kids were female and they were aged from 2 to 18. It was a very large place. I suppose there were about thirty-five kids there. I think my memory is that I was the first Black child there, and when I went there, I was obviously the youngest child. I was much petted to the extent that my first bedroom was to share the deputy matron's room. I had my cot in

---

1 Researching paternal origins and in certain instances physically travelling to their fathers' "home" lands are two ways in which the women and men with whom I spoke reclaimed denied ancestral inheritances.
2 Thelma Perkins and Isha McKenzie-Mavinga (1991) *In Search of Mr. McKenzie*, London: Women's Press, p. 18.

her room and she was a sort of substitute mum person and that
was until I was nearly 4.[3]

I stayed in her bedroom until as it happened, two other children
came who were also Black. They were Nigerian. They were full
Nigerian. They weren't mixed race, and they were there because
both their parents were studying.[4] They were there purely because
their parents were studying. In fact, eventually, they left. One was
2, one was 4. I was very very cross with them. They usurped me. I
was quickly out of the deputy matron's bedroom and into the usual
dormitory, and the younger of these two children took my place in
the cot in the deputy matron's room. They were much darker than
me, much tighter hair and people thought they were much more
authentic than I was.[5]

So I won't say I hated them, but I certainly looked askance at
them. Of course, the three of us were still the only Black people in
the place and it was around that time I do remember thinking that
I'd really rather be White. I'd had enough of being Black. I
certainly didn't get into the disturbed scrubbing my skin in the
bath with bleach or soap behavior, but I used to go up to my
bedroom at night and pray the Lord to turn me White in the

3 She describes the deputy matron as a "substitute mum person." Ruby is technically not
an orphan – both her parents are alive. However, the person tacked on at the end leads
one to believe that though this person were to take the place of her natural mother, to
whom she was not close, there was not a great deal of warmth in this relationship either.
She recalls that she was "much petted" in that her cot was in the deputy matron's room,
but Ruby fails to mention whether, as the home's pet or mascot, she was actually
nurtured in that bedroom. The term "pet" makes one wonder about the closeness of the
relationship between Ruby and the deputy matron. Perhaps young *métisse* Ruby was a
curiosity more than anything else.
4 Esther Goody (1982) *Parenthood and Social Reproduction: Fostering and Occupational Roles in
West Africa*, Cambridge: Cambridge University Press.
5 Ruby's description of the two Nigerian girls who are placed in the home because their
parents are studying is a good example of the different kind of mirroring that take place
when *métis(se)* people are describing themselves in relation to other (Black) people. Ruby
refers to herself as Black. However, over the years, she has internalized many of the racist
stereotypes about Black people. For example, in describing the two Nigerian girls, one of
whom "usurped" her place in the coveted deputy matron's bedroom, she points to their
"darker" skin and their "tighter" hair as indicators that they are more "authentic" than
she is. Given that the little girls are also Nigerian, Ruby has collapsed notions of race,
nation and ethnicity in general and ideas about Blackness and Africanness in particular.
"Authentic" meaning they are much closer to nineteenth-century/Victorian anthropological descriptions of "authentic" Black Africans. By internalizing the narrow
phenotypically prescribed possibilities for African personhood, she has cancelled her own
métisse self out. In so doing, she has then forced herself into the corners of marginality and
difference.

morning and look to see and I wasn't![6] So, I don't know, that didn't last for very long but I can remember it so it must have gone on at some point around that time.

When these other little kids came and usurped me, after some time I decided, well, I've had enough of being Black. The White kids seem to have a much nicer time of it. Us Black ones are always singled out. I went through that little period and then came to the realization very quickly that my skin was black. There was no point praying to the bloody Lord to take it away. 'Cos there was nothing to be done, that was the way it was. I think that was my first lesson in racial awareness if you like.

From that time, there's a sense in which I always accepted that I was Black. That as a Black person — even as a little girl — that I have to look out for myself. 'Cos there was nobody else gonna look out for me as a Black person. There was a sense then which I brought myself up as a Black person in as much as you can do when you haven't got a community around you or family around you or anybody around you. Only you know that you're Black and that has implications for you. So, in a sense that did isolate me a bit. I don't remember having a feeling that I was isolated but I can think back to my behavior at times.

I learned to become quite assertive even bordering on aggressive. I was often in trouble. I knew that a lot of it was because of the color of my skin and then you build up a reputation. "Oh that one — she's always up to no good you have to watch her." So, the color of your skin, the way you behave, and people's response to you gets a bit sort of muddled and molded in together.[7]

---

6 With the same results as the *métis(se)* children who rubbed themselves raw in the bath hoping to turn White, Ruby prayed before going to bed each night that she would become White. She would wake up the next morning only to discover that her prayers had not been answered. Both White-washing attempts stem from the same destructive source. Circulating in a *métis(se)* child's mind from a very early age, are public negative messages about Blackness and implicitly and explicity positive ones about elusive and illusive Whiteness. These all often shame the child into self-destruction — I heard of a *métis* adolescent who painted himself white. And rage — I know a young *métis* man who attacked all the White nurses in the psychiatric hospital that he was involuntarily admitted to.

Over time, these forces eat away at the psyche. Without ample space for self-intervention, self-reclamation and redemption, these wounds cannot heal. The number of *métis(se)* project participants, myself included, who have either attempted suicide, battled with alcohol and substance abuse, damaged their bodies with eating disorders, been admitted involuntarily or voluntarily to psychiatric hospitals or have simply been "in crisis" tells me that the seeds of self-hatred and confusion planted in childhood can bear bountiful fruits of despair and anger in adulthood.

7 After her attempts to change color failed, Ruby accepted the fact that she was Black. This realization was complicated by the fact that she was discovering her new identity in isola-

Also, around that time I started to get into an awful lot of trouble as only a 4-year-old can – 4-/5- year-old. So if we'd been out playing and if there was any bother at all, it was always me that got blamed for it. It was me that was leading others astray. There were all these big White girls around me and they'd say, "Her. That's the one." I'd get into all this trouble. I thought this was a bit unfair.

During this period my mother had stopped seeing me anyway, so I was just seeing my grandmother. I didn't know she was my grandmother. I thought she was a kind lady who came to see me. I was told that she was my auntie. An auntie could be anything – meaning that she was a kind lady or that she was a blood relative. Anything or nothing; you call lots of people "auntie." I didn't actually find out that she was my grandmother until I was about 7 or 8. I didn't find out from her. I'd actually worked something out. I thought she must be my great aunt. I'd worked out there must be a blood relation because I knew that she had some contact with my mother, whom I never saw. So I asked the matron lots of times and she must have said to her: "Look she's giving us all these awful questions. We've got to tell her something." So she eventually took me to the side, and said, yes, she was my grandmother, but she would prefer me to call her auntie. So, I always called her auntie right up to her death. She never acknowledged that she was my grandmother.[8]

What she couldn't give me in affection, she'd make up for in money. She had money. I was the richest girl in the home, so I used to get a lot of friends that way. It's like, "Can I be your friend?" If she took me out she'd say, "Do you want to take a friend?" She'd always be even-handed. Whatever she bought for me, she would

tion. At the same time, her private conception of what being Black means was constantly informed by public reactions to her perceived aggressive "Black" behavior. The two worlds collide.

8 The overwhelming shame surrounding her birth – her father was married and Black African – made it impossible for both her birth mother and grandmother to fully accept Ruby. However, like a benevolent missionary, her grandmother would visit under the guise of "auntie." "An auntie could be anything, meaning a kind lady or that she was a blood relative." In this particular context, the meaning of "auntie" is muddled. Her grandmother is a blood relative and on the surface also a kind lady. She takes care of Ruby's material needs, takes her on outings and allows her to bring friends along. But, as future events will demonstrate, she never recognizes that what Ruby really needs is a place to belong, not a place to hide. Her grandmother's public acknowledgement of Ruby as a legitimate blood relative would have facilitated the process of self-incorporation that to date, her grand-daughter has yet to complete.

buy for them too. So, they always got something good out of it. But, because I was her grandchild, she'd always give me a bit more. It does actually affect you as you're growing and you're top dog. You've always got more than everybody else has got. Though I was in a children's home, I was always materially very well catered for. My grandmother would always say, "You are not in a home because no one wants you. We pay for you to be there to get a proper growing-up experience."[9] My grandmother and my mother ran an old people's home and made quite a lot of money out of it. My mother is a trained nurse. My mother did the practical bit and my grandmother, from what I can gather, owned the place and spent the money.

I was about 8, 8 or 9, before the next Black children came to the home. In the meantime, the two Nigerian girls had left. They went to boarding school because their parents had money too. They had only ever been there because they (the parents) were studying. The next people – I'm not quite sure where they came from. Three sisters – I think they were West Indian. They were about my color; they weren't full Negro. They were about my color and their hair wasn't as curly as mine. I remember that. They stayed quite a long time. The younger of the sisters was a similar age to me. She must have been my age because she was in the same year in school, different classes though. We weren't close, but I remember we got into the habit of looking out for each other. That was really my first experience of looking out for one of mine because I knew the ropes and they didn't.

Then a couple years after that, two little Asian girls came. This time, within the children's home, social services was beginning to take off. Up until I was about 9, I'd never heard of a social worker. It was very much an orphanage in the sense that kids were privately placed by their families because a parent had died or because of a disability or whatever reason unable to take care. The child was placed in that way and usually placed when very young. So, we all grew up from babies. There was that sort of stability. When I got to

---

9 In these testimonial narratives of redemption, what is repeated is as important as what is deleted. I distinctly remember Ruby's somewhat defensive and resentful tone on the two occasions when she discusses the circumstances that brought the two Nigerian sisters to the home: "They were there because both their parents were studying; purely because both their parents were studying....They had only ever been there because they (the parents) were studying." In light of Ruby's grandmother's rationale: "You are not in a home because no one wants you. You are in a home, we pay for you to be there to get a proper growing-up experience." One could surmise that by focusing on the plight of the Nigerian girls, Ruby can indirectly justify her own situation.

about 9, kids started to come who weren't babies and who weren't
going to spend their lives there, necessarily. Or, they might do –
depending on family circumstances. They might be there for a few
weeks, a few months, few years – whatever. The social workers
started dropping in. Not like it is now, but certainly I recall these
people who were social workers would come. I was quite jealous of
that as well. I wanted a social worker who came and took me out,
who checked on me and what I needed.

These two little Asian girls came. Not sisters, they came separately. One was about 11, one was about 6. I remember the years
that they were absolutely adored. They were really pretty. People
always said nice things about them. Myself and the other three kids
– we were very much in the shadows. We were the naughties and
these two kids were the good pretty ones, but there was still that
identification that we were all Black. We were, all the five of us, six
of us including me, in a class apart from the others. That's all –
there weren't any other Black children.

I was the only Black child throughout my schooling – apart from
those other children who attended school with me. They were my
main contact for awareness that other Black people existed. Then, I
remember being an adolescent really before I saw the first Black
person on the street – independent of my household. I can
remember it was a man walking on his own up the road where the
home was and obviously I didn't know him. I remember him being
very dark and just staring at him. I can't remember more than that.
Then, I saw two or three over time, but never more. I'd always be
fascinated watching.[10]

In terms of racism, I don't think I could avert racism. I had one
teacher at school who was strictly racist, and he would call me stuff
like "nigger" – quite outrageous. There was another teacher who
wasn't so outrageous as that, but his behavior was quite racist
towards me. He always treated me very differently to any other
child in the class. He'd humiliate me in any way that went beyond
punishment to just humiliation and that nasty little way that you
couldn't quite put your finger on. I hated him too. By the time I
was in secondary school, I realized that there were ways of handling
teachers as well. If I didn't want to do something, the thing was to

---

10 This example, as well as Ruby's previous description of the arrivals of the Asian and
African Caribbean young girls, pinpoints the situational and contradictory codes of
membership and the tensions therein for *métis(se)* people. The oppositional mediated categories include self/other, insider/outsider, external/internal, public/private, Black/White,
light/dark, individual/collective and most importantly, the operational differences and
lived contradictions between self-identifications and social classification.

be good academically. If you were good academically you could get away with much short of murder.[11]

If I wanted to do it, I'd do it. If I didn't want to do a lesson, I wouldn't do it. I didn't care if they sent me out of class or not. I knew the headmistress wouldn't care. I got to a stage where I actually didn't care what they thought and I knew that it didn't really matter. I didn't sort of act out. It was more verbal. Then I finished school. I got to the stage where I was pretty well able to do what I liked by the time I left school. Not because people liked me. But because they just thought – "Oh well you know, that's just her, that's the way she behaves. If you treat her like that, she'll do that, but if you treat her like that, it's just more hassle."

I got to a stage as I got older that I would have to have quiet places. The place where I lived was a beautiful place actually. It was a huge mansion, and it was set in its own grounds. This beautiful large Georgian house with huge gardens and grounds. So there were lots of places to go hide – which I did. I had my little spaces. I did that really up until I was 14. Then, the people in the home decided that I was so naughty and I was such a bad influence on the other children that I couldn't even be trusted to be in the same dormitory as them. So they punished me by giving me my own room (*Laughter*), so I didn't need to go hide any more. I had my own room – nobody else did. So it worked for me in that way.

Then I left. I was seeing my mother by this time, infrequently in fact. When I left, I went to live with my mother, loathed it and left. I didn't hate her at that time, but I didn't like her very much so I didn't see a lot of her. I was very close to my grandmother. I used to keep in quite regular touch with her and then I went to live with her for three or four months. That period was unpleasant actually. That's the word looking back. There was an aspect that was unpleasant in that as again I have already said, my grandmother, although I felt she loved me as a grand-daughter, would never publicly acknowledge that I was her grand-daughter. During the three to four months that I was with her, if people came to the house, she would either encourage me to hide or go out. Or she would say that I was somebody that she had known for a long time – that denial. Almost like she was a sort of benevolent Christian missionary type who was kind to the Black girls. So she actually got

11 Ruby's experiences of schooling mirror those of the other *métis(se) griot(tes)*, some of whom are not featured in this book. They all learned that educational achievement was a survival strategy in what was ordinarily a hostile classroom environment. In addition, as long as they performed well in school, outside the classroom, they could also "clown around" in an attempt to garner attention and acceptance from their classmates.

extra kudos from that in some way – while not willing to recognize that I was her flesh and blood. That became very clear during that three to four months.

So, I became very adept at hiding. I was 16 or 17 – quite big, but I had actually lived quite a sheltered life. That period of time with my gran brought out very much to the fore what her attitude to me was and why it was like that. It was 80 percent because of the color of my skin; the other 20 percent was the fact that I was an illegitimate child. For my grandmother and her generation that was quite a shameful thing. But had I been a White illegitimate child it would have been very different. So as I say, 80 percent because of the color – she didn't want to be associated in the blood line with a Black grand-daughter. She was ashamed of me and her neighbors didn't know that I was related to her. She never had any photographs of me or anything like that. There was something cropped up around that time around my father and I can't remember what it was. Anyway, it's along the same sort of lines.

She was selling her house at the time so there were all sorts of people coming to the house. I remember this awful period where people would come to the house and I would do crazy things: do things like hide under the bed, in the wardrobe, hide in the bushes, in the garden all the time. It was very important that they didn't see me there so they didn't ask any odd questions about who I was and therefore embarrass my grandmother. That was very odd and really sort of sharpened up the conflict that I had with my grandmother, really up until the time of her death that in a sense never really got resolved. It became very clear to me that she was ashamed of the color of my skin more than anything else.[12]

During that period, sort of 16 to early twenties, I was in touch

---

12 The title of Ruby's testimonial narratives of redemption could easily be "Nowhere to Hide." The ideal situation for Ruby would have been a healthy home environment wherein she learned to respond to the covert and overt bi-racialized violence she was subjected to in public arenas. The desired outcome of such supportive socialization is that Ruby would have emerged empowered, full of self-love and better able to cope with subsequent difficult incidents. However, Ruby grew up in familial and surrogate familial milieux wherein she was taught that Black equals bad and hence there is no scope for the fostering and nurturing of her as a complete and unique individual. For her, there was really no separation of public and private. Even when she found places to hide, she could not hide from the painful reality that according to a bi-racialized society, she inhabited a Black skin. It is this Black African skin that makes her grandmother desire Ruby as a civilizing project. It is also this same Black African skin that shames her grandmother into concealing Ruby and denying her kinship. In a bi-racialized society, there is no sanctuary for Ruby or other *métis(se)* individuals.

with my father again, where I hadn't been up until then.[13] Which actually gave me a certain amount of strength in a very sort of low-key sort of way. After we had been to Nigeria, and lived there for a year or more, and come back, I got a great deal out of that. I did then begin to feel that I wasn't just Black in an isolated situation. There was this whole family that I had who were Black, and who supported me, and whom I could go to at any time. If life got really heavy, I can jump on a plane and go to Nigeria, and I'd have a home, and a family. That made me feel a lot less lonely, and get to a situation where I could begin to feel some pride about being Black. I didn't hate being Black before. I was always getting into trouble because I was Black, and there was nobody else to go to. I think that sort of unlocked the strapbox a little bit. It wasn't just because I was Black. There's a whole world full of Black people out there. My family is Black and they weren't ashamed of me, and I wasn't ashamed of them. So that was if you like – although I didn't see it in those terms at the time – the beginning of a developing of some sort of a Black consciousness as distinct from an awareness of being Black in a simplistic way.

Then we went back to Africa.[14] Took the kids, year after I left university. That was very good in terms of reinforcing the African connection as it were. It was nice to take the kids. That was also interesting, and had its aspects of upset. We took a White friend with us. She knew that we were going and wondered could she come for part of it. So, we said, "Okay, join in." So, we went. But what happened, particularly when we got to North Africa – Morocco, Algeria – that we would be travelling as a family and people would automatically think I was the maid – that my husband and my White friend were the man and wife, and that the kids were theirs. That was distressing. There was one particular occasion in Morocco where through a set of circumstances, the family was invited to supper by this chap. We all went along, and he had seats for everybody except for me. He didn't look at me, he didn't talk to me, he just looked straight through me. None of my family appeared to do anything about it. They hadn't picked up.

13 When Ruby turned 16, her birth mother gave her a bundle of letters from her Nigerian birth father, which she had been keeping. It was at this stage, that Ruby began to write to him.

14 Ruby, her husband and their children had already made one trip to Nigeria to meet her father and her extended family. They ended up staying in Calabar for a year or so and she and her husband worked as teachers. Unfortunately, there was not space for me to include all of Ruby's escapades, but I wish that I could have included Ruby's recollections of her time in Calabar, Nigeria. Ruby has a typical caustic English sense of humor replete with extremely vivid descriptions of all involved. I was in stitches throughout most of this portion of Ruby's performance.

They did eventually, but there were a couple of minutes when they did actually pick up what was happening. So, I remember that very very clearly, and how distressed I was about that.

Because that also implicated my family, who hadn't actually picked up what this bloke was doing. Why he was doing what he did. The so-called White friend, far from seeing it as a distressing situation for me to be in, seemed to get some pleasure out of it – it wasn't overt – but there was something about, "Oh, isn't it funny, that people see me as John's wife?" Oh, yes, how odd, how strange, what a giggle! The kids did get quite upset about it. "We know that you're our mum, and we don't like people saying that you're not."

John, I felt then, didn't make it clear enough, and so that informed my relationship with him if you like. If I want to go back to a situation where I first thought that John's attitude to the color of my skin wasn't as straightforward as it might be, I would cite that particular incident and time. It was major. Even when he saw what was going on and space was made for me at the table, he wasn't outraged, he didn't say anything, it was like "This is my wife, please get a chair." That was smoothing it down so that other people shouldn't feel upset about it, even though I was feeling very upset. Then we moved further down into Africa, and our friend was dropped off. I was very pleased when she was dropped off, and the kids were very pleased when she was dropped off.

The politics of race is different for each of us. It's one thing to me, it's another thing to John, it's another thing to each of the children. Before John met me, I was aware that most of his girl-friends had been non-English. At that time I didn't really think much of it, but after I was married to him and had lots of years to reflect, I thought, I wonder what that's about. John likes Black people. He likes non-English people. He likes non-European people. More than most people I guess. Now I know him very well, it would be very logical for him to marry someone non-White. He would be the first to admit that he gets a lot out of it. He probably gets a lot more out of it being married to me than I get being married to him – from that point of view. At the time that I married him, I didn't know any Black people anyway. So it wasn't a case of I knocked around with Black people and White people and made a conscious decision to marry a White man. It wasn't like that. It was that he was in the circle I mixed in, which was all White. 'Cos up until that time, I had always lived in a White situation. I had always been the odd token Black. So, I hadn't had any thoughts about making conscious choices about

White men or Black men or Black communities or White communities. It just hadn't come up in my life.[15]

When we had children, I fully expected my children to be Black.[16] At least to be dark, apparently non-White. My first daughter Pauline, she's about the darkest of them. She has Afro features in as much as she has dark curly hair. It's not curly like this though, it's much more like the perms Europeans go to have done – pretty little curls. She has very dark eyes, but in fact, she looks more like John's side of the family. She doesn't have particularly Negroid features, although people think she looks most like me – when they don't look very closely. Just because of the coloring that's all, because she's dark. The other two are fair, so they are not apparently like me at all.

She was born. First of all, she was my daughter, and that was the most important thing. I was surprised that she wasn't darker than she was. When the second one was born, who was outrageously fair, she had very blonde hair and looked very much like John – not a bit like me. When the third one was born, Jake, what I first thought when he came out, when I saw him, was "Oh, it's me dad." Because he just had that face. He had a very Negroid face. He's as White as the rest, but he has a very Negroid face. He does have curly hair, but it's fair hair. Well, in fact, it's light brown now, but when he was little it was very blonde. But, he has got Negroid features. I suppose it's only as they have been growing up, that it came to me. That I was the one Black member in a totally White Household.[17]

---

15 Whether *métis(se)* participants were heterosexual, gay, lesbian or bisexual, the notion that one's geographical proximity to Black, White or other *métis(se)* people or communities determines one's partner choices is a thread running through all of the testimonies. More often than not the twenty-five individuals I worked with were married to, in a long-term relationship with and/or frequently also had children with White English men or women. Regarding *métisse* women in the project, the exceptions to this pattern included Bambi, whose husband is also *métis*, Sarah whose son's father is *métis*, Yemi, whose husband is Nigerian (Yoruba) and Akousa who refused to date White men. The *métis* men I interviewed followed a similar trend. Some had White English partners. Others chose Black continental African or African Caribbean partners. Others still had *métisse* partners. At the time, no one I spoke with had an Asian partner although some had mentioned having been involved with Asian women or men in their pasts. My current partner is also *métis*. However, as mentioned, having grown up in predominantly White neighborhoods, my first relationships were with White American and Jewish men. Over time, and particularly when I moved to Northern California for postgraduate school, my relationship networks diversified considerably to the extent that my friends nick-named me the "equal opportunity lover."

16 This was a very common reflection made by almost all of the *métisse* women who had children with White English or *métis* men.

17 In describing her children, Ruby unwittingly replicates the discourse of nineteenth-century/Victorian racial typology i.e. "Negroid." Societal ambivalence about so-called

Even though it's my husband and my own children, it still left me as the only Black person in the household.

It has affected my children differently. My eldest daughter prefers really not to talk about "race" at all. I would say it would be something in her life she would find it useful to ponder on. But, she doesn't talk about "race" much. As they were growing up, they certainly had some difficulties. It was clearly as a result of them having a Black mother. To the other kids, they might be White, but the other kids would know that their mum was Black. So, that made them Black somewhere. They did get called names at school. I used to think in some respects, they wouldn't have such a difficult time, because they clearly (*Hesitation*) weren't Black, they were White.

I feel nowadays, looking back, and growing up with them as it were, that in some ways it's more difficult for them. Because, they are not Black, they are White, and yet they are Black because their mother's Black. They have that component. So some of the comments they have made to them are more snide. They are asked to choose more. Are you White or are you not? Are you with us or are you not? That sort of thing – in a way if they were straightforwardly White wouldn't happen. Then, if they were straightforwardly Black, wouldn't happen. It's the way it is. They've all had racist experiences. That they might not have been aware of, and I might not have been aware of. Looking back, I could see were.

The two younger ones went to a primary school for instance, where the headmaster was clearly racist. He hated Jake in particular, but he didn't like Rachel either. I saw him change from a happy little boy to as quiet as a mouse. He wouldn't even tell me what was happening. His sister would come back and say, "You know what Mr Throup has done to Jake today?" It would be some petty misde-

racial transgression and racial transformation is inscribed on the faces of Ruby's children. She describes them as White and yet their features are "Negroid" or "Afro." She has a White English mother and a Black Nigerian father. Her husband is White English. Yet, by virtue of the bi-racialized meanings attached to phenotype, Ruby forfeits the right to claim her White children as her own. They are White, she is Black. The pain of this realization is encoded in this statement and is exemplified by her experiences in Morocco, when she was presumed to be the family's maid. Were I to delve further into the paradoxes of "race," I would be most interested in talking with individuals such as Ruby's and Bisi's children. As children, in the public sphere, unless they are directly associated with someone Black, it is assumed that they are White. However, their home lives usually leave them pondering the existential question "Who/what am I *really*?" Upon reaching adulthood, they may choose to eradicate this bi-racialized ambivalence by disavowing their African ancestry passing permanently into the world of White privilege. Despite the attendant ridicule and disdain ("But you look White!"), in their souls, they may also hold on to the integrating notion that they are also Black.

meanor and he would lose his break or have to stay behind after-school. Looking back, the bloke hated them, and there was nothing I could do about it. Because he was racist, and the only way he could get at them – get at me – was through minor harassment at school. So, I took them out of there quick.

Rachel, the middle child, the one who looks least like me, is the one who is the most passionate about race. She curses the day she was born White. She would love to be born Black. She thinks it's really unfair that she was given a Black mother, but wasn't Black herself. She's quite racially aware, and what she doesn't understand, she wants to know. She's a quite forthright girl. She's always sitting me down and saying, "I want to discuss this." or "This has come up." "We were in a discussion and this was said." How should she react? She reacted this way. Was that the right way to react? What were the issues? She wants to know. I'd say of the three of them, she is the most aware of race issues, and the one who most wants to sort out her part in that.

Jake, the younger one, the one who looks most Negroid, he doesn't discuss race much. He lives it more than talks about it. He is very involved with street culture – house, rapping, styles of dress, ways of hanging out, being cool. He gets into an awful lot of trouble, all of the time. I think a lot of that increasingly as he gets older, it's almost as if people are saying to me if I go up to the school or something, "How dare this Black boy parade as a White boy." If you see what I mean. Because he looks Negroid, but he's White. He identifies with Black youths. But, he's White. That's the feeling that I get, "How dare you have this son playing White, when we all know he's Black." It's that sort of attitude. Now, whether that's because he's a male child as well. Maybe males can be more threatening. He's what, 14 now, so the older he gets, the more I'm beginning to see that. The girls haven't quite got it like that, but they didn't so act the part as much as Jake did. Rachel challenges in a verbal way, Jake challenges by his actions. Pauline doesn't challenge at all. So, that's the kids.

For me, I accept that I'm married to a White man, because I am. My kids are White. I'm not simply going to get some racial consciousness that is going to take me off to a Black community and away from my own people. I don't know that that would be helpful to me, my family or anybody else. What I do intend to do is put my life into compartments. Husband one, kids, family, friends, and John has his friends that aren't necessarily mine, and my friends who aren't necessarily his. When it comes to issues of race, I found myself over the years discussing it less and less with John. I went through a phase of feeling he was using the fact that he was married to me to give him some sort of extra kudos – in a weird sort of way.

It might have just been my thoughts. I might have got that entirely wrong, but that was the feeling that I had.

Well, in that case, he's gonna have to sort this one out on his own. I'm not going to talk about race issues with him any more. I find increasingly that I discuss race issues with Black friends and colleagues. I do it less and less with White colleagues. I've had to struggle to get to where I am, and there aren't any short cuts. I've felt in my life, I've been used by quite a lot of White people, in order to give them some spurious okayness in their own attitudes to race. If I talk about race with John or anybody else, I'm usually very precise about why I'm talking to them now about it, and what the limits of that conversation are. When I've had enough of that conversation, I just cut it, and refuse to talk about it.

What is Black and what is White for me? In simplistic terms, it comes down to the color of the skin as far as I'm concerned. I do distinguish between race and culture. So, I would call myself Black and I would call myself British. Britishness is my culture, but because I'm Black, I will identify more from a racial point of view with other Black people. Having said that, a lot of Black people have different cultural backgrounds. Whether it's West Indian or Caribbean, African, American, there are those differences within that. I think that as Black people, I would be very surprised to come across anybody, who hasn't had some personal experience of racism somewhere in their life, in a way that a White person could not have. There's that shared understanding; that shared culture of racism that makes me feel closer to the Black community in that respect. But, I am also British, so I guess that my values, my lifestyle, way of being are informed a lot by English culture. I used to feel uncomfortable about that at one time. But as I get older, I realize now that is the way it is, Ruby, so why apologize for it. I can't turn myself into a Black American or West Indian or something that's not who I am.

Once I came to the realization that "race" and culture are two different things, I found my own place in it more easy to define. Quite often people muddle the two together. If you're mixed race, if you're not careful, you can fall between two stalls. Where you're English, but you're not quite, 'cos you're Black aren't you? Or, you're not really Black are you, because you're English. You're not one of us. So, certainly if I'm talking to Caribbean friends or colleagues, or not even friends or colleagues, it comes up more with people I don't know. Where there's a taken-for-grantedness that I must be Caribbean in some way, and are amazed when there are facets of the culture that everybody knows, and I say, "I've never come across this before." And it's like, "Weehhh, where do you come from?" I say, "London." I've found myself in life having to explain to people that I might be Black, but I'm not Caribbean. I am English. These days I don't have a problem with that.

I remember meeting John's mother. He took me down to meet his mother – his parents. His mother was horrified – racist old cow that she is. They live down in Elthorpe. His father's fine, but his mother was absolutely horrified that he had taken up with a Black woman. When I was pregnant, she was even more horrified. I had a dreadful relationship with her for many years. When the children were born, she thought I had no right to have them. But when they were born and they were White, she wanted for the children to be hers. If she could have knocked me out and taken the children, she would have. With my eldest daughter Pauline, she did things like if we went down to stay at all, she would not allow me to do things for Pauline. She would bathe her, dress her, feed her, that sort of thing. It was like, "In my house, this is what we will do." I'd look at John and go along with it. I'd think, we're only here for a couple of days. She's the grandmother; I'd swallow my pride, and let her go on with it. Thank God we're going in two days' time. But, I didn't like it.

The fact that the grandchildren turned out White, made them acceptable not me. I was still Black. If she'd knocked me out all together, she would have. It's quite interesting actually, because years on, she said to me once when we were talking, I can't even remember the context, but I do remember her saying, "I felt that Pauline should have been my child. She took to me naturally. She should have been mine." God knows, what crazy stuff goes on in her head. She's always had a special feeling, particularly for my eldest child. Rachel, who came next, who was even fairer than Pauline, had another personality. Pauline was quite a placid child, so that was the other aspect of it. Rachel was a very aggressive child, and straightforwardly like me. So, she wasn't an easy baby. She screamed and shouted and gnashed her teeth. My mother-in-law didn't take to her so much. It was a different kettle of fish. As the children have grown up, Pauline has always remained her favorite grandchild, and she has always been in a noticeable way, so the other two see that. What has happened is it has actually made Pauline stay away from her as she's got older. She says, "It's not fair that she should give me this attention, which I don't even want and never asked for, and she doesn't give it to my brother and sister. I don't like that, and I don't like her for it. Therefore, I shan't be visiting her much." She went through a period of actively loathing her, and not wanting to be anywhere near her. She's coming around from that a bit, because the lady's getting older.

She's never had a good relationship with my children, my mother-in-law. She and I had a very bad relationship up until twelve years ago. She went through a series of amazing outbursts towards me. How awful I was. That sort of stuff. My husband, John, and his father, who I always got on very well with, let her know that she was out of line. My father-in-law did say to her "If you cause a break-up between Ruby and John because of your behavior, I'll leave you." Which warmed me to him a lot because he really laid it on the line, and he meant it when he said it as well.

But the other side of that was that they used to treat her like she was sick when she had these outbursts, which I found amazing. They'd say their bit, they'd tell me to go away and they would sort her out, and then she'd be helped to her bed. She would stay there two or three days being waited on hand and foot like she'd got flu or something. Then, I'd be told to say nothing. She'd "come round." Then two or three days later, she'd get up, matter never referred to, and just carry on as if the outburst had never happened.

Over the last years, since John's father died, as he did, she must have realized if she wasn't going to get along with me, she wasn't going to see much of her son either. So, it was in her interest to be more reasonable around me. Otherwise, she wasn't going to see her son, her grandchildren or anybody else. We didn't need that sort of aggravation. So, she has "come round" quite a lot. It's mainly because of practical considerations. On the surface, we get on quite well, but it is surface. She's quite charming some of these days, but extremely on the surface.

Anything could go wrong, or come up, or whatever, she would bad-mouth me. That's her. All those little things inform and begin to mulch away in consciousness somewhere, even though you don't do much about it at the time, you just take it on. This has happened or that. That's because of my race, it's because of my presentation, which has fitted into the format of my life.

5

SIMILOLA

"The difference comes from within me. I'm neither of those two things and both as well"

There was a wonderful informal social network operating in Thatchapee. There were a few key players, such as my artist friend Winston, and it is through him that I met an American historian who is married to an Englishman. She was very excited about my project and immediately gave me the names of some potential participants, saying she would check with them before giving me their telephone numbers. Among this group was Similola, whose birth mother is White German and whose birth father is Black Tanzanian. Similola and I took to each other immediately. We shared a belief in brutal honesty and enjoyed exercising a somewhat biting sense of humor, much to the detriment of those around us.

For our exchanges, and they were truly exchanges in that Similola asked me almost as many questions as she answered, we met alternately at her flat in Quilton or in mine in Thatchapee. I must admit that the most dazzling performances took place when we turned the tape recorder off and just chatted extemporaneously. When I left Bristol in 1992 to return to Berkeley, California to write my thesis, I attempted to keep in touch with the *griot(tes)* who had also become my friends. Similola is an excellent correspondent. Over the past five years, through her wonderful letters, I have learned of the many changes in her life, such as her Tanzanian father's passing away and Nelson Mandela attending the funeral, or about the public alterations to Bristol such as the new Empire and Commonwealth Museum, which opened recently with much pomp and circumstance. However, Similola's most remarkable revelation was the letter I received from her in 1996, when she reported having travelled to both Germany and Uganda to meet extended kin and also having finally met her German birth mother, who now lives in England.

What will become readily apparent to you, the audience, is the powerful way in which Similola carrys us along on her journey, complete with painful hurdles, towards self-acceptance and completeness.

Similola: revisiting dark days

When I was growing up, the main influence was the house mother in the children's home, who totally dominated my life up until I was 16 years old. Her views were my views. She was a very strict disciplinarian, very strong (I now realize) and also very very racist. She made me have a very low opinion of myself. She had never had any Black children in her care before. She had me when I was very very young, at age 4. They considered me to be very cute and pretty and I was spoiled. In fact, the other children used to hate me because I was so spoiled and always got my own way. As I got older – you know what children are like – they start being naughty. Then you get to be a teenager and you want to assert yourself. I couldn't do that. She'd built me up into feeling like a wonderful competent person – because of all that attention I had been getting and because I was pretty and cute and did everything I was told. Then, when I started rebelling probably from about the age of 8, she turned on me.

I'd never noticed before I was about 12 that I was that different from the other kids at school. It never occurred to me. I was always treated as being White. I don't remember being treated any differently until 12, 13, and suddenly my hair was wrong, my lips were too big, my temper was due to "the black blood in my veins."[1] Everything that I did that was wrong was somehow related to my color. I did not have friends because people didn't like me...this is what I was told. I took all this in and it was very difficult to come to terms with. It's quite a shock when you're that age to suddenly realize you are very different from everyone else and it seemed to be hitting me from all sides. I'd realize that there were teachers at school that would pick on me for no reason and I'd think well why, and of course, it started falling into place. It was because I was

---

1 As all the *griottes'* testimonies of childhood illustrate, their White birth parents or White parental surrogates' private constructions of negative Blackness function as potent instruments of bi-racialized violence. These damaging conceptions of Blackness are then reproduced by children, teachers and society writ-large within the public spaces of the classroom, the playground and the street.

different from the other kids. I wasn't White and kids started calling me names.

I'd be walking along the road and I'd get called "Blackie," and "jungle bunny" and "chocolate drop." These names cut through me. I was the only person in the whole town who was being called these names and I felt very singled out and couldn't understand it. I felt very hurt and also humiliated. When I realized what was going on, I just wanted to crawl into a shell and die. Instead of seeing the positive advantages of being mixed race, all I could see were the worst ones. I used to literally go to bed at night and cry and pray to God to let me wake up White with long blonde straight hair.[2] I used to do that because I was getting such heavy shit all around me. I'd changed from being a happy outgoing child. I became very inward looking and detached.

One day I was coming down the stairs and heard my house-mother talking to her friends. I noticed she'd stopped taking me out so much any more. I think it came up in conversation with her friend. Her friend said, "Are you taking Similola ?" or something. I heard her say, "Oh no, people might" – she must have watched a program on TV or something, because it suddenly came to her and I heard her say, "I can't because people might think I'm married to a Black man." So, she made it sound so disgusting and she never ever ever took me out after that. She never did. If I had been Black rather than half-Black, I'd either have been totally crushed or I'd have known I didn't have to identify with White people and found my own identity, because I knew I was different.[3] But because of that, she made me want to deny half of my identity. I did, I really wanted to. Why, why, why? I've been punished by God. Why do you do this to me? It's like he said, "You can have some of being White but not all of it."[4]

At that stage I started losing all my friends because all my friends were White. I felt so envious of them and I couldn't contain my jealousy enough to be with them. I was not jealous, but envious. I wanted to be like them and I found it so difficult to be with them.

---

2 Similola's bedtime wishes mirror Ruby's.

3 Here, Similola frames difference in another light and differentiates between being Black and half-Black. Presumably, in this context, Similola perceives the former to be more marginal but yet more empowering than the latter.

4 Similola's childhood experiences illuminate the ways in which she was made to feel as though being White and Whiteness were the ideal standards by which she should measure her self-worth. In the long run, she knew she could never be completely White, but being White-identified always seemed to lead to disappointment and rejection for her.

In the end I just withdrew totally. From the ages of 13 to 15, I literally had no friends. There wasn't anyone I could identify with. At that age you don't realize why you feel like that. I knew I was horrid because I wasn't White. In my eyes, I was ugly and revolting and horrible and nobody wanted to know me. It was soul destroying and there was no one to confide in. I was in a children's home and I was totally isolated from Black people or any other people like me at all. I didn't feel I could talk to anyone about it so I just internalized it all and just lived with it.

It's no good for anybody's self-esteem. I hated it for years and years and years. I hated being different. I wanted to be the same. Now I am older and wiser. Looking back, wanting to be the same is ridiculous. You'd never feel the same, but that's all I wanted. I just wanted to be White. I wouldn't even go out in the sun 'cos I thought, "Oh no! I don't want to get too brown." I'd purse my lips thinking if I look White I'll be okay. Then I realize, no, it's a mental thing it's not a physical thing. It's nothing to do with the way you look, it's what goes on in your head.[5] It took me a long time. I still haven't overcome it totally. If I feel picked on for any reason, I still think, "Oh! It's because of my color" – which maybe it's probably true a lot of the time considering the inherent racism of most people.

So many things have happened because of what I am, and they shape the way I am today. I had a very unhappy childhood because of it. I had suddenly felt my world had fallen apart. I was Black and I was brought up in a White society. I didn't even like Black people because the impression that I got from the White people around me was that Black people weren't very nice people. Not that any of them had ever had any contact with one except on the TV. They had just seen Black people on TV or maybe if they had gone off to the big city for the day. I was also very unfortunate in that I was brought up in Wales. The Welsh people are quite parochial, especially small-town Welsh people.[6] One instance which sticks very

5 This revelation is almost a unanimous one for *métis(se)* individuals who have carved out identities for themselves using the raw materials of their childhood and early adult experiences. In Chapter 10, I refer to this ongoing process of negotiation as "Additive Blackness."

6 Similola's experiences and her sense of herself would have been radically different had she grown up in Tiger Bay, Cardiff, which is the home of one of the oldest *métis(se)* communities in Britain. I visited Tiger Bay wherein I felt very much at home among generations deep of as many permutations and combinations of nationalities as one could imagine. I remember talking with an older *métis* man, Somali and Welsh, who did not seem to understand why all of the television and radio talk shows were depicting identity

clearly in my mind was when a Black doctor accompanied by his White wife came to practice in town. It caused an outcry among the women, who almost unanimously decided not to allow him to touch them.

What I found, and I think it is true generally speaking, is that they had found difficulty in accepting me. I'd be walking along the road – it would have been the same for any Black person – and they'd touch my hair. Kids would go, "Mummy, Mummy" and scream "What's that?" It would make me feel like some kind of freak.[7] When I left school I knew I had to go and live in a city where there were Black people. If I don't, I'll never feel comfortable anywhere. Even now, having been back to Wales where I was brought up and possessing much more self-awareness, I still and I will never ever feel comfortable in that town, because of the bad vibes of my childhood. I can go walk on the streets and I don't care, but immediately memories raise their ugly head and all those feelings make me lose my hard-fought-for confidence in my identity. Even though now there are Black people living there, I'll walk along the street and think, "Wow! This is great, but it is just not for me. It's far too late and the damage has been done."

Because I was different, I liked and enjoyed the attention I was given and especially in school. In fact, although I was unhappy quite a lot of the time, my school life was much happier. I found a lot of the teachers singled me out in a good way as well as in a bad way. There were racist teachers there, although I didn't realize that they were racist. I just thought they didn't like me. There were also

crises among *métis(se)* people in Britain. He then answered his own question. He realized that, like Ruby and Similola, many individuals had grown up in predominantly White settings without other Black or *métis(se)* people around them. He admitted being fortunate to have grown up in a community where "everybody is mixed."

In her important book, *Mixed Race Children* (1987), Anne Wilson points out that there is a direct correlation between a *métis(se)* child's degree of comfort with being *métis(se)* and the proximity of other children and families like them. In Thatchapee, I lived near several families with small *métis(se)* children. I witnessed first-hand the positive impact of having individuals and families who reflected one's individual appearances and circumstances.

7 Once again, here is a representation of a *métis(se)* person as a freak, an oddity, an abnormality. That is, this description suggests the subjective accentuation of the different as freakish or ugly rather than inherently beautiful. There are parallels in the representation of Black people in general where reverence masquerades as aversion. See bell hooks (1992) *Black Looks*, Boston: South End Press or Sander Gilman (1992) "Black bodies, White bodies," in J. Donald *et al.* (eds.) *"Race," Culture and Difference*, London: Sage, pp. 171–97.

ones who singled me out for attention and gave it to me and encouraged me.

I was really happy at school. I loved it. To me it was my salvation – being at school and doing school work – pleasing the teachers who seemed to want me to do well. In my first school, it was the actual headmistress. I think she was just kind of besotted with me because I was new and different and she'd never had any Black children in her school before. Luckily I managed to impress her. I was good at my work. I think they saw me as some kind of protégé so they encouraged me. For me, that was a very happy time and I was given lots of attention that came with me to my junior school. Between the ages of 7 and 11, I also got that. Unlike most mixed race children today, I wasn't even aware at that time that I was different. I thought I was the same but better than all the White people around me – because I was getting all this attention.

The secondary school was heavy. I couldn't understand why the teachers were not so nice to me any more and why some of them were just outright nasty. There were literally teachers who wouldn't have me sitting in their classroom. I don't think they could bear to look. That's quite heavy. Now, those were really unhappy times. What I remember of my childhood it was more unhappy than happy, but school was definitely my happiest time. (*Giggle*) Most people say school is the bit they hate the most. (*Giggle*) I'm totally opposite. To me it was my salvation. I used to love going to bed so I could wake up and go to school the next day. (*Giggle*)

All the other kids in the home were White. They used to keep their distance from me when we'd go out. Even at school they wouldn't want to talk to me or let other kids know that they knew me. I never really understood why. It hurt me deep down inside. Now I realize it's because I was Black and they didn't want to be seen to know me. I had quite a lot of shit at school as well, but I somehow seemed to be able to cope with it more. I just realized I'm always going to be unpopular. No one is going to like me so I might as well live with it.

At home, well at home it wasn't so bad. I don't think they realized that I was that different either.[8] I had been brought up kind

---

8 Unless Similola purposely differentiates between her public rejection by her housemates and their private acceptance of her at "home," this statement is a blatant contradiction. However, it does not take Similola long to remember the ways in which the other children subjected her to uncomfortable interrogations because she was perceived as being different.

of like their little sister. I don't think they really saw it too much in the house, because they'd been with me all my life. They'd say, "Why won't your hair grow straight?" I wouldn't know the answer and I'd go, "I don't know" and get very upset about it. "Why is your nose flat?" And they'd become personal about my appearance. That used to worry me because I didn't know. I didn't know the answers. It sounds crazy to think there's this kid who's living in this country who doesn't know, but I really didn't know the answers.[9] I can't imagine what it would have been like if I had been totally Black – a proper Black person.[10] That child would have known far more quickly that they were different from a much

9 As the testimonies of Similola and Ruby (as well as Sharon, Claudia and Zaynab, whom I mention in Chapter 7) reveal, it is not unusual for a *métis(se)* child to have an ungrounded sense of who they are in relation to both Black and White people. This disorientation is particularly problematic for young children, such as the aforementioned *griottes*, who grew up in care before the local authorities were forced by the 1989 Children's Act to pay attention to the cultural needs of children when placing them with families. However, it is worth mentioning that controversy surrounding the placement of Black and *métis(se)* children in White English in-care situations existed prior to the passing of the Children's Act (see E. R. Braithwaite (1962) *Paid Servant*, London: Bodley Head; Paul Gilroy (1987) *There Ain't No Black in the Union Jack*, London: Hutchinson; or Ivor Gaber and Jane Aldridge (eds.) (1994) *In the Best Interest of the Child: Culture, Identity and Transracial Adoption*, London: Free Association Books).

This debate also rages on in the United States in such places as Oakland, California where transracial fosterage is described in a 1993 poster campaign by the National People's Democratic Uhuru Movement Foster Care Committee as a new form of the slave trade: "They are selling our babies for profit to the White community in the name of foster care. The Alameda County Department of Social Services is selling our babies. It's a racket!! We want our babies back."

10 "Full Black" person, "proper Black" person, "real Black" person – when *métis(se)* people like Similola use these terms, they are unwittingly reflecting the sentiments of a bi-racialist society with very specific negative ideas about "authentic Blackness" and necessarily postive oppositional "Whiteness." This same bi-racialized society utilizes a very scanty vocabulary when describing those individuals who are located at the Grey interfaces or interstices. When the discussion does acknowledge the Grey area, there is either a conflation of race, culture and ethnicity or ethnicity and culture are ignored entirely.

In the public arena, I have noticed the frequency with which individuals refer to nineteenth-century anthropological phenotypic criteria – texture of hair, hair and eye color, facial features, skin color, the extent to which one's buttocks protude and other descriptions of physique – in an attempt to place *métis(se)* along the pseudoevolutionary scale. As already mentioned, *métis(se)* women and men/boys and girls have internalized these Victorian bi-racialized caricatures and have naturalized them in their everyday discourses.

While in the midst of writing the Ph.D. thesis version of this text, I had many interpersonal encounters, which affirmed much of what I was interrogating as bi-racialized theories. On one occasion, I was talking on the telephone with a new friend. He was a golden-brown African American Rasta and a physician. At one stage in the conversation, he said, "You have a lot of melanin for someone who comes from such a mixed background. You must be the dark sheep in the family…and that nappy hair." Something to

earlier age. I was actually quite light-skinned as well. My hair was incredibly short; it was so tight. In that sense, I probably didn't feel too different because my skin color was the same as all the other kids around me. It wasn't incredibly noticeable. Whereas, I think, "Oh no! What if I had been Black?" Imagine the shit and hassle. I probably wouldn't be talking about it now. I probably would be really screwed up.[11] Then you never know. Anyway that's totally hypothetical. We're talking about the reality. I don't remember any happy, happy times that stand out in my mind at all – not until I left home.[12]

In my boarding school, where I was dispatched at age 16 as the housemother could no longer tolerate my presence, I met another mixed race person. There were two Nigerian guys, a guy from Malawi, who I actually met when I was in Malawi just by chance, and there were a couple of mixed race guys from Jamaica, whose father was actually Nigerian. That was good for me; it was very very good for me. But at that time, I still really wasn't thinking about becoming Black, so I didn't take as much advantage of being with them as I could have done. It was a shame, but also the set-up in the school affected the situation. It was a boys' boarding school and they just took girls in the sixth form. We didn't live on the school premises; we lived out of school. There were only twelve of us and it was basically a boys' school. There was that whole thing – whole ratio of the sexes and everything else.

I did get friendly with one of the Nigerian guys and he terrified the life out of me. He tried to kiss me once and he had massive lips. I remember thinking, "Oh God! Im going to suffocate." He really frightened me and terrified me. I remember him grabbing me in the corridor and saying, "Oh, I really want to kiss you." I just felt really sickened by it all and thinking, "Oh! Now that's what black guys are like. They just grab you and they're really pushy." That

---

the effect that the "African" genes must have really kicked in to make me. To which I replied, "I have told you about my genotype, and you are responding to my phenotype, but you have yet to ask me anything about what it was like growing up in my family." After a pause, I added, "By the way, mixed race people come in all shades." I was seething. I had let this brother get under my skin with his own internalized bi-racialized projectiles.

11 Research involving children with two Black birth parents who also grew up in isolated, predominantly White in-care situations shows that they experience identity confusion similar to the identity conflicts of *métis(se)* children in care.

12 Similola's seemingly contradictory accounts of her reception by her peers are additional examples of the situational and necessarily conditional nature of belonging for all *métis(se)* people.

frightened me off Black guys for years.[13] He was also very big in stature and very black skinned. He was Nigerian. He was a bit, what's the word without being too rude and anti-Nigerian? He was sort of – I'm not anti-Nigerian – but he was a very arrogant sort of guy and very full of himself. I just found him incredibly intimidating, and of course he wanted to take me under his wing the minute he saw me. He really terrified me. He really scared me. I think it was partly due to the fact that coming from this little Welsh town as well, I still had this – the same kind of feelings that any White person living in that town would have had about Black people. Yet, I'm sure if he'd done that to a White girl, I mean she'd have gone screaming down the corridor and run a mile. It wasn't quite that bad, but it was pretty terrible.[14]

13 I had a similar experience in Nigeria the summer of my thirteenth birthday. After an eventful trip to Egypt, my family had been travelling around Nigeria visiting family and friends. We had stopped over at the home of a family friend. They had servants, including a houseboy named Richard from Owerri, with eyes only for me. My siblings found his attraction to me very amusing. I was quite disturbed, knowing full well what that gaze may signify.

Sure enough, when night time came, Richard aged about 23 – back then he seemed ancient – found his way to the bedroom I was sharing with my younger sister. Someone must have notified him that my sister slept like a log. She slept through the entire event. Reluctantly, I was waiting for him. That summer, in Nando, our village in Eastern Nigeria, land of the Igbo, I had just "celebrated" the year of my first menses. Mama, my paternal grandmother had made a great fuss over this biological marker of my budding womanhood.

By African accounts, I was (almost) a woman, and all I knew was that I did not want to lose my virginity with him. After all, I did not even know him, certainly did not fancy him and definitely did not love him. I could smell him even before he approached my bed – palm oil, sweat and cheap cologne. Our heartbeats quickened – his out of desire and mine from unadulterated fear. He bent over me, put one hand on either side of the pillow, and said through a heavily-accented breath of that evening's meal, "If you don't kiss me, I'll never speak to you again..."

The next morning, I did not tell my parents, for I did not want this man to lose his job. That night, Richard, the houseboy, stole a kiss and left behind with me a mistrust of my beautiful brown-skinned brothers that would take years to shake off. Like Similola, it took me a long time to feel comfortable around Black men who seemed to fit that "caricature" – full lips, "dark" skin, big in stature and muscular. It is only after years of life experience and intellectual pursuits that I can begin to understand – but neither forgive nor forget – Richard's impotent motives that hot, sticky Nigerian summer's night of my adolescence.

14 The racialized and sexualized imagery in this scene is quite powerful. Ordinarily, this would have been remembered as an innnocent kiss. However, it is the interwoven politics of bi-racialization and sexuality that have made this no longer an innocent act between two blossoming adolescents. He is a "sex-crazed Black African man" and she is an "unassuming White-identified damsel" from rural Wales. As Similola retells this encounter to me, I am taken by the symbolic significance. This is her first time away from the children's home, where she has had very little if any direct contact with Black people. With

Imagine: "It don't matter if you're Black or White."[15]

There was a time when because I felt kind of different – I thought to myself: I want to be surrounded by plain people who are just normal and ordinary. Like I'm not, sort of thing. I think this is probably at the time when I was still very much into the White thing and they were White people and therefore they would enhance my status by me being with them, which I think is bullshit now. (*Laughter*)...It just started coming to me.

Like the year when I came to college in Bristol and I told you I didn't know any Black people. I'd be walking down the road with fellow students and I used to notice that okay, mainly it was Black men originally – Black men who'd shout at me across the road "What are you doing with those honkies?" and I'd think, "Gosh! Maybe I shouldn't be with these people"...and it brought to my attention that people were noticing me being with White people – that I was different, and I started thinking about it. Thinking: "Oh maybe it's not such a good idea to be seen with them so much. 'Cos I'm not being – I'm being disloyal if you like." I started even going around on my own for a while because I couldn't decide what to do. I thought, "If I'm seen on my own, then no one can accuse me of collaborating with the enemy," as it seemed to be they saw it then. I was made to feel like that. Now of course, I don't mind any more. At that time, I was going through an identity crisis. I remember going home and thinking, "Oh, God! What can I do? 'Cos I don't know any Black people and I can't go 'round with the White people 'cos the Black people are shouting at me about it, so what do I do?" I remember being in a real quandary about it thinking, "I'll just have to go 'round on my own until I can find my niche...," and that's what I did.

Until I met this Black girl and we started going round together as it were. I started feeling odd about it. It was just the two of us and wherever we would go, people seemed to look at us. We were always standing out. So, I kept thinking if there were a few White people with us as well, we would be more of a little group. We'd balance better. I used to have little fantasies about that. (*Laughter*) I

this Nigerian fellow, she not only has her first Black embrace, but she is also embracing Blackness for the very first time. The Mirror Speaks.

15 Michael Jackson (1991) *"Black or White," Dangerous*, New York: Epic Records.

enjoyed being with her because it gave me that sense of identity. It made me think to myself that these people can now see me with a Black person and know that I'm Black – first and foremost. It was good for me at that time. Although I wasn't too sure if I wanted to be seen as being Black one hundred percent. I was just finding my feet. This is after being told that Black was horrible. After eighteen years of being told that, to suddenly cross over to the enemy camp as it were, was difficult. It took me ages to come to terms with it.

It's a very difficult thing. The thing about races mixing is it's going to produce lots of people who are going to find that problem. I really do, and I think that it would be good if there were people who understood the kind of things that transracial people are going to have to go through. I'm sure there's going to be a lot of it around. There's a lot of it around now. Not just going to be, but there will be more and more of it. I think that if you're not able to deal with it, it just leads to mental illness and things like that, and then all sorts of horrible problems. I used to think I was going mad because I couldn't decide. I used to have to think, I had to be Black or White and I couldn't decide which one I was supposed to be and which one I wanted to be. I couldn't, I didn't even think I could be either. The way I felt was I had to be one or the other. It was some-thing that I found really difficult to deal with. I used to think I was going to go mad from it. Luckily, I didn't. But, I used to think so at times, that I'd go mad. Now, I don't think in those terms, any more.

I think having been in Africa had something to do with it in the sense that most of the so called "Coloreds" that I met – this is how they call themselves – were so mixed they didn't know where they came from, therefore they didn't have the choice of being Black or White. If they decided they wanted to be one of the parts of their racial mix-up, they could be one of maybe four, or five or six – if they knew. That's what made me think trying to be Black or White is very silly. 'Cos it doesn't actually make any difference at the end of the day. The difference comes from within me. I'm neither of those two things and I'm both as well. But not that it matters so much. I came to terms with myself as an individual and I do realize, okay, because of my physical appearance it's going to affect the way people react towards me, but that's something that's going to happen to everybody in all sorts of ways…whatever race they are, whatever color they are, anyway.

So, I just think though, I'm glad I went through that process…it sounds very silly now when I think about it. You know, do we want to be Black or White? I used to even wake up and have Black days and White days. I was really stupid (*Laughter*)…I don't think I was stupid actually, because I was trying to find myself, I didn't know how to do it. I didn't know anybody else who was mixed race who was going through the same thing as me that I could turn to and say "How do you deal with it?" I didn't know anyone of my kind of background who was at that particular stage or at that particular time and I couldn't find any books on the subject or anybody to even vaguely identify with and it was really difficult for me. Of course, I couldn't talk to White people because I didn't feel they'd want to know or could understand and the same with Black people. I couldn't find anybody who would – I tried to talk to girls who had been brought up in my children's home with me, but they couldn't really shed any light because they used to say "We hadn't even noticed." So they didn't really help me either. I thought maybe it's a shame, maybe if you'd noticed, I wouldn't be going through this horrible crisis now, when I don't know what I am and who I am. I think when you're that kind of age, you want to fit in, you want to belong somewhere. If you don't feel that you do, it can cause so much soul searching, and that's how I felt. It took me years...and that's why I decided, "I'm going to have a Black day or a White day." My White day I was... (*Laughter*). I'd dress differently for starters. I'd usually wear jeans on my White days. (*Laughter*) I used to wear jeans because I thought it's more acceptable amongst White students to wear jeans. It seemed like a kind of White uniform in a way and you didn't see many Black girls wearing jeans at that time. So, I'd wear jeans, and whatever else – the bits and pieces that go with it – tee shirts, whatever. Then on my Black days, I'd wear flowery skirts (*Laughter*) and very bright clothes and people used to say "God" and I actually got to quite enjoy it. It sounds very silly at that time. I'm not sure if it affected my behavior in any way. At that phase, I was more outgoing and I tended to be a bit more – to let more of myself show, and not be so self-conscious. Because it was my Black day and I'd think: "Oh I can get away with these things in front of White people because they don't expect Black people to act like them so I can be a bit more outrageous than I normally would." In the end, I couldn't cope with both of these identities. (*Laughter*) I'd decide the night before. Not necessarily one day...sometimes it would be like I'd enjoy my Black day so much on one Monday and I'd think...it must have been all psychological. I don't think so totally, but I used to notice people treated me differently as well and they reacted towards me in a different way.

They seemed to be much nicer to me on my Black days. There weren't very many Black students there. It was mainly for White people. Because I knew I couldn't join them totally, I thought why don't I show them I'm different, but some days I couldn't handle that. Some days I'd wake up and think: "Oh, God"…'cos I'd look at the clothes and think, "Did I really go out like that?"…and just think, "Oh, my God!" (*Laughter*)…'cos even in terms of dress, I was brought up to wear very sedate subdued colors…and even the style of clothing…and I didn't. I even remember, when I used to watch TV, Black people always used to have really nice bright clothes which brought out their skin color – clothes which just enhanced them and made them look good…and I'd think, "Why can't I have my bright colors ?" and I was never allowed to – as a child. It was something I always wanted to do, but because I hadn't been allowed to, I never felt really that comfortable. I remember going out and buying a really bright red dress. I put it on, I walked outside the door and then ran inside the house and changed. I thought, "No! I can't handle it." It was that kind of thing. I found that by doing it that way, I kind of switched myself into it more. Even now though, I'm still like that, and I think that I still expect people to react to me in the same way without me thinking it. I think to myself, probably self-consciously, like even now the way I dress, to me this is my White way of dressing. Then sometimes, I also wear bright clothes and just feel more Black you know. It's not so easily defined any more because there is more of a cross-over. Now there are more grey days, I think all of them, really.

But it took me a while actually to shake off that whole Black day /White day thing. I remember loving it. I was using it as an excuse to dress outrageously, because I'd see clothes and really want to wear them and think, "Oh, I haven't got the nerve." Then, I'd think, "Yeah, I'll buy it anyway." I'd keep it in my wardrobe for a while and I'd think, "I'm gonna wear this today." I used to wear really, I mean just horrible, not horrible, but bright very gawdy clothes at one time and it was at this time I remember buying a pair of red boots – you know bright red. Even now, I cringe, but I thought I had to go to that extreme, because I suddenly thought, "I want to stand out to be seen to be confident in my clothes and to wear bright colors like White people think Black people dress." That's part of the stereotype isn't it? I thought I'd do that and then I'm immediately noticeable as a Black person. Then, of course, I started toning it down, 'cos realizing it doesn't actually suit me that much. It doesn't suit my character to be dressed in that outrageous kind of way. So I toned it down and found a happy medium where I feel comfortable. (*Laughter*) Oh, I cringe when I even think about it actually. Oh, how could I have done it? This is it, because I wanted to be totally outrageous. I was totally outrageous. It was ridiculous. I think, mainly in my eyes more so. 'Cos I mean, there are other people who dress like that and could carry it off. So it wasn't as if I was the only person, but for me it was a giant step.

To me it was something to do with acknowledging my Blackness. To me, I thought, I can't be Black if I don't wear bright-colored clothes. I had this period of going 'round dressed all in-black clothes. Before I left school, and I thought if I wore black clothes all the time, I wouldn't be noticed. It wasn't like now where people wear black clothes all the time. (*Laughter*) It was the time when black wasn't even vaguely fashionable. It was only worn for funerals and that was it. I got into this "wearing black clothes" thing thinking I'd be totally unnoticed. My whole wardrobe was full of black clothes. To me it was an even greater step to suddenly switch into really bright – 'cos I'd got so comfortable with black. Even though people do notice you, it's what you yourself feel. I used to feel that when I wore black I was totally insignificant and totally unnoticed and it suited me at that time to be like that and to just fade into the background and not be noticed for any reason. The giant leap into brightness for me was so huge that I used to dare myself.[16] I'd go into shops and buy very, very bright-colored clothing and then dare myself in the evening to put it on the next day. I'd say, "God! Are you gonna wear that tomorrow or not?" Sometimes I would, sometimes I wouldn't. Now, I don't even, I don't want to try and dress in a Black way, just because I want to identify with being Black. 'Cos to me now, that's so superficial anyway, there is much more to it then that and I don't feel the need for that kind of thing anymore. People have to accept me for what I am and the way I am, and if they don't it's just tough.[17]

16 The way Similola describes her Black Days/White Days scheme is very similar to the ways in which *métis(se)* people who are "trying on" being Black for the first time oscillate uncomfortably between the two supposedly oppositional "Black" and "White" presentations of self. Clothes supposedly being external representations of one's inner self, Similola's bi-racialized dress scheme reinforces the notion that in our society "you are what you wear"...and there is a "Black" way of dressing/being and a "White" way of dressing/being.

17 Having explored many possibilities on their journeys, almost all of the twenty-five *métis(se)* participants I worked with have reached this same point of reconciliation. That is, Similola and others like her are mindful of the everyday practices of bi-racialization and the one drop rule. However, these social facts do not disable Similola, who expresses an integrated *métisse* psyche, which has rejected distorted, essentialized and limiting compulsory exclusive Black affiliation.

6

AKOUSA

"At the end of the day, I have a White mother"

Akousa (Fante (Ghana), born on a Sunday) is my sister–friend Sarah's older sister. Akousa and Sarah's sistren relationship is analogous to my relationship with my sister Ann. We all grew up in the color-conscious English and/or American African diasporas at times feeling very inadequate about our light-skinnedness. However, color being a relative concept, despite their prominent "African" features, Akousa and Ann, being "lighter-skinned" than Sarah and I, had to manage more aggravation from both the White and the Black communities. Sarah and I were also considered to be more "beautiful" than our sisters, leading both of them later in life to confess that they felt a certain degree of resentment towards us. Having said that, there are many ways in which Akousa's experiences and personality resonate with my own. Listening to the pain in some of Sarah's testimonies connects me in profound ways with my younger sister Ann's vulnerabilities.

When I first met Akousa, I remember thinking how much she sparkled – her eyes, her smile and her presence. My responding to her sparkling smile is humorous in light of the fact that as her testimonies will reveal, until recently, Akousa has always hated her smile. Her mother is White Irish, her father is Black Bajan (from Barbados). She is a Rastafarian,[1] and yet is not seen as a typical Rasta woman. She sees herself as a Black woman and yet not everyone sees her as a Black woman.

---

1 A Rastafarian – a member of a religious group (others refer to as a "cult") which originated in Jamaica and who reject Western ideas and values ("Babylon") and regard Haile Selassie, the former emperor of Ethiopia, as divine.

102

The lack of fit between the multilayered and textured complexities of Akousa's narratives and their flattened reduction to text reinforce for me the extent to which our lived realities cannot be contained by the four sides of the page. However, with both Akousa's evocations as well as her sister Sarah's in the following chapter, I have tried as much as possible to capture and preserve their Scouse (Liverpudlian) accent, her vibrant sense of humor, her ability to "reason" (wax philosophically about life's issues) and the natural rhythm of her testimonies about "race", color, class, and gender politics. With so much rich material to work with, it was very hard for me to know where to stop when translating Akousa's oral testimonies to text. Everything she said was so profound. She spoke most candidly about the ways in which she, as a "light-skinned Black person," negotiates the paradoxes of "race" and color. Seeing Blackness as "a consciousness or a state of mind," she identifies very strongly as a Black woman. However, by virtue of her skin color and her seeming *métisse* appearance, constituents of both the White and Black communities outside the safe space of her own Liverpool community challenge her chosen identity.

Akousa: embracing Blackness as a state of consciousness

It's dead hard where to begin. I think the best way to do it is to talk about my family. My mum comes from Ireland and she met my father who was second to the chief engineer on the ship. Me dad's from Barbados. Basically, my dad wasn't a great man. He wasn't a good man. He beat me mum quite a bit. He was very – I would say Bajan in the sense that he didn't see his ancestors as coming from Africa. You know – things like that. He'd deny those kind of things.

We lived in like, one room in Liverpool, where I was born. My father would come home from ship and go out drinking, spend all his money. Basically, there wouldn't be enough money for anything else. You know he was one of those showy Black men. You know – go out and entertain all the friends and then there's no money left and they're expectin' miracles from the wife and things like that. So, I think when me mum came out of hospital either with me or our Sarah – I think it was with our Sarah, she basically had nowhere to live. My dad had gone and married another woman – an English woman, and I've got seven stepsisters and brothers. But, I don't have a real link with them. Between the age of nought up to 13, I had no contact with me father. Then, because of me brother's accident and some problems between him and me mum, me dad decided not to get in touch any more. He went off...so I didn't get on with him anyway. I didn't like a lot of his attitudes and maybe I'd seen things which I don't remember now when I was small that just didn't make any kind of link between me and me dad.

So, we went to live at me Aunt Hyacinth's and me Uncle Winston's. Me Aunt Hyacinth's from Guyana, me Uncle Winston, Surinamese. They're not blood relatives, but we went to live with them in a house, two up two down – on Salter Street – that belonged to me Uncle Desmond me Aunt Hyacinth's brother. It must have been hard for my mum living in such a small house with two other adults and three children – with us and my mum sleeping in one room. But as a child it didn't affect me. I really enjoyed living in that house.

Sunday afternoons, used to be really nice. Used to really enjoy – we'd come back from church. We used to go to a White Baptist church. But we also used to go to a small gathering with Black people who were from another church. But it was only like four or five or six people, and we'd have a little gathering – singin' and Bible reading. And we'd come 'ome from church and eat. Then, in the front room would be like me Uncle William, Uncle Lionel, me Uncle Lincoln, Mr Michael, all those people and they were all from different islands. Some were from Guyana, some were from Trinidad, some Barbados, some from St. Lucia, that side of the Caribbean also. And they'd all be sittin' in the front room, get a little rum out, whiskey out. Then they'd all sit there and talk about back home. Talk about chickens in the yard, tiefin' from the mango trees, swimmin' in the sea – you know, all those kind of things. I used to sit there and listen; I used to call it home as well. I'd be sayin', "I want to go home." My Uncle Lincoln said that from about the age of two years I was askin' to take me home with him.[2] It always just sounded like such a nice place – you know – to be, because of the wonderful times they seemed to have had there. And because I was a part of them, it was home for me. This wasn't – England wasn't home. That was where I belonged, and I want to go there. That was nice. I really enjoyed that part of my life.

2 At different junctures in their lives, "home" takes on different meanings and locations for each of the *métisse griottes*. For example, here Akousa is talking about the way in which as a child she wanted to return to her "home" in the Caribbean. Then, once she became a Rasta, Africa is her ancestral home and Ethiopia her spiritual home.

The thing I think about me Mother was she didn't let any of the problems that she was really havin' between her and me dad or even in terms of livin' in a two-up two-down house with two other adults affect us. It must have been rough. I don't feel it really affected me. I think she kept a lot of things away from us. I think she wanted us to try and enjoy as much of our childhood – 'cos she didn't have much of a childhood. She was an orphan and came from extreme poverty in Ireland. Between foster homes and the work-house side of the convent, it was pretty grim for her.

During the early stages of writing the ethnography, I was browsing through a stack of my books, of various vintages, all pertaining to "race." As luck would have it, while looking through *A Rap on Race* (1971), a classic dialogue between Margaret Mead and James Baldwin. I opened it up to the following discussion of the so-called Black community in Liverpool. However, in addition to Tiger Bay in Cardiff, Wales, Liverpool is actually the home of sea-faring *metis(se)* families, which emerged in the the late nineteenth and early twentieth century:

BALDWIN: Yes. Somebody born in Liverpool is quite another case, something different altogether. But there are comparatively very few black people, by comparison to the American black situation, born in Liverpool.

MEAD: They are very interesting though. You know, they couldn't dance.

BALDWIN: I met some of them. They can't dance?

MEAD: No, you see they have white mothers. They had white lower-class mothers who were just sort of cold potatoes; their African fathers were sailors and didn't stay at all. When our troops got to England in World War II, of course everyone thought it so nice for the black American to associate with the colored people in Liverpool – not one of whom had a secondary school education, by the way. But the thing that really riled the black American was they couldn't dance! I mean, what in thunder are you doing with black people who can't dance?[3]

---

3 Margaret Mead and James Baldwin (1971) *A Rap on Race*, Philadelphia: Lippincott, p. 82.

With her transcribed Scouse accent and intonations intact, Akousa's description of the legendary dance parties that took place every time the men came to shore certainly challenges Margaret Mead's remarks about Black Liverpudlians' lack of coordination on the dance floor. In addition, Akousa's lively conversational style engages the reader in a way that Baldwin and Mead, presumably talking about the same community, do not.

There was always a lot of people coming in and out of the house and there was always people from different parts of the world comin' in mainly Black countries. Me Uncle Desmond might come down. The ship'll dock in Liverpool and me auntie would say "He would bring half the ship with him." Which meant party time basically. (*Laughter*) There would be me mum and me auntie in the kitchen maybe doing all the cookin' for all these people. The thing I always remember about me Uncle Desmond is he used to have this donkey jacket that was black and white and he used to have a small style trilby stuck on the back of his head always chewing Wrigley's chewing gum. I used to be able to swing in between his legs. I can remember little things like that. We used to enjoy them...then we used to have parties and we used to be able to go to the parties 'cos he used to teach us to dance. You know, the little dances like The Twist and...calypso.

I always remember one time 'cos I was so much in love with me Uncle Lincoln, but then me mum said he was a rogue. Which he was. He wasn't a great man. But there was something between me and me Uncle Lincoln. Me mum says I was gullible. She said one day she doesn't know what happened between me and me Uncle Lincoln, why he was so attached to me. She thinks it was because one day in Salter Street I was crying or something from me cot. He come upstairs and me uncle come into the room and I grabbed hold of his finger and that sort of threw him. So like at this party, he was dancin' with other women. I used to grab hold of his leg. You're that small you could grab hold of his leg and he couldn't dance properly with any of the women. (*Laughter*) Here's me in between him and this woman and he's trying to dance around me. That was funny....

The other thing about my childhood was my hair was a problem for me mum. Sarah had loose hair, and you could curl it and roll it, and do anything else with it. But my hair's tough. It was murder washin' it, it was murder combin' it, and I always wanted to go to me Aunt Hyacinth's to do it rather than me mum. That was always hassle. Then I was skinny as well, which was another problem, 'cos everything hung on me. Everything would look nice on Sarah. "You're like a coat hanger," my mum would say. Everything just hangs on me. There were other things like because of the type of smile I have, I show everything, I mean the inside of the mouth. Me mum used to say to me, "Don't smile in the camera." That's given me some complexes which I haven't discussed with me mother.

The other thing was how light I was in a sense to how dark Sarah was and our Colin was. People would call me "red" and stuff like that. It didn't seem so heavy then, but it was when I was getting older – especially when I went from my community into a Jamaican community outside Liverpool. To Birmingham, this was – in the seventies. I was 17, 18 at the time. I was at the African Liberation Day, May 25, and I was gettin' told how light I was. I wasn't Black, it was this and it was that, and the other. At that age, I was startin' to get confused about things. I remember going to Wolverhampton and being in this pub with a friend and this Black guy sittin' on the pool table sayin' to me that I was like a White woman. That I wasn't Black, I was White. All this shit being hurled at me, I was thinkin', "What's goin' on here?" It was like a complete contradiction to what was happenin' at home. That brought in the whole thing about how light I was, and about me mother being White. I didn't feel like it was a real big issue for me prior to that, but now it was becoming this issue. Whereas in Liverpool, I didn't find it was a big issue.[4] I didn't find it was a big issue with family. Although people called me "red-skinned" it didn't mean I wasn't part and parcel of them, it just means that's the shade of coloring that I am. That's the way I felt anyway.

The smile and everything – that still plays on me mind. I think that was a problem that was with me mum, rather than with me. I think most Black people when they give you a smile, they give you a smile. It's weird, when I was workin' in a high-street shop, people would come up to me and say, "You've got a really nice smile." I'd say, "Go away, you can see the insides of me mouth, down me throat, front of me." You know what I mean? But then people made me realize that I did have a nice smile. They felt like it was a genuine smile and not what me mum was saying.

---

4   Much of Akousa's testimony points to the situational nature of bi-racialized labeling and categorization. She learns about the politics of "race" and color within other Black communities when she leaves the familiarity of Liverpool and visits other Black communities in England. These particular Black communities uphold slightly different criteria for full Black membership. As Akousa mentions, these chromatic standards shift according to the political climate.

There were always conflicts between me and me sister. Sarah –
everyone liked her. All the men in the family liked her, she could
twist them around her little finger for some reason. Whereas, for
me it's just me Uncle Lincoln that had this attachment, and I clung
to him out of all the family members. Whereas, Sarah – everyone
was 'round. Also, Sarah was the baby of the family and I'm the
middle. Colin's the boy. I think you become more independent. If
you're in the middle, people don't take much notice of you. I've
discussed that with me auntie and me mum at one time, and me
mum said, "Yeah, you're right because Colin is the boy he was the
first and after you were born"....There are only twenty-eight
months between me and me sister – all the attention went onto
Sarah. There's me – stuck in the middle.

I used to feel a bit jealous of Sarah. I used to think she's beautiful, and this, and look at me. As a 15-, 16-year-old teenager, I
used to think I looked awful. Clothes looked terrible on me. Sarah
would look wonderful. I used to get really vexed with myself. At
the end of the day gettin' into me late teens, I didn't think much
about meself because of all these conflicts that were startin' to come
up from the past. Also new ones that were comin' in from other
communities – Black communities – that were really shockin' me. I
mean there were times when I wouldn't show me legs. I'd go
through the summer wearing tights and socks. 'Cos I thought they
were too light and too White-lookin'. There was a lot of pressure. I
remember one day I was leanin' up somewhere and this guy said to
me, "Boy, aren't your legs White!" I just looked in horror, and felt
really sick and wanted to just run away. I was thinkin', "God, why
didn't you make me a bit darker? Why did you make me so light?"
It took me years to reconcile that.

Because of what happened in the seventies in terms of the Black
Power Movement, especially in this country, if you weren't black
like ebony, then you just didn't have a chance basically.[5] It was the
most difficult time of my life – trying to sort out who I was now.
Whereas, before, I thought I knew who I was. My family comes
from the Caribbean. I never brought me mum into question. She
seemed to take things in her stride. I kept comin' home and I'd say
to her, "I hate all White people. Tonkers, or honkies, or whatever."
There's me mum sittin' there, and I just didn't think about it. It's
hard work, but she's me mother. I don't think of her in terms of, me

---

5   Akousa discusses the Black Power Movement in Britain in terms of its direct impact on
    her "credibility" as a "Black" person.

mum she's White I shouldn't be sayin' these things.[6] But on the other hand, me mum never told me that I was "half-caste" or "half-breed" or anything like that. She saw me as a whole person. She told me, "When you go out in the street, they're goin' to call you 'nigger', they're not goin' to call you 'light-skinned' or somethin' like that. They'll call you 'black bastard.'" No matter how light or how dark you are, that's the vibe.

So, I didn't really think about it. I could think now, at certain point in time it really must of hurt her. She managed to deal with it somehow. I don't know. I think she sat back and waited for me to work my way out of that and begin to understand people more. She's got an understandin' of people, and also because of her own experiences, she kept sayin' to me, "People are basically all the same." In some respects, I can say, "Yeah." But, as a Black person, there are other issues involved. I think because of her own experiences in terms of White people rejectin' her and certain sides of the Black community. She'd go to a party with me dad, and nobody would look at her. They wouldn't serve her a drink, wouldn't say nothin'. She'd sit there at this party all on her own. She had the experiences of the Whites as well. To her, it's like, "What's the difference at the end of the day?" Basically, you've got the same kind of attitudes except comin' from different stand-points. I could see what she said, but at the end of the day with me mother and with the family, we've had more Black friends in the family and more Black people. One or two White women I would call "aunt." That was Aunt Rose, who was married to a Black man, and another woman, who used to come to visit with me mum.

School: school was an experience. Primary school wasn't too bad. There were a lot of Chinese kids and Black kids, and everyone skitzed each other off called each other "Four-Eyes" or "Fatty." It wasn't so heavy, there were certain racist undertones, but because you had other Black kids there, you had a bit of alliances with other people and things like that. But 'round the school, some of the streets we couldn't walk up. 'Cos the kids would come up, just particular streets, and call us "nigger" or "black bastard." So we never walked up that street, we'd have to go two more streets down.

It was mainly when I went to secondary school, which was like a horror story for me. I wouldn't go to that school again, I wouldn't

6　This is a perfect example of the ways in which *métis(se)* people are forced to negotiate public and private spheres which negate and acknowledge their White English parentage, respectively.

do my school career over again. People reminisce a lot over their school days. (*Kisses teeth*) My mum thought she was doin' a good thing, she was sendin' me to an all-girls' school – secondary modern school. Half of it was boys, half girls. We didn't mix, but we shared the hall, which was in the middle. I was the only Black girl there. The whole area is a White area. They called you "nigger" and "coon" and "You need to get back where you come from." All those things were goin' on in school. I remember the first couple of weeks of school and I missed the bus stop. It was only a simple thing – just one bus stop. I started cryin' me eyes out. I was totally terrified to walk up any of the streets to get to school rather than the way that I normally walked. I was frightened some White people might come out and pick on me. I never told me mum. I don't understand why I never discussed it with me mum. Why I never discussed it with me auntie. 'Cos me auntie said to me, I talked to her a couple of years ago, "Why didn't you tell us?" I can't figure out the reason why as yet. You'd go in school and people would be tellin' you that your house stinks, you haven't got any good clothes, Black people are this, Black people are that, Black people are the other. Basically gettin' called names, gettin' spat at. Stuff like that went on throughout the years of my schoolin'.

I was standing next to this White guy and he started to call this Black girl a "nigger" and I said, "Who are you callin' 'nigger?'" "Oh, you're alright Akousa, there's nothin' wrong with you. You're fine." I said, "Listen love, if you're callin' her a 'nigger', you're callin' me a 'nigger.'" And I walked away. School was heavy. Another heavy experience was during the first couple of weeks of school. There were skinheads in the area as well. There was a skinhead, and he was sittin' on the street. I'd just come from the shop up the road. He had his big boots on, and he said, "Hey nigger, come polish my boots for me." Here I am eleven and a half, and being confronted with this guy. All I could do was run.

White people are weird, man. They are weird frigging people. Towards the end of my school year we began to have discos. I remember soul – the soul walk – and the bump and all of that thing. I became popular because I could do all of the latest dances. I felt good 'cos I would teach them the dances. But they could never dance as good as me because they just didn't have the soul to dance as good as me. So I'd teach them the basics, and get out there on the floor and I'd be givin' it loads. It was the only way of gettin' one up on these people and suddenly they became friendly with me to a certain extent. I found that all really strange....

All school is school. I hated it. I stuck it out because me mum was so strict about education. Basically teachers were sayin' how good I was when I arrived at the school. How by the time I got to third year, I had changed. Now I can sit down and laugh, 'cos I've travelled the world, I've got my university degree, I've worked for the city council, I've been a director, other things like that. I think, "Yeah, man, I come out of school with nothin' and you's never did nothin' for me." I did it all for myself and the people in my community who helped me get where I wanted to go. The school never did anything for me at the end of the day. Maybe it made me stronger as person, because of what I had to deal with. It didn't give me anythin'. On an academic level, I came out with very little. But I still got to a lot of places. I had a White girlfriend and I met her on the street a couple of months ago. She just looked old. She looked like an old woman with five kids. She regretted all sorts of things. Regretted havin' children. Then, I was tellin' her about all the things I had done. I felt sorry for her. But, at the end of the day Jah will guide and what comes around goes around. School – never again. (*Kisses teeth*) I won't do it.

I did some voluntary work at Baobab Community Centre and met a Black American woman from Chicago and another woman from Sierra Leone.[7] They were workin' at this community center. Pamela was a very strong Black woman – Black American woman from Chicago. The two of them gave me and my sister quite a lot. She introduced me to Alice Walker, those people. It was when I read my first Black novel. I just ate it up. It was like, "Lie, Lie!" Finally, at last, you could relate to the stories, and you could relate to the things in the book, and the people who were writin' them. You could see yourself, images of yourself, and images of people in the community where you live. That was fantastic. She also had *The Black Book* as well, which I read through, about the lynchin's and stereotyping of Black people through cartoon characters. She had another book about Black heroes, and people who had done a lot for science. I thought, "Yeah. That was really good." Both of them really instilled a lot into us. Considerin' we were young and they were about eight years older than us, I said to her, "How the hell did you put up with us? These 18-year-olds hangin' round you practically twenty-four hours a day, never leavin' you alone." They said, "There was somethin' there and we thought we could nurture it a little bit." When my friend left to go back to Chicago, I

---

7 Consistently, at a certain stage in their lives, all of the *griottes* point to African Caribbean, African American or African women (and sometimes men) who served as their cultural surrogates. For example, they introduced them to Black literature, taught them how to cook Caribbean dishes and showed them basic Black grooming skills – creaming the skin and oiling the scalp.

couldn't stop cryin'. 'Cos I knew I was on my own. I gotta deal with me own life. I can't just run to her house no more. They helped move me in the right direction. I started buyin' a lot more Black literature – readin' a lot more widely. They got us out to theatre. I think that's where my love of culture and art now comes from. I think they started to give us a good appreciation of it.

I see myself as Black.[8] Other people see meself as bein' "half-caste" as some like to call it. Like the Greek guy who said I should have an Irish map in one ear and an African one in the other. Therefore, I should also have a Bajan one as well, and an English one, 'cos I was born in England. I could go on forever. When people bring those sorts of issues up, you sit down and you start questionin' yourself and askin' yourself, "Am I really who I think I am?" Who I've decided I am? All these people are tryin' to define who you are, tell you that "You can't be Black. Look how light you are!" "Your mother's White, so how can you be Black?"

I think at the end of the day, White society has never accepted me. They've seen me as a contamination to their stock. Diseased person, and even worse than havin' two Black parents, worse than even that. If you come to extermination we would most probably go first.[9] Nazi Germany. That's the sort of vibe, I get off White people. With Black people, generally, I know they've accepted me as I am. I've been a part of their community. I've been raised within a Caribbean culture. I don't think the way White people think. I couldn't begin to think how a White person thinks. The way they define me, I don't define myself in that way. I will be Black 'til the day I die, no matter how many White people want to tell me who I am and what I am. No matter how much society wants to put me in

---

8   Sharon is one of the original twenty-five *métis(se) griot(tes)*. She made many powerful statements including "The starting point of being Black is you." Despite antagonism from the wider Black community, Akousa's proclamation of her Black self, echoes Sharon's stance.

9   An anecdote told to me by one of the other *métisse griottes* comes to mind. This example illustrates the stigmatization of perceived bi-racialized difference. Yemi was riding on a bus up in Newcastle and she recalled that people would rather either crowd two or three to a seat or sit next to a "mentally retarded" person than sit next to her. *Vis-à-vis* Akousa's comment on the extermination of *métis(se)* people in the book, *Showing Our Colors: Afro-German Women Speak Out* (1986, Amherst: University of Massachusetts), May Opitz (ed.) reports that in Hitler's Germany, White German women who gave birth to Afro-German children were mandatorily sterilized for reasons of "racial hygiene." As adults, many of these mothers' Afro-German children were also sterilized (Opitz 1986: 50). A sad subfootnote to the above reference is that in the summer of 1996 after an insurmountable bout of depression, Ghanaian and German May (Opitz) Ayim, who co-edited *Showing Our Colors*, committed suicide at the tender age of 36.

some sort of little box which is appropriate for them, but is not appropriate for me.

I don't consider myself half of anyting. I cannot be half. When people call me that I say, "Do you see Black on one side and White on the other?" If they call me "Colored" I say, "You see me stripes?" Like I've been colored in or somethin'. There was this White woman on the coach one day and she said to me, "If you put a straight wig on you, you'd be White. You'd look White." Friggin' hell. Man, I may be light, but you can't get away from the fact that I do have strong African features. Even if you did stick a wig on me, it surely would look strange. And what makes her think I would want to wear a wig in the first place, and that I want to look like a White person rather than lookin' the way I look, which I was quite happy with? You have a lot of White people tryin' to get you to change to look White. You want to get rid of this African look that you've got. I find that really weird. That was another sort of problem that I had with White people.

The other thing they used to do to me which used to make me really cringe was they'd been on holiday to Costa del Sol and they've got their sun tans, and this was when I was workin' in a high-street shop and they love the scene of a light-skinned Black person so they can come up to you and say, "Look, I'm darker than you. I'm darker than you." Then, I'd go, "Well yours only lasts three weeks, mine lasts forever, love." That kind of scene. I hate it, I just hated it. It use to make me want to spew.

It affects me, but when I was younger it hurt. I used to wish, "God why didn't you make me darker? Why couldn't I have been dark like my sister?" When I go out in the sun, I don't go dark like my sister, I go a nice golden brown. My sister goes dark brown. She goes black, and there's me. It was a bad problem when I was in my late teens, middle twenties, tryin' to come to terms with bein' a light-skinned Black person. Some people are goin' to point that fact out to me a lot more. I thought, "Frigg it man, I am who I am. I am light. So what!" Look at Africa! From the North to the South you're goin' to find people of many shades. We come in many shades. White people also come in different shades. At the end of the day, I am who I am. That's the way Jah made me. Why should I try and change, because people want to define who I am and what color I should be.

Now, I don't care. It doesn't bother me as it did. I think I've become stronger about who I am. As I get older, I get firmer. As I read more and gather more knowledge about myself, I become a lot stronger. If a White person starts tryin', I can answer them back. If there's a Black person who has a problem with me being light-skinned, me I just raise my head up in the air, straighten up my back, and I walk proudly down the street. I don't hang my head no more, which I used to do. Especially in the seventies when it went from bein' light is the in ting to bein' if you weren't as dark as ebony, you had no chance bein' Black basically. It was like goin' from one extreme to the other.

There were other Black people where to them I was too light-lookin' and to them I was White. Also the fact that I had one White mother. In a sense you have to prove yourself that you are Black. That you are not, one, sittin' on a fence, and two, you don't think you're White. Once you get that across to them, Black people tend to accept you more because then they realize where you're comin' from. I do know people myself who have one White parent and considered themselves to be White. I also know Black people who have both Black parents, who considered themselves to be more White. I know other Black kids who were adopted into White families and consider themselves to be White. I think at the end of the day, when you look at it, Black is a state of consciousness, it's got nothin' to do with how light or how dark your skin is. It's got to do with what you are on the inside, and that's what Blackness is about.

That's why, I don't know who the poet is, who did a poem about Blacks in America, and she said, "There's more to being Black than dressin' up in cultural attire." That's what it's about. When you can find out who you are, then you can go forward. I've had some people who thought my mother was Black, because of the way I am. Had a guy in the office the other day and I told him me mum was Irish, and he was surprised. Even my stepfather's sister, the day me mum got off the plane in the States. She was surprised as she had assumed that me mum was Black. And she wasn't. She got a shock. I think the way I carry on and the way I hold meself, people must think I have been raised by a Black woman, rather than a White mother. I suppose at the end of the day, all due is to my mother. That she's allowed us to become what we want to become. That she hasn't made the decision that her children are half-caste, or that she wants her children to be White. She has allowed her children to be what they want to be and discuss and explore all of those issues to do with who they are. Lettin' them become who they want to become. That's been good.

Even locksin' up, my mum sort of looked at me, and said "Yeah, you'll be cuttin' them off in a couple years time." I said, "No, Mother, I won't." She's proud of me, and feels good about it. She goes to people, "My daughter's a Rasta, she has a degree, she's the Director of this, that, and the other." That makes her feel very proud, and that makes me feel good because I don't have to feel away with my locks. My family accepts me as I am. They don't impose their own images.

I think my mother has been good. As a White woman in this society and comin' from where she comes from, I think my mum has done really well. Because I have seen other people who have had dire problems with their White mother. Their mother has turned them against their father because their father wasn't around – he took off. I mean, my father wasn't much good, but my mum didn't prevent us from seein' him. She didn't heavily influence, how we decided our relationship would be with him.

The other thing was that me mum cooked Caribbean food. We got a mixture of Caribbean and English or Irish stew type. We got rice and peas every Sunday like everybody else, and afterwards on Monday. The soup on a Saturday sort of syndrome. Culturally me mum did take on certain aspects of Caribbean culture. She didn't have a lot of White friends around her. She had one or two. The people we knew were Caribbean people. Also I didn't have a White extended family in the same way as a lot of other people did. So, I didn't have all that to deal with. My extended family was a Black extended family rather than havin' this other White family. I didn't have those issues that other people might have to deal with within their own family structure. My mum was the only White person within the family. She took on board a lot of Caribbean culture. We went on all the trips with the cricket team and we brought our cooked rice and peas and chicken. Basically there was a Caribbean upbringin' in some respects – not totally. Because at the end of the day, my mum is not a West Indian woman. So there were certain aspects to Caribbean culture that I didn't start on, because she didn't have that. My Aunt Hyacinth provided certain aspects of that instead. I had two that were there growin' up.

7

SARAH

"I wasn't White and I wasn't the shape that a little girl should be – knobbly knees"

Sarah was one of the first people I met when I moved to Bristol. She worked in the library in one of the community centers in Thatchapee. Our friendship unfolded gradually, although like her sister Akousa, immediately I was struck by her warmth and exuberance. When she smiled, she used to light up a whole room. Her woman–child idealism and hopefulness went far in a community that was frequently characterized by despair. Everyone knew and liked Sarah.

When I first arrived in Thatchapee, I was terrified about how, or rather, where to begin my research project. I visited Sarah's library and the local public libraries on a regular basis, and for the first six weeks or so, I holed myself up in my top-floor flat, with a kitchen with a view. I existed on a heavy diet of novels by and about Black people in Britain, with a particular emphasis on Black women writers, such as Joan Riley and Buchi Emecheta. Feeling fortified, I then began the task of "doing fieldwork." Even if I was not checking out or returning a book, I continued to stop in to see Sarah at the library. If things were slow, we would have wonderful talks about everything – family, body image, racial politics, apartheid in Bristol, love relationships, food, art, etc. Interestingly enough, when I began the so-called "interview process" she was the *griotte*, with a White Irish and Black Bajan (from Barbados) father, who was the most reluctant to tell her story.

When we finally did sit down to talk, the fact that I wrote poetry and that she was about to demonstrate her own talents as a poet helped dissipate some of her nervous energy. From the drawer of a wooden bureau emerged a piece of paper that looked as though it had been crumpled up and then, at the last minute, rescued. The following untitled poem about Mama was the product:

116

Untitled

Mama, Mama, where am I from?
I know I'm from your womb
Unwelcome seed of anguished passion
Stubborn seed not wanting to die

Hot baths, whiskey, pills – nothin' would make me let go of your warm
bloody body
White flesh, Black flesh mingle to produce confused child in unwelcome world

Nigger, half-caste, mongrel, labeled – named by hatred
Stand strong, love yourself, sticks and stones may break your bones,
but names are buried deep, deep
How hard it is to claim you
Enemies of history, circumstances
How can I reconcile you as one in me?
I am neither
Love is Black, Love is White
Deep shades of Indigo

My herstories are her songs of pain
My grandmothers worked hard, bore children with pain
Who they never raised
Where are my grandfathers? My fathers? My child's father?
Their faces filled by shadows
Why weren't you there to love us?
Why aren't you here for me to reject you? Tell me your names
Where are you buried?
So that I may pour scorn on your graves
Weep for my loss.

Sarah: herstories, songs of joy and pain

I was born in Liverpool…my mother's Irish. I was the last one. She
had two others. I think all of them were a mistake, but I was a definite mistake. I remember her telling me about how much she tried
to get rid of me before I was born. She used to drink whiskey and
take loads of pills and get in hot baths, but there was no way she
could get rid of me. So, she had to really accept that I was going to
be born.

When I was about to be born, I think she just went off to the hospital by herself. She didn't really have anyone there to be with her. Then, I was born. She didn't have any…my Auntie Sheila…my family is …we haven't got any like real aunts and uncles 'cos my mother was an orphan and my father's from Barbados and so all his relatives were in Barbados. He didn't have…his mother died when he was young and his father went off to Trinidad. He had his mother's sister. His mother's sister looked after him when he was growing up. So there were no relatives there either. So all of the relatives, all of the people that I call "Auntie" and "Uncle" aren't really relatives – blood relatives. Like a group of people that have become relatives, they are from all parts of the world, and, well – mainly from the Caribbean. But, my sister's godfather was from Somalia. He's Somali. My Auntie Sheila is from the Caribbean. She made a dress for me so that my mum had somethin' to come out of 'ospital with. Like it was a real surprise for my mum as well, 'cos she brought this dress round for me.

I grew up…when I was small, I grew up in one house with my mum and my sister and my brother…and I've got no real memories of that. But, I remember me mum talkin' about that period. Saying that every Wednesday she uh – she used to have to decide what to spend the last pennies on. Whether to go out and buy some cigarettes, a few cigarettes, or to buy a little bit extra food. She said that Wednesdays always – she used to always resort to makin', you know, dumplin's, with flour and water and cookin' them on the fire. But I don't remember that point in my life.

Then after that, we went to live with my Aunt Hyacinth and Uncle Winston, which wasn't far. I'm talking mainly about houses that we lived in.[1] 'Cos this is the period of my kind of growin' up in Liverpool. I suppose we've moved about five times – from the time that I was born until the time that I was 14. So, those periods of movin' kind of brought in a lot of changes, and with each move materially we became a lot better off as well. So, we went to live with my Auntie Hyacinth and Uncle Winston from Guyana. We lived with them for five years. I don't remember much of that period of my life either. Although, I do remember how much I loved my Aunt Hyacinth plaiting my hair. I used to sit down on the

---

1 How the *griottes* remember is as important as what they remember. What is remarkable about Sarah's testimony is the way in which the bits and pieces of her life are interwoven with vivid descriptions of the houses she and her family lived in. These become veritable signposts along her journey.

floor between her knees feeling secure. She always smelled wonderful – like cocoa butter and musk.

I also remember Mama who used to live over the road. She was from Jamaica. She used to smoke a pipe, and she used to wear a wig – but it was more like a hat, 'cos she used to wear it on the side of her head –like this. It was never on in the right way. She had chickens in the back yard. She was a big woman. That's why everyone called her "Mama." 'Cos that's what people used to call big women, and she used to beat the children with a strap. She had...I think she had about seven children, and they were from babies up to 20 years old. She used to give them licks when they were bad, but we all used to get licks then when we were bad. It wasn't a matter of, "Oh you don't beat your children." That's just what you did. You beat them when they were bad.

She used to have chickens in her back yard. And her husband I used to...I could never understand him when he used to talk to me – 'cos he spoke in patois, and it was really strong. It was really difficult to understand when he talked to us. I think that was a quite nice time in my life, what I can kind of remember of it. Just like runnin' and playin' with their children, and comin' back and bein' in the house. I remember goin' for a walk with Mama, though, one day and she was pushin' one of the babies in the pram and she was sayin' to me – I wanted somethin' from the shop – "Oh! You're so selfish. You're so greedy." I felt really bad. I always remembered it for ages. I thought, "Oh! I'm the worst person." It was really bad.

Yeah, I got ran over the first time when I was in their house. 'Cos I was with Nicola, who's her daughter, and my sister, and they said, "Oh! Run across the road and ask Uncle for some money for ice cream." 'Cos the ice cream van was coming they said, "Go on! Go now, go now!" So, I ran across the road and this car ran me over, and afterwards they denied that they told me to run across the road. And they did, 'cos they didn't want to get into trouble. Yeah, that was the first time I got ran over

There used to be this man called Mr Michael, and he's from Barbados. We used to call him Mr Michael not Uncle Michael. Or did we call him...maybe we called him....Oh! I couldn't remember. But he used to always call me "Wanna," 'cos I always used to want everything. (*Laughter*) He'd say, "Oh! You wanna this and you wanna that." So, when I got ran over and I had my bad foot, he used to call me "Bongo Foot."[2] It looked really big –

2 The word "bongo" is derived from the Hausa word "bungo" meaning "nincompoop,

"Bongo Foot" he used to call me. So, yeah, I think that was a good time.

When we lived in that house, we all used to sleep in one room. We had…I think me and my sister and – I don't know – I can't remember my brother being there for some reason. But, he must have been there. I don't know where he slept. We had one big double bed where we all slept and then my mum used to have the single bed. I remember the night I used to always crawl into bed with her and she used to always wear rollers. It was always this smell of rollers and hair. I used to really like it – crawling into bed with her. I remember I used to wet the bed, and they used to say I was really bad 'cos I used to pee on my sister and get out of bed and sleep with me mum. (*Laughter*) After that we moved to – just down the road. It was like the house down the road 'round the corner – not far.

It was a big house and lots of people lived there and we had one big room downstairs and one room upstairs, and we shared the kitchen with everyone else who lived in the house. I didn't mind livin' there. It was okay. Yeah, it was okay. On one side downstairs there was a woman called Mrs Jackson, a Black woman. She's really round and she must have been 50. Her children were grown up and leavin' home. They'd left home and I remember she used to clean the stairs. She used to always wear these big bloomers and she used to wear tights up to her knees and put a little knot in them. She's a brown-skinned woman. Very proud of her brown-skinnedness. She had two sons and one of her sons had Chinese…he was like to a Chinese man. She was quite proud of that. She always used to squeeze our noses and stuff. (*Laughter*) So we'd have pointy noses and things like that. But I liked her.

Then upstairs there was a woman who lived there called, I think it was, Irene, or Marlene, or something like that and she had a few children. She was White. She used to go down to the ship some-times when the boys – the Navy boys – used to come in so she could have a good time. Me mum always used to say – she used to go off and leave the kids – "But the kids really love her. Her chil-dren really love her." It's really funny that you know, how sometimes you get a parent and they don't always do the best for

country bumpkin of unprepossessing appearance." In Jamaica, originally used deroga-tively meaning very Black, stupid, uncouth, rough. Today, also used to mean person proud of African ancestry. In the same vein, "red ibo" was a derogatory term for a "light-colored person with nappy hair or other features displaying African origin." See Sistren (1987) *Lionheart Gal*, Toronto: Sister Vision Press.

The term "red ibo" is interesting in light of the fact that a large percentage of the African slaves brought to Jamaica were Ibos from Nigeria (Ajufo 1993, personal communication).

their children or they've got a problem. It wasn't that. It's 'cause she had a number of children, and they weren't all to the same person. Maybe she met somebody like a man here and this is the one and one here and this is the one. You get pregnant. So she'd go off sometimes. 'Cos it's hard bringin' up children to have a nice time and stuff. But mum always used to say, "Oh her children really love her…"

Then upstairs, different people came in and out of the house. I've forgotten how long we lived there, but it must have been for a few years. The landlord was African –Mr John. I think he had a house over the road as well. At that time, me mum was havin' a relationship with this guy called Malik. He was from the Gambia and I always thought he was really handsome. He was really Black and slim. He used to come and visit. It was never out in the open. There used to be a gramophone in the room and he used to come and play records, and kind of just be around.

I remember the first night we moved in there, we had to get washed behind the wardrobe – the really big furniture people used to have. These few people came to help us move in. Just gettin' washed behind the wardrobe in little bowls, it was really funny. In that house, I kicked my shoe through the window and smashed the window. It was all, "Oh Mr John! We'll have to tell Mr John! What's he gonna say…uh?" But, he was okay about it.

In that house I had this experience. I don't know what happened. I remember me mum had to go somewhere and this Irish family moved in upstairs. They had this old grandfather who lived with them and he had, uh, a bit like warts –something – all over his face. Well not all over his face – it's like red patches – red patches on his face. Anyway, Mum had to go somewhere and she said, "Oh, could Sarah stay?" And he said, "Yeah." And he said, "Oh, let's play this game." It was like puttin' things into your mouth and he had to be there blindfolded and I had to put things in his mouth. I remember puttin' cold tea into his mouth, and just being really horrible. Then, when it was my turn, he put somethin' into my mouth – right? And I couldn't decide what it was. I couldn't….I thought, "God what's this?" When he took the blindfold off, he did his fly up. "Right," I said , "Oh, what was it?" And he said it was his thumb. I kept on thinkin', "How could it be his thumb, because I didn't feel any nail?" For ages I have always thought, "Did he put his penis in my mouth or didn't he?" Like I couldn't decide. That was horrible. I hadn't left primary school, so I must have been quite young – about 7 or 8 – old enough to know that it was something. That I didn't know what it was. I didn't like or want anything to do with that part of the building any more.

Then we moved from there. We went to live in Bowden Grove and it was the first time we had – it was our own house. That was really exciting – to move into your own house. I always wanted mansions. I always wanted – "Wanna!" – I wanted everything! But it was nice moving into a house, and I liked where it was 'cos it was just off Larabee Street, which used to be…I mean, now it's dead. But, when we were young, it was a really cosmopolitan street, with shops selling things from India, to the Caribbean, to Africa. Used to have loads of people comin' from different communities.

Like on Saturday, you'd have all the Chinese people, 'cos there used to be a Chinese church. On Sundays you used to have all the Indian people, and on Saturday, all the Jewish people used to be around for the synagogue. I don't know if they used to – they didn't really shop there, but they'd be around – going to their synagogue. I really liked it. I used to always love going shoppin' with me mum, 'cos you'd always meet aunties and uncles. They'd always give you some money. Like you'd walk down the street and you'd see Uncle so and so or Auntie and they'd say "Oh, doesn't she look nice! Oh, isn't she great! Mmm!" and give you some money. The men used to play a game with coconuts and you'd put a pebble underneath and twist them around, move them about, and you have to gamble on which one you think the pebble's under and things like that. Yeah, I liked it, I really liked livin' there.

It was also in that house that my dad came to live with us and to me that was terrible. I really hated it when he came to live with us 'cos it was like I was the one who slept with me mum. Then suddenly, one day, I went to go into me mum's bedroom and there's this man there. And it wasn't as if I kind of knew him before – we'd had any relationship. It was just like from that day – 'cos they didn't talk. You don't talk to children or tell them what's happenin'. That so and so's comin' to live with you's. It wasn't like that – he just was there. So, I used to be really horrible to him. Yeah, I used to be really horrible to him. In fact, I must have been younger in the other house 'cos I was still at primary school when we moved to this house.…Anyway, so yeah, I used to be really horrible to him and I think at first he used to kind of take it easy, but then he used to just hit me. You know, just smack me for being rude or, you know, 'cos I used to tell him to get out and that I didn't want him to live with us – things like that. Then he never really kind of – he liked my sister better. He was kind of in to her. Not that either of us got anything that was kind of – she didn't get any more than me in like material, but he kind of got on a bit better with her 'cos she wasn't horrible to him. I think that was quite good because when I was younger everyone used to really like me, say, "Oh, this one." But I think it balanced out, 'cos when I lived with my auntie, she really liked me. I was hers, and like my sister was my uncle's. Things always usually balanced out. It's funny how things change with time. Now me and my dad get on really well. I have a lot of deep love and respect for him. Last time he came to stay with me, we spent a day digging in the garden, laughing and chatting.

We lived there for a while, and it was there when my brother left. He went to live with my uncle in Southport. My uncle was from Trinidad – who wasn't my uncle. He had three sons in the Caribbean and he brought them over. He was a chef in Southport and he had a really nice flat with a big garden. So he said, "Colin can come live with us." Because he's always been trouble. He's one of those boys who runs away and doesn't come home when you tell him to. Real heartache – Mum never knew where he was. So, he went to live with him, but it was way before my dad came to live with us that my brother went to live with my uncle in Southport. Me mum thought it was the best thing for him – that he could get a better education. He'd be with these other boys, and stuff like that. She couldn't really cope herself – trying to keep him together. Yeah.[3]

So, then, after we lived there, we went to live in another house. That was a council house. At that time in Liverpool, a lot of Black people owned their own houses or rented houses and they were either like Victorian houses, that most of the slave owners built,[4] or terraced houses. The council did a compulsory purchase order on these houses, so that people had to sell their houses to the council at a very cheap, cheap, cheap rate. So, a lot of people started leaving –

3　There is continual debate in both *métis(se)* and research circles as to who has a "harder" time, *métis* boys or *métisse* girls? I think it is very difficult to quantify the struggles that both groups have to go through at various life stages. However, one can remark that these struggles manifest themselves differently for *métisse* girls than *métis* boys. For example, as Sarah and Yemi (Chapter 9) both observe, *métis* boys may have an easier time fitting in with a preadolescent peer group.

　　I have an African American male friend in Oakland, California who has a "Black and White" (his term) preadolescent son. This child lives with his White mother in a predominantly upper-middle-class White American community, but has regular contact with his father. My friend is aware that his son is more than "acceptable" at the moment. However, he is fearful that once his son reaches puberty, he will no longer be deemed "acceptable" in the eyes of the parents of the White adolescent girls he may want to date. It is at this stage that my friend would like his bi-racialized and sexualized son to come to live with him.

4　A powerful thought – the descendants of slaves reclaiming the houses – albeit many run-down, that the slave masters built...but then we learn from Sarah that these homeowners were later bought out by the council.

going to London and like different places. A lot of people left to go to London at that time. We got offered a house in a small housing – new houses that they built just up the road again. Eventually, they pulled down the houses on the street that we lived, which is really sad because that was like the beginning of the destruction of the community.[5] It's really terrible – terrible thing to do. Oh, yeah, I remember when I lived in that house, I remember going to visit somebody. I think it was my auntie, my Auntie Mavis. She lived in one of these big Victorian houses that she kind of had one floor with her family. I remember when she was breastfeeding her little baby, and I was sitting staring at her. She got her breast and squirted the milk at me. She's saying, "Do you want some?" (*Joint laughter*) I think I ran outside. It's really funny.

Then we went to live on this housing estate, and in between when we were in Landview Street, my brother had an accident – 'cos he joined the army when he was 17, and he had an accident riding a bicycle during training. He suffered brain damage, 'cos he went into a coma. It was just terrible. It wasn't as terrible for us, because we didn't see it. But, me mum, she had to travel to Plymouth. It was a really long way to go. She had it really hard. Because we didn't grow up with him, it was like in a way, when we seen him again, it was like we didn't know him. We used to go and visit him occasionally.

I do have memories of him, like we used to go to the park, and he'd take us into houses that were derelict. I remember going into a house with him and it was all derelict. They had these big Victorian houses, and there was like this old settee there. I remember him going behind it and like when I went to look behind it, he had just had a shit. It was all warm and sticky, and steam was comin' from it. (*Joint laughter*) Like goin' through the park and the gates were locked and havin' to climb over the gates. This policeman comin' – when we were really, really young. He used to just take us off. It was like really wild. He's about 36 – so about six years, six or seven years older.

When we went to live on Landview Street, he came to live with us after a while. He used to come and stay. He came to live in Liverpool. He stayed in like a care home, and then he used to come

5 A bit of sociopolitical commentary from a *griotte* so in tune with the community she lived in and in particular with the different spaces she and her family inhabit over the years. Through her vivid recollections of her own family's relocations, we can picture this slow destruction, one which replicated itself in urban communities of color throughout Britain.

home and stay for a while. It was really difficult. A lot of the time he used to write suicidal letters. He used to go through all this emotional stuff, but it was like comin' out. You could see me mum strugglin' tryin' to keep it together. Then he'd do things like at Christmas everyone would be havin' dinner and he'd pull the table-cloth off the table. It was because he wanted to watch *Top of the Pops*. We were all enjoying Christmas dinner, talkin' and laughin', and because we wouldn't shut up so that he could watch the TV, he pulled the tablecloth off the table. So, within the problem of like him havin' an accident, which is a tragedy, he's also got his own personality. What he's into – a lot of it, is not what I would agree with. When he used to get angry or hit out at us, we used to hit him back. (*Laughter*) If he hit us with his stick, we used to hit him back. I used to run away and he used to say, "Oh, come back." It was hard; it was a really hard time.

Then, me mum decided she wanted to buy a bigger house, so we moved again – to a house that me mum bought for herself! That was really amazing. Me mum really worked hard all her life, and really struggled. Two jobs, and stuff like this, and not havin' shoes for herself. Like she used to buy clothes for us and not have shoes to wear. She had a hard time. So, she bought her own house. That was like – "Oh, wow! Wow! Wow!...but it wasn't a mansion...(*Laughter*) So, we all went to live there.

Eventually my brother – he's gone to live in Worthing now in a home for ex-servicemen. He used to go away there for two weeks every year. He decided he wanted to stay there. Me mum was really upset at the time. Now, I think it's a good thing. I don't think it's a good thing for him. When I went to visit it, there was a lot of really old people there, been in the army and stuff. He goes horse-riding. The building's really nice, and they've got a bar there, and he's got his own room, and they've got like a crafts place where you can do weavin' and stuff like that. I still hated it. I think it's good for me mum, because I think it's just too much for her. It's like physically and emotionally really hard, because although he's had an accident, he's got a very strong personality, and sometimes he's really selfish. Sometimes he does things or says things that are really painful. But, he's just been at home for two weeks now. It is hard work. It was really hard for her. Having a child and something like that to happen to him.

So we moved from there and we lived in Emmervale Road. Oh, yeah, I got pregnant when I was there.[6] Oh, yeah, I forgot all about

---

6 There is so much of Sarah's life that I wanted to include, but there just is not sufficient space. I do not include her testimonies about pregnancy, early childbearing (she was 17

that bit of my life.…Yeah (*Sigh*)…there's loads of bits that I haven't even talked about. I have been talkin' about places that we've been livin' and kind of missin' out some of the bits that kind of went on there.[7] One bit that I remember – that we talked about later on – that was really.…When I mentioned it to the family it was like (*Gasp*) – everyone went really quiet. I remember saying, but maybe the way I did it, it wasn't good. I said – we were all together – and I said, "Oh, yeah, remember Akousa, when you used to cry when the sun, when it was, when the sun was shining?" Me mum used to go and work cleanin' people's houses, and when she came home she used to always give us jobs to do. When she came home, it was never done as good as she wanted it and she'd be really wound up. So, she used to come home and be really angry and shout at us or smack us. So, Akousa always used to cry when the sun was shining, because when the sun shines, the house looks really dusty. (*Joint laughter*) Have you noticed? If you go somewhere and the sun is shining, you see all the dust and all the marks on the walls. Even today, I mean I love the sunshine, but I hate bein' in my house in the livin' room when the sun's shinin' 'cos it's really dusty. I have to get out or I have to tell myself, "So what, if it's dusty!"

That used to be really sad. But if you mentioned it, like when I mentioned it in the family, it was because all those things are past. It's all come out of what was happening at the time and hard work. Like my mum was going through. She didn't even have time to recognize that she had feelings or value her own feelings or that what she thought or felt was important. All she was was somebody who worked here worked there. Time has allowed things to be different now. We have more time to be lovin' towards each other and to say, "I love you," and to hug each other. All those things. Before, there was love where I could go and stay in my mum's bed, but it wasn't like "Oh, I love you," on like an everyday basis. It was just like survivin' really.[8] So, that's why it's quite painful for her to

when she had her son), or the politics of gender within Rastafari. Unlike the other *griottes*' testimonies, I attenuated Sarah's narrative at adolescence, because continuing beyond this stage would have made her chapter too lengthy. This is despite the fact that Sarah's life has been full of passion and pain – her days of discovering love and sex as a teenager; nights out dancing to disco, funk and soul music; her sojourns to West and Southern Africa; her battles with substance abuse, including food; her struggles as a single mother; her creativity as an artist; and so on.

7 A bit of self-reflection. Sarah is very aware of the ways in which she is telling her story and how this approach will affect the way her "audience" receives what she has to recount.

8 Sarah and her sister Akousa both paint amazing portraits of their own-working class Irish/Caribbean family's life, the dumplin's on Wednesday, for example, (Sarah), so that

talk about it now. It's hard because like...it's hard...

When I was 16 – oh, yeah, I used to go to school. I haven't even mentioned school.[9] God, school! When we were young we went to primary school. All the schools my mum sent us to were mainly dominated by White people. But they were very working-class schools. They weren't middle-class schools. It was really awful at school because I never felt that I fitted in. I always felt odd – like really odd. 'Cos I was quite big as well. I wasn't like a skinny little girl who had knobbly knees. I always wanted to be like that and I was never like that. So, I wasn't White and I wasn't like the shape that you know a little girl should be – knobbly knees. It was really hard.

My friends at school were...I had one friend who was White, and then she moved to Mobley, which was this new housing estate that they built. I had one friend who was Indian, Esther Pajit. She was really big, very big. She was mixed race as well. She was half-Indian and half-English. Her mum was English. She had this hair that was really thick that went really down to her bum – really thick, thick, thick head of hair. She used to always have it in a thick plait going down her back. She's really big and she's quite like a tomboy – very – quite masculine. She wasn't, you know, like – huh ha hoh (*"Feminine" gesture*) – she was very – uh (*"Masculine" gesture*). Then, I used to have another friend. Let me see if I can remember her name –oh, God!...her father was Nigerian and her mother was English. I can't remember her name, may be it'll come back. I saw her when I was in Liverpool. I hadn't seen her in years. Ngozi – that was it – Ngozi. She was really tall. Like somebody who's too tall for their age. Ngozi, and she was big as well. (*Joint laughter*) And I was the smallest one amongst them. (*More joint laughter*) So, we used to hang 'round together – 'cos we were all just – we didn't fit in.[10] Do you know what I mean? All three of us were from mixed race families, and the three of us were all funny shapes and sizes – for what little girls are supposed to be. So we used to kind of hang around and find solace with each other. We did have our arguments.

---

we as the audience do not doubt for a moment the economic constraints that dictated that much of daily life was about "survivin'."

9 Out of the six *griottes*, only Similola seems to have enjoyed school and remembered attending school as the high point of her days. Everyone else is retrospectively critical of their educational experiences, which for Ruby, Akousa and Sarah verged on the racially violent.

10 Finding solidarity in difference and marginality is a theme which runs throughout all six *griottes'* testimonies.

School was quite hard. I found it really difficult. I wasn't a quick learner. I had to go to classes to learn how to read when I was 11. This woman had polio. She taught me how to read and write. She was this really sweet gentle person. She really spent time to teach me how to read and write. What else about school? I remember one day when I was in the playground – right – and we had this line. We had to line up, and these girls just came and walked in front of me in this line in school. And like I was really fed up because it was like I was totally insignificant. Do you know, like somebody could just come and walk in front of me? Like everyone else, they would have to either say something or they wouldn't do it. So, I ended up with this one girl. I just went "Bop!" and punched her right in the face. I didn't say anything to her or do anything, I just went like this. And I wasn't the type of person to fight. I wasn't a fighter or anything. I'm not very violent. I'm not good at it. But, I just punched her right in the face and her nose just started bleeding – blood everywhere. And the teacher came up to me and said, "Why did you do that?" Just punched her, and it was like I was kind of a bit meaningless. I was really insignificant.

I used to have this friend, Ellen Thomas, and she was White. I remember, I used to call for her every morning to go to school. I used to have two White friends, who were quite strong. Who were like really quite strong in my childhood, when I was at primary school. And one was Ellen Thomas and the other one was called Catherine. I used to call for Ellen, when I used to go to school in the morning. I remember one day callin' for her, and me mum bought me these shoes. This is when I lived in Bowden Grove. Me mum bought me these shoes and they were like really pointy at the end, and they were made like crocodile skin with patent leather. I was really pleased with these shoes, 'cos they were new. When I went to school, everyone was laughing. (*I laugh sympathetically*) When I called for her, she was like my friend, and she'd say, "Oh, I know...." She wouldn't laugh at me, but she was tryin' to say, "Oh, I don't know about them." Then, when I got to school, everyone gave me loads of pressure about these crocodile shoes – 'cos I really loved them.

But anyway, Ellen went to live in Mobley. Her family came to pick me up to go and visit her in Mobley, this new housing estate on the outskirts of Liverpool. It was too much. Every time I used to go out, all the children used to call me names, like really racist names. So, I only stayed for a week.

But, it was quite hard when I was growin' up, because there was like a lot of racism in Liverpool. Any time you kind of ventured out of the area, it was like you were bound to be called names by children. When we would go to Sunday school, people used to call us names. We couldn't say anything to the parents, because we knew that they would go in the house and tell their parents, and the parents might come out and call us things as well. We were very young then, but we were still really frightened to either hit these children or say anything to them in case they went inside and their parents came out and did the same thing. When I lived in Bowden Grove, I remember comin' home from school, and this Black man, he called me a nigger. I ran home and I was sayin' to me mum. Oh, I was cryin', I said, "Oh, this Black man just called me a nigger." I was really upset, 'cos it's bad enough when somebody White calls you it. But, when a Black person calls you it, you know. And me mum just started laughin', and she said, "Oh! It's only William," because I described who it was, and it was somebody she knew. But, it was the first time I came across Black people callin' each other names like that.[11] To me, "nigger" was like somethin' or somebody that wasn't anythin'. For him to call me that was...kind of...so that's what you are. All the time I've been sayin' to myself, "I'm not this idea of what they think a nigger is." Then, when a Black person – it's really upsetting.

When I was at school as well, in my last year, there was this guy in the class – Black guy. When me, Ngozi, and Esther were at school, we were never...I think me and Esther were in the same class, but I was never in the same class with Ngozi. In the last year, there was this guy in the class, Black guy, who was mixed race, and for a period we were sitting next to each other, right? In the class-room, we were sittin' next to each other. We were doin' a maths lesson, and we were really involved in this lesson. We were workin' together and we both were terrible at maths, but we just happened to get excited about it, and we were thinkin', "Oh, yeah, we can do it! We've got it all sussed." In the enthusiasm, he put his arm round me, so we were sittin' in the class and he had his arm round me. When we went to get everything marked, we got them all wrong

11 This is an issue that I still have not resolved, and I am forever battling with my African American friends over this so-called re-appropriation of racial epithets.

An English anecdote: while still immersed in the initial research project, I went to visit a friend in South London, who is a social anthropologist. We were talking about cultural identity issues and the specific parenting needs of *métis(se)* children. She recalled a friend who had adopted a young *métisse* girl. In preparation for any bi-racialized verbal abuse the child might receive at school, the well-intentioned White English middle-class family began calling her "nig nog," "chocolate drop," etc. Sure enough, the little girl went to school and one of her classmates hurled "nig nog" at her, to which she replied "How did you know my name?"

anyway. (*I laugh*) His friends noticed, and he was very much accepted by all the kids in the class.

He was very much accepted 'cos he was fashionable. When I went to school, I had to wear a school uniform, where everyone could wear what they wanted. He was very fashionable, and a bit tough and hip. He was accepted by all the other boys in the class. So, they started laughin', sayin', "Oh, look! He's got his arm round Sarah...ah, ah!..." Then, after that, every day when I used to go and sit next to him, he used to kick me. He used to just kick me and kick me. I used to go home – when I used to get washed or ready for bed, my mum said, "Where are you gettin' all these bruises from?" I'd have all these bruises up my legs. So, me mum had to go to school and ask them to move me from sittin' next to this boy. 'Cos he used to kick me.

After that, I went to secondary school. First of all, it was like an all-girls school. Half of it was all girls, half of it was boys, but still very workin'-class school. It wasn't ever easy for me, because academically I wasn't that brilliant. With the children, once again it was in a White area, and the majority of the people in the school were White. We used to suffer a lot of racism – like being spat at. Boys, they'd spit at you. The older boys in the third year, you'd go to the corner shop and like somebody would spit in your hair and say, "Nigger, come polish me boots." Stuff like that.[12] It was always like this fear of being...and I was little. It was my first year in their secondary school, and these boys were like third, fourth year.

At home, Black Power was just comin' in and my sister went to the corner shop and seen her first afro. I was with my friend Jenny whose mum is also White. My sister came home and said to us, "Oh, I've seen some afros in the shop. Oh, they're really brilliant."[13] This group of women with afros, she's sayin' how brilliant they were. At home, we were startin' this awareness of Black power and Black identity. We always related to bein' Black, because all the signals we got from when we were growin' up, we were nothin' else. We definitely were not White. I remember when Jenny's mum would get angry with her, she used to call her "Black bastard." It was always "Black this" or "Black that." It was really hard for me to

---

12 Different casting of characters. In Sarah's story, the people who say, "Nigger come polish me boots," are older boys from her school, who may or may not be skinheads. She does not mention this detail. In Akousa's version of the story, the character is clearly a skinhead. These two slightly varied accounts give the audience different spins on the particular racial climate in Liverpool at that time.

13 This recollection is an evocative example of the awakening of an emergent empowered and reconciled global/diasporic Black consciousness in two *métisse* sisters.

hear. In fact, her mum used to always say to us: "When you grow up, never marry a White man because when he gets angry he may end up calling you names." But then, the Black Power started comin' along and all the positiveness that brought at that time was like brilliant. Like somethin' we could all really feel good about....

8

BISI

"If you are mixed race you belong in two (or more) cultural traditions which may be mutually contradictory you just have to find that middle space"

I met Bisi through an American woman in exile in Bristol who by virtue of our similar backgrounds and involvement in the Arts thought we would enjoy meeting each other. However, Bristol being a very small city, Bisi had already heard about me through mutual friends. Next to Sarah, Bisi is the *griotte* I have known the longest.

Bisi is Yemi's (see Chapter 9) younger sister. Their father is Yoruba (Nigerian) and their mother is English from Northumberland. Yemi and Bisi have very different temperaments, but just listening to them for a while and looking at their faces, one knows that they are sisters. They both have four children. The father of Yemi's children is Black Nigerian and the father of Bisi's children is White English. Yemi grew up Nigerian-identified, while Bisi, who was much closer to their White English mother, grew up with a more English view of the world. Although what Englishness means to both Bisi and Yemi as well as the other *griottes* shifts, changes and is renegotiated as they progress through life's stages. Concomitantly, Bisi has matured as a visual artist. This maturity necessitates accepting the lived impact of certain Eurocentric influences, which in turn create space for artistic production, which is quintessentially a cultural *métissage*.

Bisi is the mother of three daughters and a son. What continues to amaze and impress me is the ways in which her firm and gentle hands prop up these beautiful children, who are at times confused about their identities, only because they live in a bi-racialized society which refuses to change its proverbial colors.

Bisi: a strawberry by any other name is still a strawberry

I was born in Ibadan, which is in Western Nigeria. I have two older sisters. My mother is from Newcastle-upon-Tyne in England. My sisters were born in England. They came on the boat when the sister next to me was two and Kemi was four. I was the first child my mother had in Africa, and the only child, in fact, she had in Africa.[1] I believe they were quite nervous. I was born a month ahead of time. She said, "Oh well, it seemed as though you were going to arrive. I had to set to and wash my nappies. I had nothing ready." Some woman looked after my sisters, and she was taken to hospital by somebody else on the teacher's campus. With my father following afterwards, he broke down on the way. This is a family saga. And it goes on and on. It was totally disastrous. For the next twenty-four hours, it was not very nice apparently.

I don't think my mother was working at the time, but my father was a teacher then. I'm very bad about details. When they came back from England, he came first. He was a teacher in schools like Government College. He was sent to the east, first of all to Owerri. Then he was transferred to the western region. They say that he would gradually get enough seniority so that the next promotion would have to be headmaster. The heads of schools were always the British in those days and when it got to that point, he would be transferred so they wouldn't have to promote him.

My mum is very bitter about the way they were transferred into some government boy's school in Ibadan. How she and the children were left waiting. Nobody had the keys. They couldn't go in the house. They had to drive away to a different compound and find the keys to let them in. Generally, she feels that the people in that school, where my father was going to be vice-principal, were as uncooperative and as ungracious to them as possible.

Anyhow, by the time I can remember my childhood, my father was working in the Civil Service and we lived in government bungalows, which really were very nice. Things I remember about them is there would be a big garden. Details from them — the red tile floors, the verandas, plants in the garden, wooden shutters on the windows and definitely with a smell of rain and the feeling of a

---

1 The irony is that though Bisi was the only daughter born in Nigeria, being the youngest, she was the one who was most attached to her mother — and by extension — her mother's version of White English culture. Her identification with African-ness/Nigerian-ness as different from her manifest Blackness and *métisse* sensibilities are vividly conveyed through her art practices. However, this emergent and somewhat syncretic consciousness does not occur until after she leaves Nigeria to "settle" in England.

storm coming and the way all the leaves go when there's rain coming. All the leaves sort of turn backwards and show silver instead of green. Those moody sort of things. What you remember a lot about West Africa is the weather. It's so wonderful. In English terms, the weather is so exaggerated. When you see lightning, it's real heaven-to-earth thunderbolt stuff and you can see it coming from miles off. You can see purple flashes on the horizon, and you can see it coming nearer and nearer to you. When the rain advances, its called a line storm. It's a definite bank of really enormous black clouds coming over the whole sky. The line of the rain is so definite, you can run in and out of that line as it's advancing over the ground.

My mother was a teacher. In fact, I think throughout most of my childhood she was at work. Funny enough, I don't remember any of the women who must have been looking after me at all. Absolutely no memory whatsoever. I don't think it was traumatic. Looking back then, I don't have very many early memories, really.

We went to boarding school when we were old enough. From there, we were expected to go to university, and then to go and do postgraduate studies. I disappointed my parents very much by wanting to study art. Well, I disappointed my father. My mother was about to leave Nigeria actually by the time I had finished A levels and I came to England with her. She went to Concert to get a teaching job. I went to polytechnic and I did a graphics degree.

I met my husband, got married, stayed in England and I have been there ever since – give or take a few little incidents. I have been in England for the past twelve years now. That's when my eldest daughter was born. That was a definite beginning of a totally different life.

Graham, my husband, and I met in Greece. It was after my second year of college, and I was going on holiday to Europe by myself. I had won a prize for designing something, so I had some money to go with. My mother didn't like it at all. I mean it was a real cutting of the umbilical cord. She hated every minute from when I took the decision to go by myself. That really changed something as far as she was concerned. After I left, I found she had redecorated my whole room. I think she found it quite painful and she was worried.

So, I sent off for my passport, got all these visas. Got a month's train ticket. Had a plan to go to Athens for the month. Went on the train from Victoria. It was the Orient Express. In those days, the whole line had run down. It was nothing like the Orient Express. It was just the name for a rather crappy train that maybe you prefer to be on the new one. Got the ticket. It was between £30 and £50.

Got into Athens. Met a Sudanese bloke on the train who said, "Well, I will look after you, dear girl. Come and live in my hotel." He was very sweet. I was incredibly innocent, now that I think about it. Probably that protected me. I stayed a couple of nights with this guy, until I began to think, "Well, what is he up to? Surely, nobody is as good and sweet as this. I'm sure he's going to try something on." Then I left. It was a funny little hotel in the Plaka. The woman used to call him, "Abdul. Hey, Abdul," which wasn't his name. Got on a train to Piraeus. Went to one of the islands. Stayed there about a week. Ate at somebody's home, which I paid for. It was very pleasant. I think I went to Delphi. Came back to Athens.

I came back to the youth hostel, and sort of was thinking, "What do I do now?" Also, the youth hostel wasn't very interesting. There was a bloke behind the bar serving, who had quite an interesting accent, "Do you want your coffee 'wuite' or black?" he said. He said, "I'm a 'capun.' We'll have it wuite." That was Graham. He was staying in quite an interesting hotel and maybe I'd like to stay there. Okay, I'll go and stay there. I wanted to see the Plaka. He said, "Okay, I can take you when I get off work. Would you like to do that?" "Okay, yes, I'd like to."

So, I started going 'round with him. We talked a lot. I can't remember what about at all. But I know we talked, talked, talked. We went to a wine festival together. Missed the last bus home. Stayed up on the mountainside. There were so many mosquitos there. Nothing happened. We stayed together a lot, talked and talked and talked. We had a couple of meals together. After one of them, which was late at night, he said, "If we walk this way past the park, there's a wonderful smell of jasmine." So, we walked past the park. There was a wonderful smell of jasmine. We hopped over the wall, into the park, wandered around a bit, spent the night in the park in my youth hostel sleeping bag, which wasn't very wide. I said, "I feel quite safe with you, you're not going to do anything are you?" He said, "Oh, no." In the morning, the park keeper – we were out of the sleeping bag by then – said "Tut, tut, tut, tut, tut." We went back to this other hotel, where he was staying. He had travelled about a bit, and he was just working to get the money to travel some more basically.

He said, "I know this hill, you'd really like it. You want to come up the mountain with me? We'll go camping." So, I said, "Okay, yeah." So we went up this hill. We had lots of nuts. Always remember that when you go camping you have to take lots of nuts, because they are concentrated food. We stayed up this mountain. Then we had it off, and that was that, sort of. Then we sort of stayed together. However long it was. Not very long. I think we stayed up in the hills for ages. No, not for ages. Must have been three, four, five days of camping on this mountain, whatever it was. Then came back down. Stayed a couple more days in Athens. Bought my presents, and I took the train.

We exchanged addresses and he would come and see me when I was back at college in Newcastle. I don't know if I ever expected to see him or not. But, he did come over in October, and stayed with me. We used to go to see films together, talk a lot. He didn't have a job, so he would stay at home. He had this book list he was going to read through that people had said, "Oh, you must read this." He was reading through these books. Some were good, some were crap. Being very nice to me actually – making tea, behaving like a house husband. We used to go have big Chinese meals, watch films, which were all new then, by Fellini. I remember films at college, because I saw some fairly good ones. I remember not going to see *Last Tango in Paris* because it appeared to be boring, but instead we went to see Fellini's *Roma*. That was my final year.

Then we went to Liverpool. We were still together. Then I went back to college. I had said to my father I wanted to stay a year longer in England. He said, "Okay, you can have an allowance. Here you are." College had said that I could have an exhibition after a year in the foyer of the Squires building. But, I didn't really keep in touch with them. So that all went by the board. Although I did go back once, and then it seemed that a lot of things…it was sort of complicated…it seemed that all the business I had with college was finished. There was an incipient relationship there, which I think wasn't there any longer, and that is the reason why the business of the exhibition collapsed. That's what I felt. Coming back, I don't know why, I thought, "Shall we get married then Graham?" So, we got married.

I'd been going to stay for a year. So, I stayed for that year, although the exhibition didn't happen. But, I did do some work then. Funny enough, I've sold one of the pictures I did then…was in the *British Women's Artist Diary* for 1987. I sold two of the pictures again quite recently about three years ago. So, I think the work I did was fairly interesting actually looking back. The book cover that I've done that I like best is one by a woman called Zoe.[2] Also, I like the book. There's another one, which is an anthology. It's just a picture of a woman writing, and I think it's the best

2 When I left Bristol in 1992, Bisi gave me a self-portrait in original pastels as a going-away present. In it, her hands are each noticeably painted a different color – one brown and the other white. Her hands are clutching at her mouth and her eye is seemingly

drawing I have done for a cover. It's a shame it's also been printed up the smallest. There have been five book covers that I have done.

September came. We married in September. I had bought a ticket to go home, and I went home. Oh, God, you know what it's like in Lagos. All these people came and met us off the plane. They took you to the hotel. We stayed in this beastly, tacky little hotel. It was so hot, and the air conditioning wasn't working. Then we got another plane into Ibadan, landing at Ibadan. I hadn't told anyone I was coming. Got a taxi home and it cost 5 naira, 4 naira 50. The boy said, "Give me the 50 kobo to buy a coke." I was feeling worried. These people think I have just come off a plane, so they can cheat me. So, I was feeling very defensive, and thinking 4 naira 50 is too much, which probably it wasn't. It's quite a long way from the airport to where we live.

Walked to the house. There was my dad. He was pleased to see me, though not in a very demonstrative way. "Oh, hello, Dad." "Oh, Bisi." I said, "Oh, look, I got married, here's my ring." He said, "Oh!" I think that was just about it basically. I don't know what he thought. I know one of the times I have seen him not be very pleased was after we went to Lagos to see about where I was going to be posted in Youth Corps. I ended up in Jos. There was a television station there, and I ended up in the graphics unit, which wasn't too bad at all. He wasn't very happy that it was Jos instead of somewhere a bit closer to home. Nobody said much about it. When Graham came over, people were quite nice to him. My cousin had told me, "Bisi, I thought I told you not to go and marry a White man." I said, "Oh, yes, so you did." Actually, I had completely forgotten until she said it.

I went back after I had finished College to do my Youth Corps, and then after about six months, Graham came too, and I got pregnant. That was the *fait accompli* that was going to decide what we would do next. We were going to go back to England to live. He went back and I was staying at Eleya for a while. An aunt came to visit. My father said, "Oh, she's going back to England soon to live with her husband." The aunt said, "Oh, what a shame. The one who looks most like you and she's leaving." I remember they all said when I was coming to college, "Don't go and marry an Englishman!" I said, "Oh no. Never! Who me?" So the bits that make up the identity.

searching for some recognition. This piece is a powerful emblem for all *métis(se)* people who try to make sense of their place in society. Here, Bisi has reframed the negativity that usually dominates most depictions of our lived experiences.

We ended up in Bristol, because Graham comes from Bristol. So, we came back here, had to find somewhere to live, which was difficult. In the end, we got a Council flat. He got a job as architectural technician, because he had a first degree in architecture. But, then he had to do professional practice for so many years. He had to go back to College, which he did part time, and then he finally qualified. That was the plan. It was quite difficult for him, and quite difficult for me as well. It's a really difficult thing to do with young children around. People always give up and can't face it, and put it off for a year. After he had done the degree, he had gone travelling. It was hanging over him to finish.

We married in 1977 – Fourteen years –a long time ago. We were married in Newcastle. A friend from college was a witness, and my aunt was a witness.[3] Very nice. Very nice place, very airy and open to the sun where they do the marriages. I still have the dress. It was only a little viscose dress. My daughter, Julia, who is 9, can't get into it.

It's hard to think about childhood because it's just kaleidoscoping past. It's perhaps easier to talk about coming to England when I was 17, because it was an event that was very much looked forward to. It was seeing something new – all this. Meeting my grandmother, and my uncle, and my aunt in Newcastle. My grandmother was very welcoming. Many things were a surprise. The fact that it was so cold wasn't a surprise. The way people were used to being poor. That was a bit unfamiliar. There's very simple things like buying the cheap-brand washing-up liquid that doesn't actually work well.

I was about seventeen. My father's step-mother died. His mother died when he was little; this is one of his father's other wives. She was very ill, and she was the last person remaining of their generation. When she died, it was going to be a very big event. It was older brothers and sisters – in fact there are five of them – two girls and three boys. They all contributed to make a feast, because she was very old. So it was a cause for a big celebration, because she had been so old. So we were all giving thanks that the person had a long full life. My father had built a bungalow in his village with a wall around it. He had been allowed to use the land. I don't think he bought the land. The land had been given to him, and he had been permitted to build on it. Because there was already a family house in the village, that had belonged to the grandfather, then, he was allowed to put his bungalow, which not everybody was allowed to

---

3 I never did find out from Bisi where her mother was on the day of the wedding.

do. A cow was killed. This massive party was had. People came from all the towns; they dispersed to Lagos, Ibadan, even Kaduna, all those places. The whole village, and really cousins of cousins came to the event. It was quite an event for me in a way.

We were a bit separated from what was happening in the village, because we were in this bungalow place getting dressed. People would come up and visit us sometimes. Then, when they were bringing the body from the mortuary to the village, there was a police band escorting them that sounded a bit out of tune, very loud and brassy, with a strong sort of marching step. So, we knew something was happening, and we all had this great feeling of expectation. I was the only one of my sisters who actually saw the body. That took me by surprise. I'd never seen a corpse before. They brought her in front of the house, and all the little kids were peering in "Oh what's this?" before they were going to put the lid on. The surprising thing and the shocking thing was that the body is nothing. It's just like a piece of cardboard. It doesn't really matter. There's nothing there. Neither before nor since have I had that realization that this is just clay basically. I was a bit upset about it for a while. It had been something of a revelation. They put the lid on and she was buried actually in the compound of the family house.

The event, which would show something of our position in that family was, people would come to the house and say, "Oh, hello. How are you?" There's a long sort of greeting ritual. I don't actually speak Yoruba, though I know some of the appropriate things to say. Some of the people that came were just coming out of curiosity to see the house. One old woman came up and by this time I'd just gotten sort of fed up with somebody who had been there just to while away their time. So, I was a bit off-handed there, and she said, "Do you know who I am?" I said, "No, I don't." She said, "I am the mother of your father's mother." Which meant I should have really showed her a great deal of respect. So, I apologized and I greeted her properly, and so on.

But, that sort of shows that we are really apart from the family. At least, I certainly was. There were so many things that I should have known that I didn't know, plus I didn't speak the language. It was really hard actually. I would run a mile from having to go in there and display my ignorance, where it would be laughed at, say all the wrong things. It's at the heart of this big family do. That, I think, shows how much I wasn't really a proper part of the family in spite of the fact that people were actually very considerate of us. Considerate of us in the sense that they would make allowances for me, because, for instance, I was the youngest, so I was really closest to my mother.[4] So, I was all the less absorbed into Yoruba culture.

Here's an incident from the other side – Newcastle. After we got up there, where my grandmother was living had actually been condemned. The whole village was being knocked down and most of it had gone. Then there were these three rows of houses left,

4 The relationship between the gender of the Black continental African or Black African Caribbean parent and the extent to which *métis(se)* children acquire knowledge of their particular continental African and African Caribbean cultures in all their multilayered complexities and diversities is fascinating. Since I have not encountered much social science literature that addresses this issue, I intend to tackle this topic in future research. In the meantime, I have provided substantial illustrations from the six *griottes'* testimonies, which enforce what I refer to as "the impress of the White English mother or White English mother surrogate on the fundamental formation of cultural identities." (Also refer to Chapter 10 of this book.)

With the exception of Yemi, who refers to herself as "her father's son," all of the *griottes* highlighted talk about their fathers, not as insignificant influences, but rather as individuals who played a very different, perhaps even marginal, role in their lives compared to the everyday and sustained influences of their White English birth mothers or White English mother surrogates. This raises profound and untapped issues regarding the socialization of societally deemed Black daughters by White mothers. It is from a White woman that these young girls are learning about burgeoning womanhood, yet our bi-racialized society denies *métisse* daughters the opportunity to embrace and socially identify with that same source that gave them life and sustained them. This is one of life's profound cultural paradoxes.

Regarding the reverse situation, wherein the mother is Black and the father is White, the psychosocial circumstances are different. I spoke with and spent time with a middle-class married couple with two young sons. Joan, who is Black Nigerian (Yoruba), and Simon, who is White English, met in Nigeria nine years ago. It is readily apparent from the food that is eaten, the language that is spoken as well as the fact that Joan takes her children "back home" to Nigeria every summer that she and necessarily Simon have ensured that their Black Nigerian and White English sons are not deprived of their Nigerian heritage.

This bicultural preservation strategy is, of course, mediated by social class. I recall a conversation with my colleague and friend Samba Diop, who is Senegalese. I was addressing the aforementioned example and he was questioning just how much of their parental culture first- or second-generation working-class Senegalese children living in France either acquire or retain. In the aforementioned example, Joan and Simon have the material resources and, most importantly, the time to provide a bicultural environment for their children. On the other hand, regarding the latter example, many Senegalese parents have two or three jobs. Their labor may generate enough income to send their children home to Senegal for the summer. However, it does not afford them the day-to-day luxury of interacting with their children around the dinner table or in other familial milieux where much of culture is transmitted. I would argue that this 'diasporic angst' plays itself out in other African diasporic locations wherein either retaining questionable notions of cultural authenticity or celebrating cultural hybridity must submit to the daily demands of economic survival in the globalizing metropolises we tentatively name as home. See Smadar Lavie and Ted Swedenburg (1996) (eds.) *Displacement, Diaspora, and Geographies of Identity*, London: Durham University Press.

where people who had refused to move or didn't want to move rather. Then they had been written a letter saying, "You'd better buy your house otherwise who knows what will happen." Stuff like that. So it's like two-up, two-down small houses, big gardens, and beautiful, beautiful countryside. Never seen anything like it. Really beautiful. My granny with all her sort of accumulated paraphernalia of how many years. How many years since the war? Thirty years? All the stuff she's accumulated since that dreadful experience of the war when you had to hang on to everything. So, there's all this junk that you really don't feel you can get rid of yet, but you know it's useless. There was a whole generation in England, who have been forced into that mode. They are old now.[5]

My aunt had a daughter called Amanda, who's about three years younger. Blonde girl, very big. I had the flu. I was sat in the rocking chair, and my granny got this red woolen shawl, which was new, out of it's box and I had the shawl on. Frankly, Amanda, my cousin, sulked afterwards because she'd recently had a cold and no one had given her the shawl.

The landscape in England in a way was like if you have heard Doris Lessing talk about growing up in South Africa. She says, although she's there, the earth is red and what she sees in her mind's eye is like fairies, and little green fields and daffodils, because she's brought up with those fairy stories. England becomes the mythical prototype of land, of country.[6] Maybe it's the land beyond the rainbow. Right? You can only get to heaven if you just like England. Okay? Things my mum said about being homesick like, "Oh, well, I have never heard the birds singing like what they do in England." I know they just make the same twittering noises. I try hard not to say to my children, "You're calling this grass? Wait until you see the grass in Nigeria!" – because you're just going to

5 Bisi has framed her English extended family's experiences in sociohistorical terms. We learn that her grandmother was alive during World War II and that this accounts for her need to accumulate "useless junk." Adding a bit of social and historical commentary, Bisi then situates her grandmother's idiosyncrasies amid a "whole generation in England, who have been forced into that mode...and are old now."

6 The configuring of England in both the colonial and the post-colonial imagination is a topic about which I could write an entire book. The ways in which Bisi compares and contrasts her two "homes" are consistent and generally involve the natural world – the weather, the landscape, birds. However, what is most compelling is her description of the way in which she anticipated her first taste of an English strawberry. As she notes, the strawberry then becomes a powerful metaphor for England itself. Neither England nor her first strawberry – first envisaged as a "quintessential mango or piece of ambrosia" – completely lives up to her ten years of expectation. Her final verdict was "rather watery, with a good flavor, but not a great deal of taste."

give a reinforced impression. "Call this rain? You haven't seen rain yet. Wait until you see hot rain, real lightening, like they have it in Ibadan!"

So there was that sort of sense of expectation of coming to England the Promised Land, where milk doesn't come out of tins, it comes out of cows – where you can buy strawberries – strawberries or things like that – where actually, if you had ten odd years of looking forward to this fruit called a strawberry, by the time you get to the strawberry it's not going to be like you imagined. By that time, you imagine the strawberry like a quintessential mango, like a piece of ambrosia, not like the sort of rather watery…it has a good flavor, but not a great deal of taste that it really is.

I think the first thing about it was, in the train going up to the North, was the smell of smoke in the air, which always makes me paradoxically think of freshness and this sort of wet, light airyness that we have here. I was surprised about things like the sun stays very low on the horizon, something I don't notice now. The fact that you're not very conscious of night sky, because there's light all over the place. Street lighting.

Teachers? Well, there was always this sense of Europe as this wonderful place. I had a very nice art teacher, a Scottish woman, Mrs Campbell, a very tall blonde woman. All the things she would bring to her pupils, seem to be like gifts from another culture, another country. In Nigeria, first of all if your daughter is going to be educated, then you want her to be a professional. She is going to go beyond O-levels. She will become a professional of some sort – a doctor, lawyer or maybe even a research scientist. Not somewhere in the arts, which was not a very serious subject. The fact that she took the subject seriously seemed to be very fine. Even more paradoxically she did more than any other teacher I had in primary school with the means of expression most of her pupils had.

All the conscious input I had about art until very recently was from Europe. It's only now that I have been in Bristol and I am much more conscious of a Black identity in myself than I was then – very much more conscious. I have been able to see a relation in the way I'm thinking and the tradition of African art – to be able to see that there is a real, not a false relationship, an organic relationship – that I'm influenced by these things rather than something I was really impressed by and thought, "Gosh! I must learn how to do this."

If you're a mixed race child growing up in an African country, you are told in no uncertain terms that you are White. White is what you are and will remain, and there is nothing you can do about it. It doesn't matter, even if you did speak the language, even if you did wear the right clothes, even if you had nothing distinguishing culturally – you still know very well that White is what you are.[7]

Whereas, coming to terms with a Black identity in Bristol. You have a lot of things within you to cope with. One of the things you have as a coping mechanism is your identity as a member of a family, as a child of a family, who has been given a name more or less by the head of the family. You have a place there. You have that, which is actually not a part of your racial identity. What the "race" of the family is is incidental. The fact that it was a Black African family has certainly...let's see, supposing I had grown up in Britain, except I had a White extended family and I knew my place in that family. I had been given a name, say, by my mother alone, which my grandmother had then changed, say, to a pet name. Then I think a Black identity would have been a lot more problematic. One gets to the point where one realizes that you cannot a hundred percent identify with a White culture.[8] You have to go and look and find and seek that Black culture from somewhere. If you can't find it, then you have to synthesize it, which I think many people here have done.[9]

---

7 In her stories, Bisi's sister, Yemi, recounts several examples wherein she was treated as a White woman. The most comical and ironic incident, since Yemi speaks and understands Yoruba, occurs when she and her White American friend go to the local market to buy haberdashery. A young Yoruba woman, speaking in Yoruba, is making a play at the darkness of her own skin and the lightness of theirs – these two "White women." This example illustrates the ways in which many Africans have internalized the colonial complex of Black inferiority and White superiority.

As Fanon states: "Out of the blackest part of my soul across the zebra striping of my mind surges this desire to be suddenly White." See Frantz Fanon (1967) *Black Skin, White Masks*, New York: Grove Press, p. 63.

8 Like many *métis(se)* people, Bisi has reached that critical point wherein she can recognize the ways – both within her family as well as in society at large – in which White English culture has been privileged. She also knows for the most part that White English society does not notice nor rather care that her birth mother is White English. This biological fact has no cultural capital in a bi-racialized society, which designates entitlements on the basis of phenotype. Unless, of course, as she mentions, they are looking for a token "good nigger," then as a "light skinned" woman with a White English husband and four "White" children she is more acceptable than someone deemed "full Black" by appearance. In short, she is considered less threatening than a person with two Black parents. Most importantly, Bisi's individual awareness of endemic bi-racialization in England in general and Bristol in particular has also made her collectively conscious of the ways in which English society writ large systematically denies her and other Black people access to certain resources – jobs, education, utilization of the arts, etc.

9 Bisi's notion of a "synthesized" Black culture corresponds with my ideas about "Additive

Sometimes when you talk about being Black it's directly in opposition in a sense to being White. I didn't have that. I had the knowledge of my family name, I'm a member of the family, I look like my father. I'm half-African and half-do I say English? Or rather half-Northumberland, 'cos that's also quite a specific culture, which I didn't really and probably still don't know that much about. It just appears that I did. So, I think I know what my mother's culture is because I see it through her.[10] Actually she's not at all typical of her culture. I've come to realize.

Gradually, I realized just how racist this culture is, and how many people it excludes – how I found I was excluded from very many areas. Which isn't really so because, if you want to, you can actually claim to be, you can sort of assimilate yourself into this culture on sort of fairly decent terms if you are willing to. You can do it if only you are willing to take on its prejudices. How can I be more specific? You can get into there on the terms of you're the one "good nigger." Right? You can actually do it. I think. So, I have come to the realization that sometimes actually sussing it out that when someone is being friendly to you, they're doing it because they are so relieved that they have found a Black person that they can relate to. Now, I do have actually, in the oppositional sense, a Black identity, which I certainly didn't have before.

People who are aware of the history…before, one would have said as an African, "Oh, well, slave trade, that has nothing to do with me. I know where my roots are. It's just hard cheese really if you come from the Caribbean and you don't know your roots. You're not

---

Blackness," which I will develop further in Chapter 10. That is, many *métis(se)* people, as well as perhaps those who have grown up in care, or in predominantly suburban areas, have grown up in a social context wherein Whiteness is qualitatively and quantitatively valued at the expense of Blackness. When the forces of bi-racialization and the one drop rule, leaving home or other transformative factors lead a person to question their predominantly White English upbringing, that individual frequently reacts by seeking out what they perceive to be an oppositional at times "hyper Black" identity. However, this act of reconciliation is most successfully accomplished after the individual has accepted the fact that their psychocultural starting point has been White English. Unfortunately, many *métis(se)* individuals feel they must abandon both their White English parentage as well as their White English cultural roots in order to "become Black." When in fact, most of the *griottes'* testimonies reveal that a formulated Black identity with an acknowledged White English reference point – a "synthesis" as Bisi says – is generally in less conflict with the over-all process of self-transformation than a process wherein White English parentage and White English cultural influences are denied.

10 Here Bisi reinforces the notion of the impress of her mother's culture and how "she sees it (and necessarily experiences it) through her." Yet, over time, she realizes that her image of her mother's culture, as seen through her mother, is in fact Bisi's own construction.

going to feel African are you? Hard cheese! Ha! Ha! Ha!"...being more aware of all the things that created history.

Where I would call home is very difficult, because now I have been here. Well, I came when I was 17, and then I went back for a year, so I'm, right at the middle. I'm 36 now, so, I've lived as many years here as I did there. I know I grew up there and yet, how can I call that home? It's a very fond experience to grow up, you know. But I had my children here, and I changed a great deal through that. So, I don't know where I would call home.

My passport expired some years ago. Because I was born in Nigeria, I have a Nigerian passport. I don't have a British passport. I wasn't entitled to one.[11] So, my passport expired and it's just a real hassle to renew a Nigerian passport. It's just so awful. You go down one day, and meet someone who doesn't like you, tells you to come back in two weeks time. I didn't want to get a British passport if I was to apply. I knew I could apply for nationality, 'cos I had been here and I am married to an English person. But I couldn't decide and just didn't have a passport for years. My father kept coming over. He has visited me here about three times, and each time he says, "You must get a passport, dear." Once he actually did all the stuff for me and I got it. But it was only for two years. So, it has expired since then.

I went down to London, and I didn't get any joy. That was last year. So, I decided I would just go for nationality, and get a British one. It was really like a quandary to decide which one to go for – and be treated badly by people who definitely don't want to see you there. The woman at the Nigerian passport office gave me a dirty look.

11 Given that Bisi's mother is English, it is not clear to me why Bisi is not entitled to a British passport. We were never able to clarify that. The passport application process and the passports themselves come to represent tugs-of-war involving citizenship, nationality and ultimately belonging. She is straddling British and Nigerian worlds. In Britain, she was supposedly ineligible until she married an Englishman and had established residency. The bureaucracy and the blatant hostility in the Nigerian passport office turn her away from applying for a passport. Her geopolitical struggle is exemplary of those of many transnationals who may or may not be *métis(se)*. However, the world is changing rapidly and in Europe alone, there are many countries – Britain excluded – who will soon be allowing constituents of other EU countries across their borders without passports. However, this "hospitality" does not extend to Black Europeans in general and Black British in particular, who are frequently treated with contempt, hostility and suspicion at various European "border check points." See Nozizwe (1991) "European Fascism: cult of the master race," *Spare Rib*, November, pp. 42–4.

By the way, I still have a key to my father's house. He wrote a letter recently saying, "Why haven't you learned to drive?[12] While you are away, you should really do this and that." Like, I'm gonna be back![13]

I don't even know if I've got a community, honestly. Sarah said I was middle class, which for her is obviously an insult. So many things are contradictory. For instance, I have had a lot of privileges. I don't have to go to work. I'm married to a man, who is doing very well. He drives a company car. He's a man who is in a "muddy-welly" profession. He's an architect; he's on site a lot. I'm not really living a lifestyle as his wife. Because I'm not being very wifey, very much of a couple, like we don't go places together. There's that there.

When you have a child, you've lost a lot of self-determination, and you're very much under the State's control. Which was the first time for me, because of all the hospital stuff, and the notes that are taken, and you have a health visitor visiting you, and all this. You don't have personal freedom. In fact, the lack of personal freedom was so immense basically that I have only just begun now to look back and see how immense it was. You lose a lot of status – instantly. Basically, the society's view of a woman who has to stay at home with the children is that she is a complete idiot. You do suffer quite a loss of self-confidence because of that. I'm fairly sure most young mothers here do feel that.[14]

Having children affects such a lot of your life. It affects your housing, the sort of housing that is going to be okay for you to live in – the fact that you're responsible for somebody else and you have to care for them and all this, which is quite a big shock for a young person. Having a child brings out a lot of things in a relationship. It changes the relationship very basically. A lot of tensions that have been there or that have been in the background, suddenly come to the fore. A lot of unresolved stuff people have about family, about family relationships, and the status of the relationship between them and their mother suddenly comes into play once there's a

---

12 Since this conversation, Bisi has taken driving lessons, resuscitated the car her mum gave her, acquired a driving licence and has become *chauffeur extraordinaire* for all of us with either the pavement or the bus as our only mode of transport.

13 The ways in which Bisi's father barks orders to her as if she is "gonna be back" is in keeping with – as Bisi's sister Yemi tells us – the way time is frozen in their mum's bedroom. Everything is as she left it years ago as though any day she, too, would be walking in the door to resume a life which had simply been suspended.

14 As we are talking about motherhood, in the background, Bisi's youngest daughter is shrieking "Mum! Mum! Mum!..."

third person in the marriage. There's more around having children that changed the marriage.

After you've lived here for a bit, you get aware that, in fact, there's a whole load of stuff that gets involved in mixed relationships. Which maybe one would choose not to take on board. A friend of mine once mentioned how complicated it is. How people might have a bad opinion of you. How you've got so much explaining to do, which is totally boring. Once this couple walked past. It was a White guy (with a Black woman), and he was saying to her, "Oh, and do you do your hair like that all the time?" That sort of curiosity about personal characteristics is first of all extremely rude and was just obnoxious. Do you always have hair up your nostrils or? It is rude, how dare he! These assumptions of what's strange and what's not – all that is a lot more theoretical. Once you've got children, then perhaps the real stuff is gonna make the other stuff not matter so much.[15]

Had I been brought up in Bristol, I don't think I could have got off with Graham at all – if we met in Bristol and I had some knowledge of Bristol. But, we didn't. We met in Greece, which was far from home for him. Theoretical things like will I be compromised as a member of the Black community? That's theoretical. It takes a lot for two people to stay together.

A lot of the modern consciousness I have of being African and being Black, which is not the same thing, is probably in spite of my mother. Being Black in the sense that I feel now, that would be in spite of her. It's not something she agrees with. But you must remember that when she went to Nigeria, she was in her twenties. She spent her formative years there not here. She has very little knowledge of how racism operates and how it affects people, and she doesn't really have any sympathy or understanding of the kinship between people – American, Caribbean, and African. The sort of feeling that there is the unity there, consciousness. One can

---

15 Bisi's reflections reinforce my conceptualization of the public and private domains which *métis(se)* individuals and their families frequently negotiate. In the public domain, she, her husband and perhaps her children must contend with bi-racialized and sexualized politics as well as the conflation of "race" and culture in their communities. No one stops Bisi and her husband to ask them about their shared interests, passions and values. Disapproving gazes only register a sexualized couple who are marked by their apparent bi-racialized physical differences. However, at home, Bisi and Graham must contend with the everyday task of living, which includes raising four children in a declining British economy. While I was in Bristol, Graham was made redundant (laid off). However, he was quickly able to find his feet. He decided to follow his dreams and started his own architectural firm.

get something from it and one owes something to it. She would say things, "Why do you want to put yourself on the side of those who are feeling victimized? Put yourself on the winning side." She would stress this to us very much – that we have an English family and English roots, and some heritage from them as well which is bannered.[16]

It's funny though, when I started relaxing about it and owning that there is quite a lot of English in me basically – when I could come up with that admission, then that's almost when I started making Mbari,[17] and really finding that, "Yes, there is a lot of English, but there is also a lot of African."[18]

16 In so-called multicultural Britain, White English culture is still seemingly pervasive and privileged over other cultures. Hence, there is a strong argument among cultural nationalists that Black and *métis(se)* children's education should be infused with a heavy dose of the cultures of their "minority" parents – Black continental African, African Caribbean and South Asian. However, this perspective meets with much resistance, but especially as it pertains to *métis(se)* children. Parents, educators, among others, shout for parity, not wanting to accept the fact that in mainstream English culture, there is ample validation of their child's White English heritage and it is the "Black" African/Caribbean/Asian diasporic cultures and histories that need a "banner."

As previously mentioned, throughout this book, I have neglected the other permutations and combinations of diasporic *métis(se)* that exist in England. Juxtaposing such multiple and complex experiences would have downplayed the social and cultural complexities within and without interwoven diasporic communities. Moreover, especially now, in the age of globalization and as we approach the millennium, those of us of essentialized African origin are still at once revered and feared. This mixed reception is despite the fact that there have been longstanding *métis(se)* communities in Liverpool, England and Cardiff, Wales since at least the end of the nineteenth century. Black African mixed with White British is still viewed by the general populus and politicians alike as problematic. The words of White English politician Enoch Powell's 1968 "Rivers of Blood" speech warning White English people of the evils and dangers of "race mixing" ring true today and such ideas are evident in much right-wing propaganda.

Consequently, Bisi's mum's remarks are not surprising to me and are actually words I have heard uttered countless times before. The common assumption is the fact that a White person is married to a Black person liberates both parties from bi-racialized prejudices. However, I have found some of the most bi-racialized people to be those individuals who have supposedly transgressed racial borders. In fact, one could argue as have Hernton (1965) and Fanon (1965) that it is rationalized "Black" desire for "Self" annihilation and rationalized "White" hunger for immolation of "the Other" that subconsciously provoke certain "inter-racial" unions. See Frantz Fanon (1967) *Black Skin, White Masks*, New York: Grove Press; or Calvin Hernton (1965) *Sex and Racism in America*, New York: Grove Press.

17 An Igbo art form, primarily practiced in Eastern Nigeria. The artist erects shrines to placate the Earth goddess. Bisi uses Mbari to "describe a new artistic impasse." According to her, "It is not static; it absorbs new ideas."

18 The African influences are most apparent in Bisi's art. In Bristol, I attended a lecture wherein Bisi spoke about her latest exhibition. What she creates is a successful synthesis of "two extremely different cultures" of "the traditional and the modern" and of "tradi-

I'm very aware of being self-conscious all the time – speaking to have an effect and what the effect will be. I have been aware of that since childhood – to find that I could relax and it would just happen – I wasn't expecting, and it was a nice thing to happen. Being self-conscious is so hard to escape from. Because of that, everyone is constantly repressing things. When you do escape from things, it's nice to find that, "Oh, well! What was I afraid of?"

You just see what a middle-class activity it is to have anything to do with art. My definition of middle class: somebody who speaks English without a regional accent, whose parents have prioritized their education, rather than their going out to work – that's a big element of it – while they were growing up, had music lessons, gaining a skill, whose experiences of education have probably been pleasant and positive. Black people can be middle class. It all goes down to your need to live in a middle-class area – go to a middle-class school, though that's not necessary. Your parents could send you to a rather bad school, because they've got this social conscious thing. They want schools to improve, and give it support. All those children have a lot more privilege. If they do very badly, they'll get coaching; they'll get lessons. They'll not be written off as stupid. Sarah uses "middle class" as an insult. I think I'd guess that she means when you have assumptions that you own stuff, or think you can do stuff or take stuff for granted.

The question of what race are my children? What do they think? How do they feel? It's difficult as well. I think Elizabeth said, "I'm one-quarter Nigerian (very specific, very precise), but I'm three-quarters English, Mummy." Which is true. I ask my son sometimes, "Do you think you are White?" I don't know whether he says it to please me or not but he says, "Well, no, not really." And they use this dreadful term – "half-caste," "'alf caste." They say, "You are, aren't you Mum?" I say, "What kind of a word is that? Half of what? How can one call oneself half of something?" I don't think that's made any impression on them

---

tional and Western art." Having attended art college in England, she acknowledges that "most of the cultural influences she was exposed to were greatly products of Europe." Moreover, as previously mentioned, "a child takes a great deal of culture from their mother." In this case, the culture is English. This is despite the fact that Bisi grew up in Nigeria. At a critical point, she decided she needed to find out "what I have from Africa only." She "didn't know she had the figures in her psyche." I refer to Bisi's retrieval of her African roots as "cultural memory." I have also been able to "retrieve" aspects of my neglected "African/Nigerian" heritage and express these influences in dance, poetry and the visual arts – painting and photography.

basically. Because it's the basic term they use at school, and everyone knows what it means. "I'm 'qua'a- (quarter-) caste' aren't I Mum?" "What do you mean 'caste?' Do you know what it means?"

Of course, Julia looks completely English. What are they to feel? Julia's probably the child who'd have the least problems adjusting to a new country.[19] She hasn't got this terrible sense of normal Elizabeth has. She's outgoing. Actually they are all quite shy, funnily enough, apart from Emma. Julia is more sociable than Elizabeth, that's why. She would have less problems. You can't actually feed thoughts into your children. They are aware that they are not completely British. Let's put it like that. I don't know how far that goes. The words I put it in then are negative. They are aware that they are not completely English.[20] Is that being aware of something positive or not? It's only through talking and discussing that I know what they think.

Being aware that one's system of ideas isn't absolute. It isn't the absolute, the one above all others. There are many and they are all sort of parallel and contradictory. If you are mixed race, you belong in two (or more) cultural traditions, which may be mutually contradictory, you just have to find a middle space. As I said, this other woman who is Irish, her culture is something that will support her personality and at the same time oppress her. To come to terms with the ways in which it does that. The stuff about, you're never completely invisible or at home, you are always a bit of a stranger. Same status as strangers. My children are all English, and I still call myself a stranger.[21] Anywhere at all. I used to think, oh, maybe one could go to South America and just be able to walk down the street and not be a stranger – because of my appearance. It's not so bad actually, there are places one could walk and not look out of place –

---

19 Bisi's observation that her one child who looks completely "White" English is the one child who would have the least difficulty adjusting to another cultural context is consistent with Ruby's ruminations about her children. Obviously, in a world that still glorifies "Whiteness", those who are closer to "it" or even embody "it" are going to have an easier time with life.

20 Note shift from usage of the term "British" to "English."

21 Running like parallel lines throughout the six testimonies are the twin themes of empowerment, which locate *métis(se)* people as cultural bridges and political agents and of hopelessness which highlight the intermingled psychosocial sensations of not belonging, being marginal and being (in)visible. Without either putting words into the mouths of the *griottes* or ignoring their cumulative and collective pain, my autoethnographic challenge was to create a sociocultural context and a safe space for them to re-frame the negativity that usually dominates most depictions of the lived experiences of *métis(se)* people.

like Thatchapee, actually. In many ways, it's gettting better in that sense over here. I think Black people are more visible and more vocal. You don't have to conform to any idea of a Black person any more, which is very nice.

9

YEMI

"I am my father's son"

Out of all of the six *métisse griottes*, Yemi is the most powerful epitome of an English–African Diaspora daughter. As her testimonies will illustrate, she may not necessarily feel as though she belongs everywhere she situates herself and/or her family, but she has definitely learned to negotiate her different worlds and the disparate roles she plays within them. She eases into life in Nigeria, where her husband lives and works, where she spent her childhood, where she and her children return each summer, and yet where she is still frequently an outsider or rather "not one of them." For nine or so months out of the year, she shifts gears and tolerates Raleigh, a closed predominantly White English community a few miles outside Bristol, whose inhabitants will gladly and repeatedly accept Yemi's invitations for coffee or tea, but yet they never seem to reciprocate. She raises her four children here during the school year and as I have already mentioned Yemi and the four children return to Nigeria for the summer months to spend time with their father, who is also Yemi's husband.

Yemi is the elder sister of my friend Bisi. I first met her at one of Bisi's famous gatherings. I was impressed by her self-confidence and by the related fact that she seemed to have something intelligent or humorous to say about everything we discussed that afternoon. I would later learn from her that earlier stages of her life had been an emotional checkerboard of pain, protest and passion. Her troubled relationship with her English mother drove her to attempt suicide. The silver lining under this failed attempt was that she became "her father's son." In so doing, she learned the Yoruba language, customs and culture, all of which her two sisters, still bonded to their English mother, did not.

Before we begin our first conversation, Yemi is giving me a "personal inventory" of her home. It is full of beautiful wood carvings, most of which she buys from a Hausa man in Ibadan, Nigeria. However, something on the mantel catches my eye. There are some beautiful watercolor paintings, illustrating some Nigerian folk tales. They were intricately painted by her sister Bisi.

Yemi: there is no place like home

African art and plants and cane make the house seem tropical. To give it some light and warmth, you need things that look tropical. At least to remind me of home anyway.[1]

My father was born in 1920 in a village in Ijebuland (close to a town called Egba), which is called Oduduwa. My mother was born in 1927 in a village called Hamsterley – Hamsterley colliery, which is close to a town called Concert on the outskirts of Newcastle. Where they met was at the University of Durham. My father was doing a degree there in Physics and my mother was doing a degree in English. She was about eleven miles from home. He wasn't. He was on scholarship. He was one of the people chosen by the government to do a degree in England – I suppose by the Federal Nigerian government – to come back and be part of the middle-class indigenous work force – because by getting this training they would go into either teaching or the Civil Service with their degrees. At that time there wasn't an educational institution that gave a degree in Nigeria. There was a Lagos School of Technology or something like that, that he'd been to, where you actually do a degree course. He did a degree course, and after it he got a diploma. So, he came here after he got this first degree if you like, to do another degree in Physics.

He married my mother. He went back first and worked with the Government College. I have a feeling it was in Enugu. She joined him there after eighteen months. She joined him after my elder

---

1 Before I left for the "field," Carol Stack, the Co-Chair of my Ph.D. dissertation committee, passed on several useful fieldwork tips. One of her suggestions was that I ask each participant to provide me with an "inventory" of their living spaces, which also included an acount of the significance and origin of each important item. Yemi was the only one of the twenty-five participants who took me on a very detailed tour of her home. What seemed most significant was the importance for Yemi of creating an atmosphere reminiscent of home, which for her was Nigeria. Incidentally, since this original project was conceptualized most of the twenty-five *griot(tes)*, including Yemi, have moved locations.

sister and I were born. She was born in 1950. I was born in 1952. I was born in Shortleybridge, which is near Hamsterley. My elder sister was born in Edinburgh. For some reason they were living in Edinburgh at first, and then they moved to where my grandparents were. I was born. He went back to Nigeria. She stayed there, continued with her studies, and when she finished her degree, she joined him in Nigeria. At first, we lived in the east, and then we lived in Oyo, close to Ibadan in the west. He had then joined the Civil Service, and she was teaching. Then, Bisi was born. After some years in Oyo, he was posted to England with the London office for the Nigerian High Commission. He worked there for a while, so we were all going to school here. Then he was posted back to Nigeria to Ibadan, and that's where we lived ever since.

We all went to school there. Both my parents were socialists politically, both coming from fairly humble upbringings, both scholarship children. They place a very high value on education, but they don't place a high value on exclusiveness. At that time, when we went back to Nigeria from England, there were three free primary schools just started as an experiment by Awolowo. He was one of the people in the political forefront before independence and also after. He was also a Socialist and he wanted to prove to the people and to the government that free primary education would work. There was this feeling that if something has no value, if you don't pay for something, you don't really appreciate it – education should be paid for – then that meant education is exclusive. It's those who can afford to send their kids to school who will. So he started these three free primary schools. One was in the University of Ibadan – Abadina Primary School and it was actually placed inside the campus, which is fully residential. We went there.

We were at home with our mother and our father. Although my mother worked, she was the primary influence in our house – culturally. We didn't really know very much about Yoruba culture. We just didn't. We didn't speak the language. We didn't have any of the taboos. My father always spoke to us in English. He kept Yoruba as the language he spoke on the telephone secretly, so that we didn't know what he was saying. My mother used to get quite irritated. She'd pick out the English words and string them together and say, "We do know what you're talking about."

At home we used to eat a mixture of semi-English/semi-Nigerian food. If we had a steward, we would have things like pounded yam. If we didn't have a steward to pound it, we would have mashed yam. We would have groundnut stew or bitter leaf stew, but we would have sausage and bacon and fried eggs for breakfast. We never had things like yam for breakfast. Some things we never actually ate at home. Although my father attempted to introduce them, nobody liked them. Like *eckaw* or *ogi* – cornmeal fermented slightly and it can be little triangles almost like a cold savory blancmange, or it can be warm like a very thin porridge. It's pap and it can be tough or it can be cold. We would never have that. Nobody liked that. We would have porridge. We would have sausage. We would have eggs. We would have chickens.

As a family, I recall my childhood days as being very happy.[2] We had a dog. We had chickens. We had turkeys at one point. A cat. There were usually animals. The animals were always my responsibility. We had ten chickens and a rooster. It may have been less – five or ten chickens and a rooster. I must have been 8 and my older sister would have been 10. My father proposed that we sell the eggs and keep the money and feed and water and have our accounts. Anyone who came to the house, we were free to sell them eggs. We were also free to sell eggs to the household at so much per dozen. The money was ours, so that he had worked out a way of not giving us any pocket money and we assumed serious responsibility. This was for both of us together. I did the watering, the feeding, the collection of the eggs and the numbering. I put the date on in pencil. My sister did the accounts. This is how she was. She had the money. She doled it out, and I did all the work. This is me.

They provided a very very stable environment for us. We had access to any information that we wanted, because both of them collected books – especially my mother, because she is an English teacher. She also has a very broad spectrum in her mind. So we had books on everything – psychology, geography, on all sorts of things. Many, many scientific books from my dad. There was a book, locked in the cupboard, that you had to really search for the key called something or other about sex. I can't remember what the title was, but this "magic book" – if one could just lay one's eyes on that book![3] All sorts of information – books and glossy books, picture books about geography or places in the earth, poetry and wonderful prose by contemporary writers. So, we almost had a little clue into the world.[4] The house was tapped into the whole world for us. It

2 Yemi contradicts herself here. According to her testimonies, her childhood was less than idyllic. Then again, memories of the times spent selling eggs or hunting down the key for the 'Sex Book' may have made the more painful experiences seem less significant.

3 I recall a radio interview with the esteemed Nigerian writer, Ben Okri, who confessed to having similar adventures with a book in his father's library. I wonder how many middle-class Nigerian children could recount the same tale?

4 From some of Yemi's and Bisi's descriptions, their childhood and their home seem like worlds of enchantment: farm animals, a variety of books giving Yemi, Kemi and Bisi "a

was a very happy place. I'm not an indoor person. My sister is. She would always be with a book, even at the age of 5. If you're looking for Kemi, you'd find her somewhere with a book curled up. Whereas, I'm not. I prefer to be outside. I was the tomboy – often mistaken for a boy. People would think, "Okay, those are the girls, that must be the boy then." I played with my cousins, the boys. My best friends, my cousins, were all boys – none of the girls. The girls were awful. We would climb trees, we would go and catch frogs. We played very well together. I tried to play with the boys at school, but I had an enemy, who was the boy who sat next to me. We looked very much alike. We were almost the same except he was one year older. He was very very fair. Very beautiful smooth – almost like a Chinese face – marvelous oval kind of face. He was very naughty and disruptive. Apparently, so was I. So the teachers used to put us together right in front in the middle of the class, so they could actually see. We were not friends. We weren't very good friends. I was okay when I got there, because I was allowed to play cowboys and indians. The girls used to play skipping games and clapping games – all sorts of dancing games where you put your feet out, and you've got to count how many – three, then two then one, whether left or right. I didn't know any of those games, but I did know cowboy games. I used to play on the yard with boys.

One day in the classroom – you have to hide. Some people are escaping from the people with guns. You can shoot each other like the Cisco Kid. I got him in the classroom. He was all alone. He was not aware that I was behind him. I said, "Bang, bang, you're dead!" He turned around and said, "No I'm not!" I said, "You are dead." He said, "No, I'm not! You're a girl!" That was the end of my cowboys and indians. He said, "I'm not playing with any girls. Why do we have to have any girls?" This is my partner at my desk.

Then, we went to our own house from government quarters. We were living in a place called Elele. This coincided with my sister and I starting secondary school together. We'd always lived with our family. In St Agnes', we were at first day students. My mother was

little clue into the world." Bisi remembers the times during power cuts when they would make shadow pictures in the kitchen with a candle and sing sea shanties around the piano. Yemi vividly describes Saturday trips to the market.

These are depictions of *métis(se)* family life that rarely, if ever, appear on the pages of sociological or even ethnographic studies. Yemi's and Bisi's remembrances are excellent examples of what is possible if we disaggregate "race" and culture as analytical categories. At the same time, their accounts of relationships with their mother, their father, each other as sisters, as well as their interactions with the "real world" place gender at the center and distort the perfect picture of family life which they both could have seduced us with.

teaching there. She was actually teaching me as well. So she would take us every morning, bring us back every afternoon when she finished her work as a teacher. She got another job. She couldn't bear the teaching in St Agnes' any more. She got a job in another school.

She could sometimes give us a lift, but my father hit on the idea that we could go by taxi – which was cheap, only a 6 pence. But you have to change. It's in two laps. You change in the middle of town in Dube market. So my sister and I would start this in the morning. Get a taxi down to Dube market, walk across the big roundabout to the other side where the roads go in the direction of the school and get another taxi there. It's almost like a Raleigh taxi and a Bristol taxi, you try to get one for the appropriate area. That was an adventure, because sometimes, for instance, in the market-place, there would be some kind of a disturbance. The biggest cause of these disturbances was a mad man, actually very mad, who might attack girls, molest them. This would echo through the market. "So and so is around!" Most of these people with a psychosis, who are crazy like this, they have what's called a "marijuana psychosis."[5]

They've gone bananas, but they used to be hemp smokers. So, they belong to the group of boys, like vandals almost, sitting about smoking hemp. You see these small boys – they are not so small – they're young men, but they're jobless, and they're bored, and they all have their names – like RJ and everybody knows RJ. Your mother will be calling you, "RJ's around! RJ's around!" and you'd have to run and hide inside the market stalls until RJ has paraded through and gone away – 'cos of course he's crazy, and he loves it – see all these people scattering.[6] We never had any problems going to school or coming back.

5 In England, there was and still is uproar within the African Caribbean community over the excessive diagnosis of African Caribbeans (primarily men) as "suffering" from "cannabis psychosis." The debate continues. A Bristol-based Trinidadian social worker, Stephanie Gabriel, wrote a scathing article responding to a White English psychiatrist who had written an article on cannabis psychosis. According to Stephanie Gabriel, the symptoms of cannabis psychosis are not unlike psychological reactions to racism. See Chris Ranger (1989) "Race, culture and 'cannabis psychosis': the role of social factors in the construction of a disease category," *New Community*, (15) 3: 359–70; Roland Littlewood and Maurice Lipsedge (1993) *Aliens and Alienists: Ethnic Minorities and Psychiatry*, London: Routledge; Suman Fernando (1995) *Mental Health in a Multiethnic Society*, London: Routledge.

6 Irie, one of the residents in Thatchapee, from whom I learned a great deal about the politics of stigmatized difference, seemed to have a similar effect on this community. However, what most people neglected to recognize were the myriad ways in which Irie manipulated and negotiated his role as one of the "local mad men." See Erving Goffman (1963) *Stigma: Notes on the Management of a Spoiled Identity*, Harmondsworth: Penguin; Erving Goffman (1959) *Presentation of Self in Everyday Life*, Harmondsworth: Penguin

By the time I was 13, my mother and I started to have very serious head-on collisions. The situation couldn't be ignored – it had to be confronted. She is a violent woman. She just is. It's her nature. She's aggressive. She used to give us tasks to do. We'd have to do the washing up or clean the sitting room. Or she would say, "Peel the potatoes." Or, "Peel the yams." She would come into the kitchen and start ranting and raving and eventually she would hit you. She would just come in and say, "Where are the potatoes?" Or, "Why haven't you washed the dishes? I'm sick of this. You children are so lazy. I asked you to do it and you haven't done it." On and on like this. Then, you'd say, I'm pretty sure that's what we'd tell her, "We're doing it." Or, "We're just about to do it." When you'd open your mouth, she would then hit you. She would hit you across the ear. Bam! Or she would hit you with a wooden spoon. Back! She just always would. It seemed to be becoming a pattern. God knows what was wrong with her. She'd be in this crazy mood. She'd come in, then she'd start yelling, and then she'd hit you.

I started not being able to stand it, and I also noticed that when she was looking at me, I was looking at her eyes without looking up. I was 13 then. So, to get her to stop hitting me, one day I picked up a knife. She had the wooden spoon. I said, "You take one step closer to me, I'll kill you." She said, "What are you doing? Don't be so stupid." I said, "I'm serious. Take one step closer to me and I'll kill you." So, she shouted and shouted and shouted and she drove me out of the house. "Get out of my house. I don't want to set eyes on you. You disgusting creature." But, she wasn't able to hit me again, because each time she would come and strike me, I would bring a knife out and threaten to kill her. She would drive me out of the house. She would mention that I wouldn't come in until my father came home from work at five o'clock. So, my father would come in and say, "Where is everybody?" And he would say, "Why is Yemi outside?" "I don't want that revolting girl in my house," she would say. "Now then, Thea, let the girl come in. At least let her go in and go to her room." "I don't want her in my house," she would say.

The long and short of all this is I attempted suicide around that time. She liked to exclude me. She tried all sorts of things. She played the piano. She would be playing the piano downstairs in the living room. She'd say, "Come on everybody come and sing sea shanties. Come and sing this or that musical." She had a big thick book of songs you could sing. Some were hymns, some were sea shanties – all sorts of different things we could sing. We would come down and start singing, and she'd say to me "Go away you're spoiling the song with your voice." I wouldn't be trying to spoil the song. Maybe I was singing too loud or off key. Who cares.

She picked favorites. Bisi was her favorite. Bisi could do no wrong. Bisi was also small and delicate. She was asthmatic. Bisi – precious little darling. The reason why my sister Kemi wasn't in the middle of all these confrontations in the kitchen was as soon as she would start yelling, she'd just turn her nose up and go upstairs. She wouldn't chase after her the way she would chase after me. She would leave her to go upstairs and face me. I was the one who was always being yelled at.

She let me sew. She was trying to teach me how to sew. She let me sew an outfit, a skirt and a top. I suppose it was fairly stupid, very stupid – clothes. It was a skirt in green. The top was red with frills of green. I made this thing and she said to me, "It's beautiful, it's really, really nice." Then, that particular Saturday, she said to me "Get ready, we'll go to the shops." We would go to the shops on a Saturday…we'd buy all sorts of things – treat things, like big pita breads, fresh butter, and salady things – something to go with the pitas – and come back and eat it. Also, there were clothes shops we'd go to and we might get something nice. She saw me coming down the stairs in this outfit I had made, which she had said was nice, and she said, "You're not coming with me dressed like that." I said, "But, I am. I want to wear it." She said, "Not with me you're not." I said, "But, I want to wear this, and anyway you said it was nice." She said, "It's revolting." I said, "Look, you said it was nice, and I've got it on. Let's go!" "No, you're not coming with me." She took the other two and said, "Come on let's go!" and left me behind. So, I searched the whole house for what I 'm going to take to kill myself, because I had had enough. I felt, she didn't really love me. It seemed as if I was in the way. She seemed she'd be much happier if she had her precious Bisi and her darling Kemi and not that horrible Yemi. This is how my mind was working. It's one of the reasons why I try not to pressurize my kids, because if you go into a downer, you can't see anything good happening. The more negative things happen to you, the worse it gets. It gets until you feel so oppressed. I didn't believe that there was no after-life or something like this. I felt like my life was now a nuisance. My presence in the house was one that was causing unhappiness. The best bet was to get out of there, and the only way to get out of there was to actually die. I felt she would be happier.

My parents take no drugs. The only thing they take is aspirin. I looked everywhere, but there was nothing but this bloody aspirin. And there weren't even very many aspirins There were only about sixteen aspirin and about five or six Anadin – 'cos my mother had period pains. That is what she takes. Everything I could find I took. It was just aspirin. I wrote a note, took off my clothes, and put on my dressing gown. I have a feeling I must have taken off those clothes to change. Because there's no need to take off your clothes. So, I must have thought, I'll change, and then thought I'm not changing. I know there must have been more. They were supposed to be out for hours. What she said we were going to do was not just shop, 'cos I know they were supposed to be out for a long time. When they came back I was so shocked, and I thought, "YEEH! They're back already and I'm not dead." So, then, the car came back. I was standing at the back door watching them. The little one came out, Bisi. "Look what we bought for you." I thought, "Oh look, they bought something for me. They must love me after all. See, she must love me after all. So, I better tell her." So, I told her. I couldn't see properly. Obviously I thought I was dying. I had been writing a long good-bye letter, but I gradually stopped being able to write. Not before I had written anything that I wanted to write. I knew that I was being very weird.

I told her. "Oh, you idiot," she said. "Get inside the car. You're nothing but trouble, you." She put the other ones in the house, got inside the car and drove me to our family doctor – an old man called Doctor Runshewe, who had been our doctor since I was a little, little girl. He took me quickly to his own bedroom, gave me a emetic to make me sick. He gave some salt or soap. I don't even know what it was. It tasted like soap. I was sick. I told him, "She doesn't love me. She'd be much happier if I wasn't there."

The result of this was that she had very little to do with me after that. My dad took me every evening, when he came back, to my uncle's house. Every single evening! When he was going out, he didn't actually leave me with her ever again. He took me whenever he went to my uncle's. He took me when he was going to his farm, he took me when he was going to Ijebu or when he was going on one of his trips. My dad and I became very close, which was very good. My mother and I can't actually get along very well. It's now that I see her that I realize I'm not the crazy one when I was young. I was in no way disturbed. She's the nutter. She's the difficult one and she picks favorites. It's not reasonable to have more than one child if you have this mentality of picking favorites and having the others as horrible. Also, because of this change with my father, I got very close to my cousins. So, I am closer to my cousins than my other sisters – very, very close. They are all boys. So, I now get to know how to speak Yoruba – Yoruba morals, the life itself – better than my sisters – ostensibly, because I was actually flung out by my mother, or I stepped away from my mother.[7] Then all of these things were more accessible to me.

'Cos as I say, our house was secure. It's not a house where people are coming and going. Some people used to come and stay with us – cousins used to come and stay with us, older women. Older girl cousins would be sent to my mother's to help them with their exams. For instance, one of my cousins stayed with us when she had failed some exam or other and my mother was tutoring her to do something else. She was also giving her typing lessons and all the rest of it, but they were quite a bit older than us. They were also fairly unhappy staying there, from having to work too hard or what-ever and finding it unfair. Because in a household with children there's a lot of work to do. When you step in from another house-hold it seems as though you're being asked to do everything, because you don't know what the others are doing.

The end result of all of this was I was then sent to boarding school. Both of us were. Kemi was going into Form V, I was going into Form IV. She decided enough is enough, somebody can take this lot over. "I'm not doing any more, mate!" We were then boarders. In the boarding school is when I suppose I realized that it isn't everybody, who for instance, sleeps on beds, eats with knives and forks, and so on and so forth at home. It's not immediately obvious, because everybody has a bed and everybody has a locker. But I was remembering that there was one day, there were these two girls, very close buddies – Abigail Adewale and Allison Adebayo. Abigail was a Yoruba girl, Allison was from the Midwest. They were good buddies, but one day there was some trouble. They were in the same room, I think, in the same dormitory. There was a little bit of an altercation. Allison was particularly upset. She was

---

7 What Yemi has to say about her family of origin does not really differ from family dynamics that play themselves out in contexts which are not *metis(se)*. As such, Yemi succeeds in normalizing *metis(se)* family life and strife. However, her narrative is also in keeping with a prevailing theme, which is the impress of the White English mother or the White English mother surrogate in the transmission of White English culture in all its variations. Even if the Black father is physically present, as was the case in Yemi's family, White English cultural codes are frequently reified at the expense of Black African or Caribbean referents in all their complex manifestations. From linguistic silences to dietary omissions, more often than not it is Black/African/Caribbean culture that is subverted. The privileging of White English culture in *metis(se)* households has serious dialectical implications for *métis(se)* identity formation since it is a bi-racialized essentialized and socially constructed Black/African identity that society at large imposes. In Yemi's case, her squabble with her mother puts her in a position wherein she now has access to Yoruba culture, which had previously been perceived as male and from which she had been excluded.

shouting and screaming outside at Abigail, 'cos this is the way girls fight. They yell and cry and shout. She was saying, "Look at this Abigail, eh? Look at what she's doing to me, eh? She says we no have beds in our house." What had happened was somebody wanted to rearrange the dormitory and Allison said, "I want my bed here." Abigail said, "I don't know what your fuss is all about, you don't even have a bed at home. So what are you making this big deal about the bed for? You're not even used to beds." That's her close buddy. So the girl was so annoyed. She was annoyed for two reasons. One, here she had discussed her home environment with Abigail in confidence, because they were best buddies. Two, she thought it was disgraceful that she was being disgraced – showing the whole school that she was one of the people who slept on a mat at home. I think a lot of people did. A lot of people would have, 'cos a lot of the boarders when they would actually go home, they would be in completely different circumstances. You don't know where they come from.

Bisi and I didn't have a good relationship at all. Bisi was the little pet. My mother and Bisi were close, very close. She used to talk to Bisi and keep Bisi with her. Bisi didn't have to do any housework for some reason. The people who had to do the housework were the girls, Kemi and I. Bisi would always be sent on errands. "Go and ask those girls if they've finished doing the dishes." "Go and ask those girls to bring their lazy selves down for supper." We were the girls and her daughter was Bisi. So, at any opportunity, I would fight with Bisi. I was really, really mean to her. Always trying to fight with her and my dad would step in. His point was, if she was sent on an errand by mother, we should treat the messenger with the respect we would give...it was bullshit anyway, 'cos she'd say, "Girls, Mum says have you finished the dishes? ""Get lost, creep!" It's amazing that Bisi and I are such good friends now because we used to be enemies. I certainly felt that she was something to get at somehow.

I suffered very severely from rage – before this thing with my mum came up. This was one of the things. When she would send me upstairs, "You're not singing with us. Go away!" Once I hit my little puppet with a scarf. It shattered. I must have been really really furious. Another time, a huge wooden bed – I went upstairs I looked at the bed and heaved it over. I sat there and cried and cried and cried, cooling down, 'cos it takes half an hour to calm down – looked at the bed. "Hell! Where am I going to sleep?" Tried to pick it up. The bed was stuck. I could not move that bed. How did I push it over, then? So, I had to put books underneath, gently, gently trying to heave it up. It was really, really heavy. I suffered from rage, terrible, teribble rage.

As for my sister Kemi's life, her life is sleeping and eating. She's not really bothered by all of this. As far as she was concerned, it was between me and my mother, and had nothing to do with her. Also, later on, my stance with my mum was that she was not going to tell me what to do. She could try. My sister wasn't social. She didn't like going out. She didn't have a need for it. If she had a book, she was fine. She was in another world. She didn't see the need for things like parties, or picnics, with one's friends rather than with one's family. I was the one who had to break down all the barriers for all that stuff in our house – everything – plus, having a boyfriend, going to parties, having friends to come in, men to come in. I'm the one who had to do all the work with my parents, 'cos my parents didn't see the point of having social interaction with other people. Maybe they were both oddballs.[8] I think they were simply contained and content with what they actually had. Some people have a very social household, where everyone is coming in and going out in droves, and in the middle of it, two parents totally unflustered. In our house, my parents actually felt a sense of intrusion, and closed ranks to make sure that the house wasn't destroyed by this intruder whoever it may be. They didn't really want us out there either. They felt that the big wide world was dangerous. Especially since I didn't have my mother's ear.

Most of my later adolescence and young womanhood was certainly spent in privacy, because I didn't have parents with whom I was going to exchange any information or ideas or ask advice from. I had to do it myself, 'cos I didn't have an older sister who was already there to give me any, and my younger sister was too little. So, I've always felt, I'm on my own, I'll do it my way. The mistakes I make, I make them. I have yet to find the day when I need to look to somebody else to ask their advice. Having struggled through adolescence – those are turbulent times – you often find yourself in situations that you wish you hadn't put together. You have to get your legs out of there. If you put your feet inside boiling water, you jump out, right? What else do you do?

Of my extended family in Newcastle, there was my grandmother. She was lovely, very nice, very dogmatic, very practical

---

8 This statement, among many Yemi makes about her parents, challenges many popular ideas about why couples from so-called different races come together. In her narratives, Yemi attempts to show us just how much her parents share.

too. She was the matriarch, because my grandfather had died in his middle fifties. I think he died when he was 54. Then, there' s my aunt, my mother's younger sister. She's seven years younger than my mum. Then, there's my uncle who's thirteen years younger than my mum. We are close, because I spent one summer with my grandma, staying in my grandma's house, when I was a student. I think I was going from first to secondary. I stayed in the house. I had a bedroom. There were three bedrooms in the house. She took me everywere that she went. We went shopping, down to the village, went to go buy butter and cheese together. She took me down to her friends showing me off, "This is our Thea's daughter. Hasn't she got lovely long legs!" – the way only a grandmother can do. With Grandma, you do automatically believe everything she says.

I told her about my mother – not in great detail, because a lot of the details I had shoved to the back of my mind. It wasn't important. It was past. It wasn't significant. In no way did if affect me. Whereas, now I know it does affect you. It's not as if I'll be going and crying every day, but it affects me, for instance, in that I don't think suicide is a bad alternative to despair. Somehow or other, trying to do it and knowing as I know now that I would be dead if they had only had something else apart from aspirin or maybe more aspirin rather than just twenty. I didn't have trouble with trying to swallow all the things. I just looked at them and thought, "Are you enough?" But, there was nothing else, so if there had just been sleeping tablets or something like a painkiller, a muscle relaxant, rather than aspirin, then I would be dead. So, I'm not meant to take the easy way out. I have to wait. Also, you have time in order to fix things.

Those days they're not really discussed. But, I tell you what. I went home last summer and I'd been home for about three weeks and my sister tried to kill herself. My elder sister. She claimed she was tired. She took six Lagat pills. She claimed she was sick and tired, and she just thought, "I'll take these six Lagat pills. If anybody comes to look for me either today, tomorrow or the next day, the most anybody can ever tell is she's sleeping." When her husband noticed that she was walking funny, he questioned her first. Finally, she said she took some Lagat pills. "How many?" She said, "Three." He immediately went running to my dad and said, "She's taken three Lagat pills." My dad said, "Oh no!" and went there. He asked how many she took. She said, "Six." So then, they called all over the place. She was in hospital, and then she was undergoing psychiatric treatment for a little while. What she did was, not intentionally ask for help, but seek help through weird means, if you like.[9] If you feel you need help, isn't it easier to face what the problem is, and then seek help – rather than doing it in such a roundabout way? "I'm throwing myself into the well. Oh! Put one leg in. Oh! Now, I'm putting the other leg in, and now I'm throwing myself into the well. Oh!" So, they can come and ask you, "Okay, what's wrong?" Half the time, I won't even ask you. "Okay, throw yourself in, if you have to do it." How many times can you make such an extreme gesture of despair and needing help? You can't do it every day, can you? It would be difficult.

My grandfather on my father's side died in 1952 in March – the year I was born. I was born in April, he died in March. My grandmother on my father's side died when my father was 7. So, we've never known any of them. His eldest brother, Tunde, was like a father to him. My dad's 70, and the old boy is 86. So, he's sixteen years older. He is the one who sent my father to school – to secondary school, to primary school, sent him to that technical college where he got his first degree, looked after him, gave him all the advice he needed as a young man. He still has quite a lot of say in the family. I'm very close to him, I like him very much. You should meet him one day. Honestly, Jayne, he's marvelous. He has an innate calm serenity, which is mirrored in everything he says. The way you feel when you have been with him for a while – no matter what on earth was wrong with you, he can calm you down. He is in a position of complete and total leadership of the entire family. Anybody with a problem, no matter what it is, goes to Tunde, and he sorts it out. He gives the advice. He may not give advice *per se*, because during the course of the discussion, what he'll do is ask two or three questions. You, yourself will begin to see things from a different angle. Just asking you questions, so that you can change your perception of events. Frustration comes from tunnel vision. So that if you change perspective, you can usually see something different about the picture, and the frustration starts lessening immediately. He's very very nice to me. He always has been.

They say, those women in the family that like me, that I am my father's son. I am the one who will do things for my father. I am the one who is most like a son to dad. 'Cos we have two sisters, so he hasn't actually got any sons. My husband says one day these sons will appear and they will be big and strong and they'll say, "I'm

9 This is an ironic statement in light of Yemi's previous recollection of her own suicide attempt as a teenager.

your brother." My dad tends to refer – this is one of the things that used to drive my mother mad – decisions to my uncle. Our names? My uncle is the one who named us. He sent a telegram, "Oh, Thea's had a baby girl." My uncle sent the names back. She should be called such and such. It was only in Bisi's case, my mother was so fed up. There's no way that he should give her a name as well. So, Bisi is not just Bisi, but also Thea, which is my mum's name.[10]

My mother is back in England now, and my father is still in Nigeria. She moved back to England twelve years ago. She had terrific problems with depression and menopause. She was crying for months. She wasn't able to go to work any more. She felt like everything was closing in on her. She felt like she was dying – that she was dying in Africa and she didn't want to.[11] Every time she has a problem, she leans very heavily on me. She would cry, kneading my skin, or whatever. I took her to the doctor who put her on some tablets, that were supposed to help. He was trying to raise the estrogen level. Of course she hadn't had a period for nine months. She really hated that. So, I was helping her. Helping *her*, helping *her*! She left the country, and never felt as if she wanted to come back. She feels, she's done her stuff. She'll stay here now. My parents are still officially married. My father still has all my mother's clothes hanging in her wardrobe.[12] He has all of her bottles of perfume on the dressing table, all of her shoes still there, everything. Just dusty. As she left it.

I went with an English girl to the wholesale market to buy haberdashery, sewing machine things. They started speaking in Yoruba. There was a girl there, thin girl, very black, young girl, and she said to the others, "Let me show you how black I am. I'm going to stand next to these White women." They had lumped us. She and I were both White. "I'm going to stand next to these White women, and you'll see how black I am!"[13] She stood next to

10 This is in keeping with Bisi's position as "mother's pet."
11 This is a powerful admission and one that raises certain questions about the permanence of nationalism for Yemi's English mother. She is married to a Nigerian, she is living in Nigeria and has made earnest attempts to absorb the local cultures. However, now that she is aging, unlike her daughter Bisi, she can reaffirm where "home" really is for her. It is England.
12 I have a very vivid image in my mind of these remnants of a marriage that Yemi's father has preserved like a frozen memory.
13 This anecdote is interesting on two accounts. First, it exemplifies the situationally constructed concept of race. Second, it reinforces the notion of skin color as a relative concept. For example, among my friends in the Nigerian Diaspora, I have noticed an unhealthy residual colonial obsession with skin color. The internalized hatred of dark pigmentation is further augmented by their cultures of location in Europe and North America. However, what is seemingly baffling is that the individual who is being

us and compared her skin and said, "You see now?" It was unbelievable.

I had a Black American friend in college, who was quite dark. He was really, really dark. He was not black very black. He was quite dark and he looked a bit like a Yoruba boy. His name was Anthony and he had a friend, William. William looked like a half-caste, he was tall, had an afro and was yellowish. He was really tall and slender, like a basketball player.[14] Anthony was short and squat and muscular like *abekiti* man. Like a farmer's muscles on his legs. They call it *ishu* – yams. He and William would go to the market. They'd be asking "How much is this? How much is that?" and asking questions – like tourists or Americans would do in a market situation in Africa. "Mama, how much is this one?" The market women would be abusing Anthony. "You stupid boy, because you are with this Negro – they called Black Americans Negroes then – "You are pretending you don't speak your language any more. You useless boy! Speak to us in Yoruba." Anthony would almost be in tears, "Mama, I'm from America." "You see, you useless boy!"

Whereas, William was okay, because William obviously was not a typical Yoruba boy. But, poor Anthony. We're talking about the early seventies. This great balloon of Black consciousness.[15] So, they would wear tie-dyed shirts or something like that to the market instead of American clothes and have maybe leather bags – you know, proper African – sort of thing. There's Anthony trying really hard to look like an African, but unfortunately the women think that he is one![16] So, is he happy or not? He wasn't very happy. He

dismissed as too "dark" is frequently the same shade of brown as the individual hurling the insult.

14 Albeit stereotypical, an interesting cultural referent and most definitely emblematic of Yemi's African Diaspora(s) consciousness.

15 Like Yemi, almost all of the *griot(tes)* seemed to have some awareness of the Black Power Movement in the United States and its global impact on people of color in general and Black people in particular. What I find fascinating is the different ways in which the *griottes* featured in this book contextualize and articulate their first encounters with Black consciousness. Whether it is Sarah's remembering seeing her first afros or through her cultural surrogates becoming involved with politics, or Akousa linking her own burgeoning politics to her struggle as a "light skinned Black person" to find a place in a movement which at times seemed to exclude her, or Similola's and Ruby's attempt to understand and embrace Blackness in social and cultural contexts devoid of sites for the affirmation of Additive Blackness or Bisi, who begins to understand Black consciousness through confronting racism within her family and her immediate surroundings.

16 Whether we locate ourselves in Nigeria, England or the United States as examples, the ongoing existential crisis of belonging persists. Who is African? If one no longer resides on the African continent, can one still claim to be a "true African," if such an entity

never really used to enjoy being told – they used to really tell him off – because teenagers can have an identity crisis and want to be somebody else. So, it's possible. He could have been, but he wasn't. He wasn't a Yoruba boy at all.

I have never wanted to be other than who I was. I find that because I like to look at people, I've found that it wasn't very easy for me to wish to be White definitely not especially in a Black society where within a peer group things would happen at school and they'd think that you're not going to understand or that you know nothing about it anyway. There are certain undercurrents, for instance, the belief that everybody has in *juju* or black magic. Obviously we knew nothing about it. Not that we had a little knowledge, none. If it was about something to do with *juju*, we would automatically be excluded. Once you realize you don't know anything about what they're saying. You don't know anything about the words they use to describe what's going on. You don't know the names that everybody knows. It's like talking about tampons to a collection of rubgy-playing Eskimo bachelors. They don't know what you're saying when you say, Lilacs or Tampax. They say, "Hmm, interesting." Frames of reference would just be completely different. We would hear things like fables, and everybody else is taking them very seriously. As far as we are concerned, isn't that just a fable? We couldn't actually get into it. You can't contextualize it, and you can't see it from the other person's point of view. You don't really know what they're saying. You don't understand that they're telling you a warning. You don't understand anything. You think they're just chatting to you. We were not Black enough.

The only thing I wished for was my bust to be smaller. That was all I ever worried about. If I could just have a smaller bust, I'd be fine. But that never happened so I guess it's not going to. That was my terrible thing as a teenager. I was like everybody else. My breasts started to grow at 11. They just didn't stop. Everybody else's breasts stopped growing at eleven and a half. Mine went on growing. When I was 13, I was 38 inches in D cup. I didn't know anybody with a bust this big that was a grown-up. It was terrible. It was really, really terrible. My mother didn't understand. She would say things like, "When you get older it will settle down." Settle down to what? My mother wasn't large-breasted – not as big as I was. She's a fatter person, and I was thin with this bust. Just a

exists. This former question is the cause of a great deal of angst among both the more recent as well as the older constituents of the African Diaspora(s).

bust and some glasses. You'd see me coming. You'd see the boobs – the glasses on top. Finish! That's me!

The only good thing was that the hips were wide. So that 38 was 38 also in hips. All the things you can't imagine that I couldn't wear. You can't go without a bra on. The funny little skimpy tops with just a little strap that every teenager had on, I couldn't wear them 'cos I'd have this massive bra strap. The fact that Kemi had a large bust didn't really help because her's wasn't as big as mine. She was 36, which was still human. I was 38. This could have been the reason why I got a lot of unwelcome attention. At least my friends, my really really catty friends at university used to say to me, "It's the boobs!" There was a wealthy man who owned a pharmaceutical company. He was also married to a Swiss girl, who he was going through a divorce with. He decided to fixate on me. He met me once and decided that he wanted me to be his girlfriend. He used to come for me and take me out to dinner, trying to chat me up. He was quite accommodating when I said "No, I don't want to go to bed with you." One of my friends drew a cartoon of the attraction – in this case is the fact that his eyes were just level with my tits. "That's all he sees Yemi. That's all he sees."[17]

17 Yemi's expressed discomfort with the size of her breasts serves as a powerful critique of one-dimensional approaches to the very complex sociocultural phenomenon of identities politics. In so many words, she is saying: "Being *métisse* is not an issue for me, I can manage the situations I find myself in." Now, having large breasts is a different matter altogether. However, interestingly enough, the popular assumption is that being *métis(se)* is a tragic condition, which requires sympathy and pathologization. Very few social science studies have actually attempted to normalize and contextualize the everyday complex lived realities of *métis(se)* individuals and their nuclear and extended families.

10

LET BLACKNESS AND WHITENESS WASH THROUGH

Competing discourses on bi-racialization and the compulsion of genealogical erasures

I searched but could not find myself, not on the screen, billboards, books, magazines, and first and last not in the mirror…I longed for an image, a story, to speak me, describe me, birth me whole. Living in my skin, I was, but which one?

(Evaristo 1997: 69)

white and black represent the two poles of a world, two poles in perpetual conflict; a genuinely Manichean concept of the world; the world has been spoken, it must be remembered – white or black, that is the question.

(Fanon 1967: 44–5)

If you don't honor your ancestors in the real sense then you are committing a kind of suicide.

(Sam Shephard "Interview," *Bookmark*, BBC2, London September 1997)

In the first part of this text, in their own voices and from their own emblematic experiences, six *métis(se) griottes* speak against the generalizing and subjugating tendencies of discourses on Blackness and Whiteness which contain, exclude and silence them. In this chapter, to substantiate their critiques of essential Blackness and normative/naturalized Whiteness, I have culled extracts by under-represented *métis(se)* authors from disparate literary and social science sources and varied geopolitical and historical contexts. Collectively, these *métis(se)* discourses stage debates which do not resolve but rather elucidate both the discursive and political problematics of Blackness and Whiteness. Their evocations function as agents of change, shaping and molding critiques of particular bi-racialized societies and demanding a revision of a double caste system, which binds all Black people both economically and socially.

White (English) mothering, Black daughters?

The relationship between mother and daughter stands at the center
of what I fear most in our culture. Heal that wound and we change
the world.

(Levins Morales 1981: 56)

In the first part of the book, aspects of six women's testimonies remind us of
painful psychosocial consequences for *métisse* women, whose lived realities
defy the false one drop rule. That is, at different life stages and across age,
class, ethnicity and locality, at times, the six *métisse* women subject themselves to self-destructive regimens of physical and emotional torture in an
attempt to position themselves in a racially polarized society, which denies
them full womanhood – whether it is performing "Black" and "White"
subjectivities through oppositional dress as Similola did, or attempting
suicide as Yemi did – all the narratives speak to a desire for "racial" reconciliation and an integrated sense of self, which can embrace both maternal and
paternal sociocultural inheritances.[1]

In the following two sections, I intend to shed light on paradoxes of identity and affiliation for *métisse* women, whose White British or White
European mothers or mother-surrogates have been central socializing influences.[2] "Racial" regulation, in the form of the one drop rule, collapses ideas
about "race" and culture in general and disallows White British or European
maternal and cultural influences in particular. As they mention, the six
featured *métisse griottes* all have White English, German or Irish mothers.
Akousa and Sarah, and Bisi and Yemi were raised by their White Irish and
White English birth mothers, respectively. Ruby and Similola, were raised
by White English women, who were the matrons in the children's homes
where they spent their formative years. However, based on locality, family
circumstances, social class and ethnicity, the two sets of sisters and the two
women who grew up in care all deploy different strategies to make sense of
the process of becoming (Black) women.

Feminist analyses are replete with, at times, ambivalent recognition of
the primacy of the mothering role in the social rather than biological
reproduction of gendered identities (Chodorow 1978; Rich 1977; Nakano
Glenn *et al.* 1994; Collins 1994). However, to appropriate Rich (1977),
the "great unwritten story" is that which critically acknowledges the fact
that, at times, young *métisse* girls first witness the complex world of
womanhood through everyday interactions with White female caretakers.
Through the psychosocial processes of White English mothering, the
primary culture the women I spoke with inherit is White English.
Societal assumptions based exclusively on their physical appearances
frequently deny this reality. Furthermore, society tells them that they

must deny this socializing fact and remember that they are "just Black." As Yemi remembers:

> We were at home with our mother and our father. Although my mother worked, she was the primary influence in our house – culturally. We didn't really know very much about Yoruba culture. We just didn't.

Similarly, Similola recounts:

> When I was growing up the main influence was the {White English} house mother in the children's home, who totally dominated my life up until I was 16 years old. Her views were my views.

As Bisi recalls, despite their best intentions, sometimes White mothers do not completely understand the extent to which their own White privilege separates them from the "everyday racism" (Essed 1991) which their Black daughters face:

> A lot of the modern consciousness I have of being African and being Black, which is not the same thing, is probably in spite of my mother. Being Black in the sense that I feel now, that would be in spite of her. It's not something she agrees with....She has very little knowledge of how racism operates and how it affects people.

Furthermore, as Ruby describes, White grandmothers of Black granddaughters grapple even further with their own White daughters' "transracial" transgressions, which "contaminate" allegedly "pure blood lines":

> That period of time with my gran brought out very much to the fore what her attitude to me was and why it was like that. It was 80 percent because of the color of my skin; the other 20 percent was the fact that

I was an illegitimate child. For my grandmother and her generation, that was quite a shameful thing. But had I been a White illegitimate child, it would have been very different. So as I say, 80 percent because of the color – she didn't want to be associated in the blood line with a Black grand-daughter.

One could argue that from the cradle, *métisse* women who have been mothered by White women are potentially equipped with the social tools for understanding White feminists and building coalitions across the Black/White feminist divide. Yet, amid all the feminist academic attention paid to mothering and mother/daughter relationships, very little if any textual space attends to this strategic political possibility. Both Black and White feminists have also neglected the specific problematic of the bi-racialization of White mother/Black (*métisse*) daughter dyads. Perhaps, like many theoretical innovations, this critical issue must begin its life on the pages of (auto)biographies or in the creative arts before continuing its journey with textual treatment by critical/social/cultural/feminist theorists. For example, in the following excerpt from the 1990 autobiographical film piece *The Body Beautiful*, English–Nigerian film-maker, Ngozi Onwurah, declares her allegiance to her White English mother. In this scene, she and her mother are lying naked in bed together, pink and brown skins mingle, youthful and aging bodies lie side by side:

A child is made in its parents' image. But to a world that sees only in Black and White, I was made only in the image of my father. Yet, she has molded me, created the curves and contours of my life, colored the innermost details of my being. She has fought for me, protected me with every painful crooked bone in her body. She lives inside of me and cannot be separated. I may not be reflected in her image, but my mother is mirrored in my soul. I am my mother's daughter for the rest of my life.

At the same time, this impress of maternal circumstance can be misperceived as a weakness by those espousing a Black separatist feminist standpoint:

My apparent collusion with white women was significant because I am mixed and because ill-founded alliance with white people is part of the historical guilt of a people mixed with the white race. Although all people have been betrayed by their own, because of the history of colonialism, any perception of betrayal is particularly profound for people mixed with white.

(Paulse 1994: 46)

Nevertheless, unfortunately, in the long run, any solidarity which *métisse* filial loyalty may cultivate is usually over-ruled by the bi-racialized trappings of the White feminist privilege which the one drop rule perpetuates:

> They (White women) can assure themselves that they are good "feminists" helping out the cause against colonialism....Later this year, I discovered that the redhead who held us at the door is pregnant with a mixed child. I thought about her disregard and disrespect toward black women and wondered how she would eventually treat her child if she were female.
>
> (S. R. W. 1994: 255–6)

Overall, this psychosocial splitting breeds *métisse* confusion and motivates women to seek compulsory Black legitimacy when in an ideal de-racialized world, the more sensible existential project should be that of psychic and social unity:

> I was pleased that I had been a target of racism. The REAL kind, the blatant kind, the kind that regular people mean when they say "racism." I was pleased because this was proof that I really was a woman of color, no matter what anyone said. I had my credentials. I had my badge. I counted.
>
> (Kinsley 1994: 121)

When we look into each other's eyes, our war torn souls communicate in their silences.

"Other-mothers," Black cultural surrogate sisters, and male/African daughters

> My mother raised me, she loved me, but upon reaching adulthood, I've never realized that there was something very important my mother could never give me – a culture which matched my color. If women are the bestowers and the keepers of culture, the ones who pass on language, nuance, myth, food, spiritual teachings and values to children, then I have been culturally malnourished.
>
> (Hernandez-Ramdwar 1994: 3)

For the most part, all six women had other Black continental African, African Caribbean or African American safety nets into which they could fall when identifying exclusively with White English maternal culture either led to "malnourishment" or in Yemi's case resulted in a suicide attempt. For example, Akousa and Sarah fondly recollect the pivotal role played by "fictive kin" in the form of Black "other-mothers." Fictive kin are not related to individuals by "blood, " however. They perform the same functions as these family relations (Stack 1976; Stack and Burton 1994). For example, Sarah remembers:

All the people that I call auntie and uncle aren't really relatives – blood relatives. Like a group of people that have become relatives, they are from all parts of the world, and, well – mainly from the Caribbean. Auntie Hyacinth was from Guyana....I do remember how much I loved my Aunt Hyacinth plaiting my hair. I used to sit down on the floor between her knees feeling secure. She always smelled wonderful, like cocoa butter and musk.

Similarly, Akousa pays homage to the dual role her mum and this same Aunt Hyacinth played in her successful passage from girl to woman:

Also I didn't have a White extended family in the same way that a lot of other people did....My extended family was a Black extended family rather than havin' this other White family....My mum was the only White person within the famly. She took on board a lot of Caribbean culture....Basically there was a Caribbean upbringin' in some respects – not totally. Because at the end of the day, my mum is not a West Indian woman. So there were certain aspects to Caribbean culture that I didn't start on, because she didn't have that. My Aunt Hyacinth provided certain aspects of that instead. I had two that were there growin' up.

Akousa and Sarah point to two Black women, one African American and the other from Sierra Leone who acted as Black cultural surrogate sisters. In so doing, these two older women nurtured their younger surrogate sisters' emerging Black feminist consciousness. Akousa recalls:

I did some voluntary work at Baobab Community Center and met a Black American woman from Chicago and another woman from Sierra Leone. They were workin' at this community center. Pamela was a very strong Black woman. The two of them gave me and my sister quite a lot....They helped move me in the right direction. I started buyin' a lot more Black literature, readin' a lot more widely. They got us out to theater. I think that's where my love of culture and art now comes from. I think they started to give us a good appreciation of it.

At the age of 13, a falling out with her mother led Yemi closer to her father's Yoruba Nigerian culture and turned her into what Amadiume (1987) would refer to as a "male daughter:"

The result of this was that she had very little to do with me after that. My dad took me every evening, when he came back, to my uncle's house....When he was going out, he didn't actually leave me with her ever again....My dad and I became very close, which was very good....Also, because of this change with my father, I got very close to my cousins. So, I am closer to my cousins than my other sisters, very, very close. They are all boys. So, I now get to know how to speak Yoruba – Yoruba morals, the life itself – better than my sisters. Ostensibly, because I was actually flung out by my mother, or I stepped away from my mother. Then, all of these things were accessible to me.

Ruby and Similola became African daughters when they travelled to Nigeria and Tanzania, respectively, to meet their African fathers and extended African families. In fact, Ruby describes her connection with her African relations as a source of strength and pride:

After we had been to Nigeria, and lived there for a year or more, and come back, I got a great deal out of that, I did then begin to feel that I wasn't just Black in an isolated situation. There was this whole family that I had who were Black, and who supported me, and whom I could go to at anytime. If life got really heavy, I can jump on a plane and go to Nigeria and I'd have a home and a family. That made me feel a lot less lonely and get to a situation where I could begin to feel some pride about being Black.

Renaming and reclaiming

This is the way the American [and British] system works: if you have one parent or ancestor with African origins, you are black. You are not a member of the white family that might also claim you. That family must renounce you, and you must renounce it. You are in the black family, as will be all of your children and your grand-children and your great-grandchildren. It is by thus redefining "family" to exclude their black family members that white Americans [and White British] keep themselves and their "family" white. The notion of "family" in White America [and White Britain] has very controlled borders: "family" stops where "black" begins.

(Scales-Trent 1995: 62–3)

Black is the totalizing term that names us and which we claim as an act of political resistance (Brah 1996). Heidi Mirza, editor of the new anthology, *Black British Feminism*, defines Blackness in Britain by the fact of common bi-racialized locality so that "being 'Black' in Britain is about a state of 'becoming' (racialized); a process of consciousness, when color becomes the defining factor…is to share a common structural location; a racial location" (Mirza 1997: 3). However, the facts of designated ethnic minority status and shared bi-racialized locality do not create consensus as to the anthropological and sociopolitical criteria, which determine the classification of *Black*. In fact, the term Black has become an essentialized political term lacking both dynamism and fluidity and frequently confused with ethnicity and nation-ality (Modood 1988; Modood *et al.* 1997).

The Official Census classification system clearly embodies this rigid fixity of terminology (Owen 1998; Aspinall 1997). The first time the British government Census attempted to calculate the number of *non-White* people in Britain was 1991. Out of a total British population of 54.9 million people, just over 3 million or 5.5 percent are designated as ethnic minori-ties. The major "ethnic" subheadings of the 1991 Census are White, Black-Caribbean, Black-African, Black-Other (please describe) Indian, Pakistani, Bangladeshi, Chinese, and Any Other Ethnic Group (please describe). This classification system is flawed in its conflation of race, ethnicity and nationality, discriminatory in its homogenization of peoples from continental Africa and the Caribbean, and problematic in its presumption that White is the normative homogeneous category (Aspinall 1995; Owen 1998). However, in response to focus groups and critical research, preparation for the 2001 Census involves the consideration of new classifications such as a disaggregated "White" category, "Black British, " "British Asian," and "mixed ethnic origin," and a category for religion (Dixie 1997; Aspinall 1998, personal communication).

At the moment, this official categorization scheme is most problematic when accounting for the ethnic origins of *métis(se)* people with multiple ethnic affiliations (Phoenix and Owen 1996). For *métis(se)* individuals, self-description is highly subjective and variable. For example, Aspinall's health survey research findings indicate that:

> about half the respondents answering in the free text fields used collective terms like "mixed" and "mixed race;" the others wrote in a more detailed description, giving two or more races/ethnic groups or sometimes descriptions like "half"...or "quarter" (i.e. declaring only part of their mix/).
>
> (Aspinall 1998: 1)

The terms used by others, including official agencies such as the census, the state, health practitioners and social workers, academics and the media are also many and varied (Aspinall 1998).

In general, there are at least two significant and interlocking factors at work. First, the prevailing and inconsisent social and political stance that anyone who does not look phenotypically White is classified as Black impinges on identity construction for many multiethnic *metis(se)* people, particularly those who have been raised by a White British or European mother or mother-surrogate (Ifekwunigwe 1997). Second, in specific temporal, spatial, and sociocultural contexts, the complex processes of self-identification for this group may or may not coincide with the aforementioned classifications. *Métis(se)* people often negotiate several different identities depending on "where they are" both physically and psychologically and with whom they are interacting (Phoenix and Tizard 1993). Anne Wilson's (1987) study of mixed race children, Phoenix's and Tizard's (1993) work with mixed parentage adolescents and my ongoing research with adults all coincide with Okamura's (1981) notion of an ethnic identification, which is by nature operationally situational. In other words, on the night of the Census, for simplicity's sake, an individual may have reported themselves as Black-Caribbean when in fact they have one White English parent. In another context, that same individual could just as adamantly identify or be identified as *metis(se)* or, at times even, White. Once again, Aspinall's findings support this situational identification: "In the 1991 Census, most people of mixed race/ethnicity eschewed the predesignated categories and utilized the two free text fields to describe their mixed origins. 230, 000 persons used the free-text fields in this way" (Aspinall 1998, personal communication).

Since I completed my initial research in 1992, the Policy Studies Institute has published some interesting statistics regarding demographic changes in the ethnic and racial composition of British families. Among their findings were that "as many as half British born Caribbean men and a third of women, had chosen a white partner...for two out of five children (39 percent) with a Caribbean mother or father, their other parent was white" (Modood *et al*. 1997: 27). These seemingly striking results motivated *Guardian* journalist Gary Younge (May 22 1997) to report: "Beige Britain...a new race is growing up. It's not black and it's not white and it's not yet officially recognized. Welcome to the new mixed-race future." I would argue that there is nothing "new" nor particularly hopeful about these statistical revelations. First, the same study reveals that only about 1 percent of the indigenous White British population had a partner who is not White (Modood *et al*. 1997) With the rigid enforcement of British rules of bi-racialization, even if they reside with only their White parent, usually their mother, these "beige" children are socially absorbed by Black not White communities (Zack 1993; Small 1994). In addition, a disproportionate number of "beige" children end up in care. Barrister and social worker Margaret Boushel reminds us that although:

> most will grow up happily, valuing their identity as black or mixed-parentage people and the opportunities it affords to understand diverse cultures, there are some mixed-parentage children whose experiences give cause for concern. These are the very young children who are two and a half times more likely than others to spend part of their childhood in local authority care.
>
> (Boushel 1996: 2)

Third, contemporary African Caribbean communities are perpetuating a historical tradition of racial and ethnic intermingling, which began centuries ago during their enslavement in the Caribbean and Britain (Gerzina 1995; Ramdin 1987; Fryer 1984). These current statistics obscure this important historical custom of so-called inter-racial mixing (Banton 1967; Young 1995; Hall 1992). What is also significant is that the Policy Study Institute study completely ignores continental African communities in Britain, wherein there is also a longstanding legacy of intermarriage and interethnic mating (Killingray 1994). Finally, as Policy Study Institute analysts admit: "a problem for all currently used methods of classifying ethnic groups, including our own, is that they do not deal adequately with people of mixed parentage" (Modood *et al*. 1997: 14). Hence, as I mentioned earlier, individuals may have self-identified as Black continental African or

Black African Caribbean, when in fact they also have a parent who is White British or South Asian, for examples.

To remedy the Census classificatory confusion that manifests itself both in the United Kingdom and the United States, there have been lively political and academic debates over whether to introduce separate "mixed ethnic" and "multiracial" categories, respectively. In the United Kingdom, most of the discussions have been amongst academics, politicians and other government officials (Phoenix and Owen 1996; Aspinall 1997; Jones 1994; Root 1992). However, in the United States, a full-fledged nationwide new social movement has erupted with attorney and political activist Carlos Fernandez as its most vocal spokesperson:

> the failure to accommodate what are regarded as interracial relations and people in the United States is at the heart of an unresolved American identity crisis, a dilemma that perpetuates ethnic and racial disunion and makes the resolution of the general race problem virtually impossible. The failure to recognize that some people transcend traditional communal boundaries based on race or ethnicity is equivalent to enshrining those very same boundaries and thereby preventing even the concept, let alone the reality of national unity.
>
> (Fernandez 1996: 28)

My position is that an intermediate "multiracial" or a "mixed ethnic category" perpetuates false ideologies of "racial" purity and "racial" pollution within social contexts such as the United States wherein most African Americans already have at least partial White American or Native American ancestry (Haizlip 1994; Katz 1986, 1993). On a more immediate note, one needs to address the political ramifications of either a "multiracial" or "mixed ethnic" category for the political power base of Black communities in the United States and the United Kingdom, respectively. That is, we would be creating an official tripartite system reminiscent of South Africa, wherein this intermediate racial group is simply a powerless albeit more privileged buffer community (Kuper 1974; Head 1990; Head 1974). However, the most convincing argument comes from Lisa Jones whose African American testament is as relevant to those of us in the English–African Diaspora:

> To say that biracials have been cold-shouldered by African-Americans throughout history, as some activists have suggested is selective ignorance. Black communities have always been shelter to multiethnic people, perhaps not an unproblematic shelter, yet a shelter nonetheless. Black folks, I'd venture, have welcomed difference in their communities more than most Americans.
>
> (Jones 1994: 60)

These transatlantic separate census categories debates provide a useful platform for political critiques of Blackness and Whiteness and their paradoxical legislation and regulation via identities politics. In other words, the different ways in which *métis(se)* individuals self-identify or are categorized create contradictory meanings of "race," gender, generation and family.

By invoking the "zebra" as a metaphor for the paradoxical nature of *bi-racialized métis(se)* existences, I intend to destabilize conventional "racial" thinking, which is trapped in the constrictors of a one drop rule compulsory Black mandate. At the same time, I hasten to add that this "mixed metaphor" is not devoid of problematic nineteenth-century zoological/science fiction connotations of "racial breeding" (Zack 1993; Griffin 1913; Tegetmeier and Sutherland 1895; Ewart 1900). Akousa's indirect critique of bi-racialization also finds fault with the "zebra" metaphor:

I don't consider myself half of anyting. I cannot be half. When people call me that I say, "Do you see Black on one side and White on the other?" If they call me "Colored", I say, "You see me stripes? Like I've been colored in or somethin'."

Nevertheless, wanting to test the limits of the personal, the political and the categorical as they pertain to Black and White identifications, during lectures and other educational engagements, I often ask unwitting audiences my "zebra" question: "Is a 'zebra' black with white stripes, white with black stripes or...?" Respondents frequently think this is my subversive way of discerning their "racial" politics, when in fact I am more interested in the extent to which individuals can envisage zebras as being *both* black with white stripes and white with black stripes. Most of the responses are variations of the question. However, astute University of California, Berkeley sociologist Troy Duster replied, "essentially striped." This answer turns conventional bi-polarized notions of Blackness and Whiteness on their heads. He said "striped" as opposed to "Black and White," indicating the colors are dissolved and just the pattern remains. However, because of public ideologies which dichotomize and hierarchically rank socially constructed notions of Blackness and Whiteness, *métis(se)* people learn to live with Black and White factions at war within themselves. Some days they are Black with White stripes, other days the stripes are Black and they are White. Some days they would like to be either Grey or perhaps neither. Similola recalls the emotional turmoil she felt once she recognized the power of these seemingly fixed bi-racialized designations:

So many things have happened to me because of what I am, and they
shape the way I am today. I had a very unhappy childhood because of
it. I had suddenly felt my world had fallen apart. I was Black and I was
brought up in a White society.

The transgenerational psychic damage of global and historical processes of
bi-racialization is meted out equally to all socially designated Black
constituents of the African Diaspora(s) as well as to those living on the
African continent and results in skin bleaching, cosmetic surgery and other
remedies to alter Black African physical features so that they more approximate to a White European appearance (Mama 1995; Weekes 1997; Jones
1994; Chapkis 1986). Not surprisingly, almost always *métis(se)* individuals
with immediate both Black continental African, African Caribbean or
African American *and* White continental European, British or North
American parentage join other constituents of the African Diaspora(s) in
paying far too much covert and overt lip service to what Russell *et al.* refer
to as "the color complex: a psychological fixation about color and features
that leads Blacks to discriminate against each other" (Russell *et al.* 1992: 2).
Others refer to this preoccupation with skin color and the privileging of
"paler" skin as shadeism or colorism (Mama 1995). Frequently, these
unhealthy externalized obsessions with skin color and other facial features
extend to White family members of *métis(se)* individuals:

> It is terrible to say this, because I am talking about my own chil-
> dren and I love them, but because I am white, if I'm on my own, I
> can walk anywhere, I feel free, nobody bothers. But when I have my
> children with me, I am a prisoner to how people feel about me and
> the children. Once I was walking through the market and I
> remember thinking "Thank God it is Terry – who is light-skinned
> – who is with me and not the other two, who look quite dark."
> (Alibhai-Brown and Montague 1992: 222)

In households with *métis(se)* children, public racial politics govern private
family realities. *Métis(se)* siblings with the same biological parents but with
different physical appearances will be spared or subjected to the psychological injuries of a social hierarchy that privileges individuals with paler skin,
straighter hair and more "White European" facial features.

In general, in the English–African Diaspora, all psyches have been
wounded by individual and collective experiences of racism and other forms
of discrimination.[3] In particular, for Black/White couples and their *métis(se)*

children, the one drop rule disrupts conventional notions of kinship and stigmatizes the ordinary institution of the family (Alibhai-Brown and Montague 1992; Benson 1980). Yet, by virtue of genealogy and domestic circumstances, most *métis(se)* individuals, including the women featured in this text, can actually become whole at the precise meeting point of the same White British or White European *and* Black continental African or Black African Caribbean social borders, which the one drop rule fights fiercely to protect:

> It is not simply the relationship of oppressed to oppressor, of master to slave, nor is it motivated merely by hatred; it is also, literally and morally, a *blood* relationship, perhaps the most profound reality of the American [and by extension the British] experience, and we cannot begin to unlock it until we accept how very much it contains the force and anguish and terror of love.
>
> (Baldwin 1955: 42, my emphasis)

In other words, as *métis(se)* children many have been nurtured, supported, by White British or White European carers. As adults in close quarters, many recreate family with White British or White European partners.[4] Within both private spaces and in the public domain, the particular challenge for multigenerational *métis(se)* families remains recognizing and negotiating the invidious signs of bi-racialization while not falling prey to the demands of genealogical erasure. That is, it is possible to equip *métis(se)* children with the psychosocial tools to recognize and cope with prejudice and discrimination without forcing them to deny their natal origins. In the long term, both the specificities and complexities of *métis(se)* subject positions demand a re-fashioning of the constricted and bi-racialized criteria for both citizenship and belonging in the English–African Diaspora. In the short term, I suggest "Additive Blackness" as a survival strategy for *métis(se)* individuals who are unwilling or unable to sever ties with their White British or White European origins.[5]

From "compulsory heterosexuality" to compulsory Blackness to Additive Blackness as a *métis(se)* survival strategy

In a classic essay entitled "Compulsory heterosexuality and lesbian existence," American feminist Adrienne Rich dares to challenge what she refers to as "the erasure of lesbian existence from so much of scholarly feminist literature" (Rich 1986: 24). The critical theoretical framework within which she worked is that of the "political institution" of "compulsory heterosexuality, " where "heterosexuality is presumed 'the sexual preference' of 'most women' either implicitly or explicitly" (ibid.: 28). In 1980, she suggested that heterosexual and lesbian researchers bring the same critical insights gleaned from studies of motherhood to feminist studies of heterosexuality. Although groundbreaking at the time, Rich's critique homogenized the different "race," class and ethnic experiences of women in general and lesbians in particular. Interestingly enough, a year before this essay was published, in dialogue with Audre Lorde, Lorde asserts:

> There are different choices facing Black and White women in life, certain specifically different pitfalls surrounding us because of our experiences, our color. Not only are some of the problems that face us dissimilar, but some of the entrapments and the weapons used to neutralize us are not the same.
>
> (Lorde 1996: 151)

Nevertheless, this criticism does not detract from the potential potency of Rich's concept of compulsion as an analytical tool for understanding the politics of Blackness. Hence, to extrapolate, compulsory Blackness is a political institution wherein it is presumed that identification with Blackness is the implicit or explicit personal preference of most *métis(se)* women or men with one Black continental African or Black African Caribbean parent and one White British or White continental European parent. However, with just one exception, in my research project, the parental combination was exclusively, Black father and White mother.

More specifically, in the previous section, I discussed the lack of consensus in the English–African Diaspora as to "Who is Black?" and the concomitant problematic official census minority "ethnic" classification scheme. At the center are minority intraethnic disagreements over what constitutes Blackness as well as who can legitimately claim an authentic Black identity. Canaan adds:

> The enemy is brownness and whiteness, maleness and femaleness. The enemy is our urgent need to stereotype and close off people, places, and events into isolated categories. Hatred, distrust, irresponsibility, unloving, classism, sexism, and racism, in their myriad forms, cloud our vision and isolate us.
>
> (Canaan 1981: 236)

Since genotype has little bearing in a society that discriminates based on phenotype, the differential push by Black and White people to encourage *métis(se)* people to identify as Black is supposed to provide what *griotte* Bisi refers to as "protective coloration." In other words, "color is only the symbol of imagined difference" (Maja-Pearce 1990: 60). With the criteria for Black membership as limited as they are, society at large generally "sees" *métis(se)* people as "just Black."

On the other hand, what one's family and life experiences have been as well as the cultural constitution of one's household account for very little in a bi-racially confused world:

> The color of my skin shows that the line was crossed. Someone fucked someone who should not have been fucked. When people ask what is my mixture, they are trying to find out who those persons were. My origins do not haunt me. Attitudes about my origins do.
>
> (Paulse 1994: 4)

As a *métis(se)* person, aligning oneself with Blackness is supposed to provide a cushion against the inevitable blows of bi-racialization. In the long run, I maintain that embracing an exclusive Black identity – as a political strategy – is counterproductive. In the name of elusive solidarity, this monolithic Black identity masks the many differences that exist across cultures, nations, ethnicities, classes, religions, gender, regions, and generations. However, what this recommendation ignores is the indelible impress of individual circumstance, which makes the process of identifying with Blackness, Black people and Black culture painful, mystifying, and gradual for many *métis* men and *métisse* women. Black children who have grown up in care or in predominantly White suburbs also struggle with these issues (Boushel 1996; Gaber and Aldridge 1994).

For *métis(se)* individuals, many of whom have grown up in primarily White English environments, this form of "Black-washing" also threatens to erode a substantial part of their psychosocial foundation, which at the contested time is often exclusively socially and culturally White and *métis(se)*. I refer to this moment of identification as "The Day of Reckoning" or "When the Mirror Speaks." In this chapter, mirrors are a useful motif, since *métis(se)* individuals' images of themselves are frequently distorted by the bi-racializing, objectifying and exoticizing gazes of a zebra-driven society.

In part, affirmation of one's Blackness necessitates the reification of nineteenth-century bi-racialized hierarchies based on skin color, hair texture, and eye color (Mama 1995; Weekes 1997). From Nigeria to Brazil, from New York to Bristol, barometers of Blackness – hair texture, skin tone, width of nose, fullness of lips, rise of buttocks – travel. Carol Camper, Canadian editor of *Miscegenation Blues: Voices of Mixed Race Women*, recalls:

> In my attempts to understand race and mixing I began to search for faces like mine in my immediate world. I had no idea how dangerous that could be. In grade eight my discussions with a apparently – White Gayle about what her full lips and broad nose could mean, led to her grandmother's instruction to slap my face the next time I dared to say such a thing. I had ventured into forbidden territory....I had

learned that we could not meet at the place of our Blackness, but only at a place where her race could not be spoken.

(Camper 1994: xvii)

To paraphrase *griotte* Sharon, one of the members of the original group of twenty-five project participants – we can try to deprive ourselves of our realities but in the darkest hour of the night when no one else is around and we have gone to the loo to spend a penny, we must look in the mirror. Eventually, that moment comes when we look in the mirror and we see what a bi-racialized society tells us we must see – a Black woman:

As a girl and woman with little self confidence, the external gaze, intrusive as it was, perhaps offered the solace of definition: I am seen, therefore I exist. Without that gaze would I still know who I am?

(Majaj 1994: 60)

For many this closer scrutiny is sparked by someone pointing out to them or reminding them of either their physical sameness or difference – that is, their Blackness. *Griotte* Claudia, another *métisse* voice from the original group, recounted an incident to me. She was in a club in Liverpool with a group of her White English friends and a Black man kept shouting out, "Hey, Black Sister." At age 27, she went home that night looked in the mirror and cried.

Psychologists refer to this as "negriscence" – coming to terms with one's Blackness, or becoming Black (Mama 1995). Though their model is a cumulative one, its typology of Black traits seems to suggest that there is both an essential Blackness and an illusory Whiteness, which *métis(se)* people can strive to embody, but they can never completely attain. This paradigm also does not stress the qualitative importance of the starting point of the journey. Once a *métis(se)* person recognizes the ways in which the one drop rule designates them as "just Black" in society, I refer to the process of coming to terms with one's Blackness as both affirmative and as a source for social discrimination as "Additive Blackness." That is, an individual must start with her or his familiar social foundation and build forward without having to sever ties with her or his often White English roots. Bisi's notion of a "synthesized" Black culture corresponds with my formulation of "Additive Blackness":

coming to terms with a Black identity in Bristol. You have a lot of things within you to cope with. One of the things you have as a coping mechanism is your identity as a member of a family as a child of a family, who has been given a name more or less by the head of the family. You have a place there. You have that, which is actually not a part of your racial identity. What the "race" of the family is is incidental. The fact that it was a Black African family has ....Let's see, supposing I had grown up in Britain, except I had a White extended family and I knew my place in that family. I had been given a name, say, by my mother alone, which my grandmother had then changed, say, to a pet name. Then I think a Black identity would have been a lot more problematic. One gets to the point where one realizes that you cannot a hundred percent identify with a White culture You have to go and look and find and seek that Black culture from somewhere. If you can't find it, then you have to synthesize it, which I think many people here have done.

However, many *métis(se)* people, as well as perhaps those who have grown up in care, or in predominantly suburban areas, have grown up in a social context wherein Whiteness is qualitatively and quantitatively valued at the expense of Blackness. When the forces of bi-racialization, leaving home or other transformative factors lead a person to question their predominantly White English upbringing, that individual frequently reacts by seeking out what they perceive to be an oppositional at times "hyper Black" identity or what my colleague Peter Bond (1998, personal communication) would refer to as a "compensatory Black identity."

"Racial" reconciliation is most successful accomplished after the individual has accepted the fact that their psychocultural starting point has been for the most part White English. Unfortunately, many *métis(se)* individuals feel they must abandon both their White English parentage as well as their White English cultural roots in order to "become Black." When in fact, most project participants' testimonies reveal that a re-formulated Black identity with an acknowledged White English reference point – a "synthesis," as Bisi says, is generally in less conflict with the overall process of self-transformation than a process wherein White English parentage and White English cultural influences are denied.

When I used to walk along the streets of Thatchapee, I was aware of the fact that many people did not make eye contact. However, whenever I came face to face with [another] *métis(se)* person, there was a particular way in which they did not make eye contact. That made me wonder where they were on their journey of self transformation:

When I see your faces, I cannot help but remember the war.

The illusory state of Whiteness: transforming the naturalized and normative properties of Whiteness:

An anthropologist friend of mine tells me the story of a Haitian statesman who was visited by an official from the United States during the 1930s. "What percentage of Haiti's population is White?" asked the American. "Ninety five percent," came the answer. The American official was flustered and assuming that the Haitian was mistaken exclaimed, "I don't understand – how on earth do you come up with such a figure?"
"Well – how do you measure blackness in the United States?"
"Anyone with a black ancestor."
"Well, that's exactly how we measure whiteness," retorted the Haitian.

(Williams 1997: 50)

(Bi)-racialization entails ascribing symbolic and frequently oppositional meanings to perceived or real (i.e. physical) differences (Miles 1989; Anthias and Yuval-Davis 1993; Omi and Winant 1986). In other words, in the same way that specific societies and cultures attach differential meaning to female and male and to woman and man which then creates the category gender, Western European-centered societies have created "race" as a construct which in general defines the White European or Anglo Saxon self in relation to the nonwhite nonEuropean nonAnglo Saxon object (Fernandez 1996). Hurtado and Stewart confer: "Whiteness, like maleness was viewed as background; being of Color, like being female was understood to shape and define one's personality, as one's life" (Hurtado and Stewart 1997: 298). In particular, the binary opposites are Blackness and Whiteness as they are differentially defined in specific geopolitical contexts (Dyer 1997). Blackness and Whiteness co-exist in symbolic opposition (Frankenberg 1997). Yet, until recently, in social scientific circles, Whiteness has been represented as a naturalized, vacant, normative, empty category:

Whiteness remains a relatively underdiscussed and underresearched "racial" identity...while the history and categorization of "non-Whiteness" has been frequently subject to debate, it is only in the past few years that a comparable discussion has begun on the subject of Whiteness. One of the most important consequences of this relative invisibility has been the naturalization of Whiteness for White people; whiteness tends to be far more visible to non-Whites.

(Bonnett 1997: 173)

By our very exclusion, those of us branded as "non-White" are regularly reminded of the infinitely mutable ways in which Whiteness is as laden with meaning and as marked as the varying connotations and symbols of Blackness. bell hooks reminds us that:

> although there has never been any official body of black people in the United States [or I add anywhere else in the African Diaspora(s)] who have gathered as anthropologists and/or ethnographers whose central [explicit] critical project is the study of whiteness, black folks have, from slavery on, shared with one another in conversations "special" knowledge of whiteness gleaned from close scrutiny of white people.
>
> (bell hooks 1992a: 165)

New books and articles on Whiteness are being published as I write, however, to date, *White Women, Race Matters* by Ruth Frankenburg is one of the best feminist ethnographic analyses, which addresses the complex interplay of race, gender, class and ethnicity in the construction of subjectivities. In particular, Frankenburg's "exploring, mapping and examining the terrain of whiteness" is an important starting point for dismantling bestowed normative and naturalized properties of Whiteness (Frankenburg 1993: 1). There are other contemporary White/Whiteness pioneers who continue to historicize and thereby challenge the essentialist and exclusive association of ideas about "race" with Blackness.[6]

In the real world, constructions of Blackness and constructions of Whiteness coexist are inextricably linked and at this stage cannot be separated:

> For the color line does not merely divide and separate; by a contiguous logic, it also binds, defines and shapes. The meaning of being black is determined through an active process which defines white as much as it does black; in historically specific ways, the discourses of race simultaneously separate groups of people *and* mobilize them, creating both stereotypical clichés and complex cultural–political identities.
>
> (Mohantey 1989: 21–2)

The theoretical focus of much of my research is discerning the interlocking and interdependent relationships between the taken-for-granted but extremely malleable categories of Blackness and Whiteness as they are manifest as identity diffusion for *métis(se)* individuals in the English–African Diaspora and by comparison the African–American Diaspora (the United States). In Chapter 1, I argue in favor of the dismantling of "race"-based social hierarchies altogether. At the same time, we must abandon the one drop rule, which mandates that the racial categorization of *métis(se)* individuals with partial Black African ancestry is completely determined by "only the lowest status racial category," which of course is Black African (Zack 1995). It is this law of "hypodescent" that has created essential "inferior" Black Africanness and normative and naturalized "superior" White Europeanness. Being or becoming White is never presented as an option: "Lara, lovey, so long as you're of negroid stock, diluted or not, you're black" (Evaristo 1997: 76). *Métis(se)* individuals are never entitled to address the ways in which they are also White. As I discussed at the beginning of this chapter, the cry for unification on the basis of compulsory Blackness also situates *métis(se)* individuals in a precarious position *vis-à-vis* their so-called White kin. Russell *et al.* mention "the White mother martyr syndrome, when a White mother informs her racially mixed children that they are Black, she must renounce her own Whiteness" (Russell *et al.* 1992: 76).

Soundings from the bloodlines frontlines: on *métis(se)* existences or the skins we are in

When we break that silence, we find community and that is reconciliation.

Ultimately, I am interested in the re-humanization of all experiences. The answers are not to be found in discerning which are Black issues and which are White, but in attacking and eradicating institutionalized racism and discrimination. After abandoning the hegemonic qualities of bi-racialization, perhaps we can attend to the seemingly insignificant concerns of humanity. To let the Blackness and Whiteness wash through is to embrace – among others – a re-defined identity that is crafted from the annals of each *métis(se)* person's particular multidimensional histories. For *métis(se)* people in particular and all people in general, one's subjectivities are multiple and not singular. Rather, we negotiate and narrate our experiential selves through disparate and hybrid manifestations of diaspora(s), cultures, classes sexualities, religions, ethnicities, nations and gender:

> Since identity is process, what we have is a field of discourses, matrices of meaning, arratives of self and others, configurations of memories, which once in circulation, provide a basis for identification. Every enunciation of identity, whether individual or collective, in this field of identifications represents a reconstruction.
>
> (Brah 1996: 247)

This sense of multiple and migratory subjectivities forms the foundation upon which *métis(se)* subjects construct their particular individual and collective narratives of self:

> It is a critical reflection on the self-and its history or its becoming – that may dramatize the unstable but determinate relation between the subject and its others. Auto-biography may write its subject only insofar as it renders its subject a subject, that is an embodied and located entity, which is representable only through its partial negation or loss. As a writing of the subject, autobiography may traverse that impossible distinction between the psychic and the social.
>
> (Ahmed 1997: 154)

Frequently, it is a life event such as getting married, the birth of a child, or the death of a parent which hurls the *métis(se)* individual into a heightened state of bi-racialized self-consciousness. However, the face-to-face and situational encounters comprising daily life can just as easily trigger bi-racialized contemplation. For example, *griotte* Akousa is sitting next to a White English woman on the bus, who says something to the effect that "If we put a straight wig on you you would be White." At times as in the previous example, gendered Blackness is at the contested center at other times, Whiteness is interrogated. On other occasions, *métis(se)* affiliations, ethnicities or nationalities are challenged. In other instances, they may all collide at once.

Borrowing from Native American cosmology, Scales-Trent would refer to this situational mutable shifting and shaping of subjectivities as "skin-walking:"

> When I think about how we all 'skinwalk' – change shapes, identities, from time to time, during the course of a day, during the course of our lives. I think about how we create these identities, how they are created for us, how they change, and how we reconcile these changes as we go along.
>
> (Scales-Trent 1995: 127)

Griottes Sarah and Akousa grew up in an African Caribbean community in Liverpool with their White Irish mother and a certain degree of consistency around being *métisse*, Black but not White, and Caribbean. Yemi and Bisi grew up in Nigeria with a White English mother and a Black Nigerian father and many contradictions around "race." As Bisi says, "If you are a mixed race person in Africa you are considered White." Ruby and Similola grew up in isolated predominantly White English settings with an imposed Black consciousness. Both their experiences and their relationships with others illuminate the different and complex ways in which, over time, they have forged identities that are neither necessarily essentialized nor exclusively bi-racialized. Their perspectives challenge the homogenization of Blackness as political strategy as well as the exclusionary practices of normative Whiteness. The affirmations and celebrations of *métis(se)* cultural influences provide alternative paradigms for other constituents of the English–African Diaspora who are also exploring the political possibilities of critical multiculturalism (Brah 1996; Goldberg 1994; Malik 1996).

As Zhana asserts in the anthology *Sojourn*: "…I want to get to a place where we are our own point of reference, where we form our own collective subconscious, where we set our own terms" (Zhana 1988: 12). These selves-transformations involve the re-appropriation of differences and marginalities and their re-working in a positive light. At the center is the interrogation of the taken-for-granted constructs of "race," nation, culture and family and their confluent relationships to gendered identities. The narratives of the *griottes* reveal dynamic articulations of selves. They also account for the situational ways in which bi-racialist societies attempt to situate those of us who have already been named.

Notes

1 Ruby and Similola were raised exclusively by White English mother surrogates, while Akousa and Sarah were raised by their White Irish mother and Black Guyanese "other-mother." Yemi and Bisi were raised by both their White English mother and their Black Nigerian father. With the exception of Yemi's adolescent bonding with her father, all of the women's testimonies speak to the important socializing influences of the women in their lives. With gender, class, ethnicity, religion, sexuality, locality and bi-racialization as important mediating variables, future research on *métis(se)* individuals and their families should focus on the differential agency of "majority" and "minority" parents, i.e. White mothers and fathers or Black mothers and fathers.

2 The geopolitical focus of my research has been specifically English. However, in this chapter, I also incorporate writings by Canadian and American *métisse* women authors with White mothers. Yet, recognizing the historical, cultural, social and political specificities of these varied experiences is essential. Nevertheless, across generations, time and space, comparative feminist research and theorizing on the differential dynamics of bi-racialized/multiracialized mother/daughter relationships is long overdue.

3 An interrelated and important fact which in part destabilizes my critique of compulsory Blackness is that bi-racialization does not disaggregate and racism equally discriminates against all segments of minority ethnic communities whether South Asian' African Caribbean, continental African or Chinese. One only has to examine the results of the Policy Study Institute's survey on crimes of racial violence and harassment perpetrated against minority ethnic communities to be convinced of the salience on the one hand of strategic collective Black political identification:

In a twelve month period between 1993 and 1994, there were about 20,000 people who were racially attacked, 40,000 people who had been subjected to racially motivated property damage and 230,000 people who were racially abused or insulted. Over-all then, the survey results would suggest that over a quarter of a million people were subjected to some form of racial harassment in a twelve month period

(Modood *et al.* 1997: 267)

4 As I will discuss later on, due to the fuzzy and slippery nature of official ethnic/racial categories, there are no demographic statistics available which track the actual relationship patterns or reproductive activities of specific multiple generations of *métis(se)* individuals in the English–African Diaspora.

5 I will discuss and define the concept of Additive Blackness later on in this chapter.

6 Vron Ware (1992) *Beyond the Pale*, London: Verso; Catherine Hall (1992) *White, Male and Middle Class*, Cambridge: Polity; Richard Dyer (1997) *White*, London: Routledge, p. 64; David Roediger (1994) *Towards the Abolition of Whiteness*, London: Verso; Alastair Bonnett (1997) "Constructions of Whiteness in European and American anti-racism," in P. Werbner and T. Modood (eds.) *Debating Cultural Hybridity*, London: Zed, pp. 173–92; Peter McLaren (1994) "White terror and oppositional agency: towards a critical multiculturalism," in D. Goldberg (ed.) *Critical Multiculturalism*, Oxford: Blackwell, pp. 45–74; David Wellman (1977) *Portraits of White Racism*, Cambridge: Cambridge University Press; Michelle Fine, Lois Weiss, Linda Powell and L. Mun Wong (eds.) (1997) *Off White*, London: Routledge; Phil Cohen (1997) "Laboring under Whiteness," in Ruth Frankenberg (ed.) (1997) *Displacing Whiteness*, London: Duke University Press, pp. 244–82.

EPILOGUE

Beginnings by way of concluding remarks

> Until the philosophy which holds one race superior and another inferior is finally and permanently discredited and abandoned; Until there are no longer first class and second class citizens of any nation; Until the basic human rights are equally guaranteed to all without regard to race; Until that day, the dream of lasting peace, world citizenship and the rule of international morality will remain but a fleeting illusion to be pursued but never attained.[1]

In this book, Ruby, Similola, Akousa, Sarah, Bisi and Yemi bear witness to the ways in which, as a major cleavage, the mis-philosophy of "race" and social hierarchies still prevails. Their collective stories highlight the fact that we need no longer look exclusively to South Africa as an exaggerated reminder that we still live in a (bi)-racially polarized world. Bristol, the temporary setting for the retelling of these narratives of home, is also one of many unofficial apartheid zones in the English–African Diaspora. In England, bi-racialization takes flight and form in discriminatory social practices, such as:

- housing allocation
- employment opportunities
- immigration and asylum legislation
- substandard education
- police harassment and brutality
- over-representation of certain groups in psychiatric facilities and prisons
- and in sustained racially motivated hate crimes including murder, among other indicators of structural inequalities.

Although ethnic monitoring for the 2001 Census is expected to remedy this, at the moment, among other discrepancies, most government bodies and their official statistics have not adequately accounted for the existence of differential *métis(se)* communities in the United Kingdom. With the one drop rule mandate, more often than not, an individual with one Black continental African or African Caribbean parent and one White British parent is seen as "just Black." Social, historical and political forces as well as the thirst for power have created bi-racialized discrimination in England. It is the persistence of this same bi-racialized hatred that gives salience and lends credence to Black as a political affiliation for *métis(se)* people.

The everyday plights and acts of resilience of *métis* men/boys and *métisse* women/girls reflect the heightened angst of all constituents of the English–African Diaspora. Hence, as (in)visible one drop rule casualties, they are more than likely overrepresented in bi-racialized institutions of violence, which dictate the multiple, complex and contradictory ways in which the popular folk concept of "race" takes on dynamic and real meanings. In other words, in part, English society is stratified on the bases of flimsy science fictional criteria. In varying amounts, power, prestige and privilege are apportioned to those designated as White and English. Those labeled as Black or Other are often devalued, discriminated against and, in certain instances, physically and psychologically damaged.

Mediated by gender and class among other structures, it is these fundamental realities of social inequality which are derived from the manufactured social facts of Blackness and Whiteness.[2] The psychic by-products of such fabricated social science fictional engineering manifest themselves as episodic grief, confusion, rage, despair, resentment, resilience, resistance, brilliance, creativity and innovation in the everyday lives of so many of the multiple generations of *métis(se)* warriors I have encountered, listened to, spoken with and learned from during my two-year sojourn in Bristol in particular and over thirty-four years of living in general. Ruth Behar describes the potent and transformative possibilities embedded in the naming of one's experiences as "testimonies of redemption:" "Telling her story, turning her rage into a story, is part of her quest for redemption, the redemption of her past and the redemption of the present she is actively seeking to understand and forge."[3]

When released, this arsenal of sentiments, actions and reactions will continue to reverberate in both wider interwoven English–African Diasporic communities wherein *métis(se)* individuals are located/locate themselves as well as increasingly in the "Whiter" British society writ large.[4] Unless and until there is an armistice, we remain *métis(se)* survivors:

> Thus, the mixed-race self that invents itself on paper is a refugee to the life of the mind. Only on the printed page at this time can one begin to lay down the parameters of mixed race identity and explore criticize [and I add transcend] them.[5]

We are all implicated.

We are all trapped in the crevices of our skins.

Notes

1 Cited in Horace Campbell (1985) *Rasta and Resistance From Marcus Garvey to Walter Rodney*, London: Hansib Publishing, p. 142. In 1963, Hailie Selassie, then Ethiopian monarch, gave this address, entitled "What Life Has Taught Me" to delegates of the United Nations, White English and Black Jamaican, Bob Marley, who died of brain cancer at the tender age of 36, is probably the most famous contemporary *métis griot*. Before his death, he spread his messages about world peace, love and understanding through his unique ever-evolving and timeless brand of reggae music. One such anti-racist anthem was "War/No More Trouble," which Marley created by taking the words of Selassie's speech and setting them to music.

2 Unlike the United States, in England, critical "mixed race" theorizing is still in its infancy. "Indigenous" work by *métis(se)* scholars ourselves is still almost non-existent. Among other pressing concerns which I have already addressed, this ongoing analytical project must become global and comparative. We also need to address, critique and challenge dominant binary Black/White discourses, which exclude and marginalize individuals who identify as "mixed race," but do not have White parentage.

3 Ruth Behar (1990) "Rage and redemption: reading the life story of a Mexican marketing woman," *Feminist Studies*, 16 (2): 233–58.

4 The emerging critical "mixed race" research community is slowly beginning to redress the bias, my own work included, which focuses specifically on continental White African/African Caribbean and White British and continental European "crossings." For example, in the future, more scholarship will be produced which addresses the lived experiences of *métis(se)* sons and daughters of (South)Asian/White British or (South) Asian/White continental European unions. I would also hope that we will learn about the unspoken lived realities of *métis(se)* individuals who are (South)Asian and Black continental African or (South) Asian and African Caribbean among other multiethnic and transnational affiliations.

5 Naomi Zack (1995) "Life after race," in N. Zack (ed.) *American Mixed Race*, London: Rowman and Littlefield, p. 299.

SELECT BIBLIOGRAPHIES

1 Cracking the coconut: resisting popular folk discourses on "race," "mixed race" and social hierarchies

Ageyman, Opoku (1985) *The PanAfricanist Worldview*, Independence, Missouri: International University Press.

Ahmad, Ajaiz (1995) "The politics of literary postcoloniality," *Race and Class*, 36 (3): 1–20.

Ahmed, Sara (1997) "'It's a sun tan isn't it?' Auto-biography as an identificatory Practice," in H. Mirza (ed.) *Black British Feminism*, London: Routledge, pp. 153–67.

Alibhai-Brown, Yasmin and Montague, Anne (1992) *The Color of Love*, London: Virago.

American Anthropological Association (1997) *Draft Official Statement on "Race,"* Washington: American Anthropological Association.

Ang-Lygate, Magdalene (1997) "Charting the spaces of (un)location: on theorizing diaspora," in H. Mirza (ed.) *Black British Feminism*, London: Routledge, pp. 153–68.

Anthias, Floya and Yuval-Davis, Nira (1992) *Racialized Boundaries*, London: Routledge.

Anzaldua, Gloria (1987) *Borderlands, La Frontera: The New Mestiza*, San Francisco: Aunt Lute Press.

Appiah, Anthony (1997) "'But would that still be me?': Notes on gender, 'race,' ethnicity as sources of identity," in N. Zack (ed.) *Race/Sex*, London: Routledge, pp. 75–82.

Aspinall, Peter (1997) "The conceptual basis of ethnic group terminology and classifications," *Social Science and Medicine*, 45 (5): 689–98.

Bachman, John (1850) *The Doctrine of the Unity of the Human Race Examined on the Principles of Science*, Charleston, South Carolina: Canning.

Back, Les (1996) *New Ethnicities and Urban Youth Cultures*, London: UCL Press.

Banton, Michael (1967) *Race Relations*, London: Tavistock.

Barth, Frederik (ed.) (1969) *Ethnic Groups and Boundaries*, London: Allen and Unwin.

Beauchamp, Kay (1979) *One Race, The Human Race*, London: Liberation.

Benedict, Ruth (1940) *Race, Science and Politics*, New York: Viking.

Benson, Sue (1981) *Ambiguous Ethnicity*, Cambridge: Cambridge University Press.

Bhaba, Homi (1994) *The Location of Culture*, London: Routledge.

Brand, Christopher (1996) *The g Factor*, New York: John Wiley and Sons.

Broca, Paul (1864) *Phenomena of Hybridity in the Genus Homo*, London: Anthropological Society.

Burley, David, Horsfall, A. and Brandon, A. (1992) *Structural Considerations of Métis Ethnicity: An Archaeological and Historical Study*, Vermillion, South Dakota: University of Dakota.

Camper, Carol (ed.) (1994) *Miscegenation Blues: Voices of Mixed Race Women*, Toronto: Sister Vision Press.

Canclini, Néstor García (1989) *Culturas Híbridas*, Miguel Hidalgo, Mexico: Grijalbo.

Chanady, Amaryll (ed.) (1994) *Latin American Identity and Constructions of Difference*, London: University of Minneapolis.

Colker, Ruth (1996) *Hybrid: Bisexuals, Multiracials, and Other Misfits under American Law*, London: New York University.

Comaroff, Jean and Comaroff, John (1991) *Of Revelation and Revolution: Christianity, Colonialism and Consciousness in South Africa*, Chicago: University of Chicago Press.

Davis, James F. (1991) *Who is Black?* University Park, Pennsylvania: Pennsylvania State University Press.

Davidson, Basil (1992) *The Black Man's Burden*, New York: Random House.

Day, Beth (1974) *Sexual Life Between Blacks and Whites*, New York: William and Morrow.

De-costa-Willis and Bell, Martin (eds.) (1992) *Black Erotica*, New York: Anchor.

Degler, Carl (1971) *Neither Black nor White: Slavery and Race Relations in Brazil and the United States*, New York: Macmillan.

Delaney, Martin (1879) *The Origins of Races and Color*, New York: New American Library.

Diop, Cheik Anta (1991) *Civilization or Barbarism: An Authentic Anthropology*, New York: Lawrence Hill.

Dominguez, Virginia (1986) *White by Definition*, New Brunswick, New Jersey: Rutgers.

Dyer, Richard (1997) *White: Essays on Race and Culture*, London: Routledge.

Ferguson, Russell, Gever, Martha, Minh-ha, Trinh T. and West, Cornel (eds.) (1990) *Out There: Marginalization and Contemporary Cultures*, New York: New Museum of Contemporary Art/MIT.

Fine, Michelle, Weis, L., Powell, L. and Mun Wong, L. (eds.) (1997) *Off White: Readings on Race, Power and Society*, London: Routledge.

Fisher, Jean (1995) "Some thoughts on 'contaminations'," *Third Text*, 38: 3–7.

Frankenberg, Ruth (ed.) (1997) *Displacing Whiteness: Essays in Social and Cultural Criticism*, London: Duke University.

Fraser, Steven (ed.) (1995) *The Bell Curve Wars: Race, Intelligence and the Future of America*, New York: Basic Books.

Freyre, Gilberto (1956) *The Masters and the Slaves: A Study in the Development of Brazilian Civilization*, New York: Alfred A. Knopf.

Fryer, Peter (1984) *Staying Power: The History of Black People in Britain*, London: Pluto.

Galton, Francis (1870) *Hereditary Genius*, New York: Appleton.

Gerzina, Gretchen (1995) *Black England: Life Before Emancipation*, London: John Murray.

Gilroy, Paul (1987) *There Ain't No Black in the Union Jack*, London: Hutchinson.

——— (1993a) *The Black Atlantic*, London: Verso.

———(1993b) *Small Acts: Thoughts on the Politics of Black Culture*, London: Serpent's Tail.

Gist, Noel and Dworkin, Anthony (eds.) (1972) *The Blending of the Races: Marginality and Identity in World Perspective*, New York: John Wiley and Sons.

Goldberg, David Theo (1993) *Racist Culture*, Oxford: Blackwell.

Goodwin, Brian (1994) *How the Leopard Changes its Spots*, London: Weidenfeld and Nicholson.

Gordon, L. R. (1995) "Critical 'mixed race'?" *Social Identities*, 1 (2): 381–395.

Gossett, Thomas (1965) *Race: The History of an Idea in America*, New York: Schocken.

Gould, Stephen Jay (1994) "The geometer of race," *Discover*, 15 (2): 64–9.

Haizlip, Shirlee (1994) *The Sweeter the Juice: A Family Memoir in Black and White*, New York: Simon and Schuster.

Hannaford, Ivan (1996) *Race: The History of an Idea in the West*, London: Johns Hopkins University Press.

Hashim, Iman (1996) *Mixed Up or Just Plain Mixed? An Examination of the Construction of Identities in Individuals of Mixed Heritage as a Means of Exploring Debates Around Multiple Subjectivities*, Discussion Paper in Sociology, Leicester: Leicester University Press.

Henri-Cousin, Pierre (1994) *Diamond French Dictionary*, London: Collins.

Hernton, Calvin (1965) *Sex and Racism in America*, New York: Grove Press.

Hill Collins, Patricia (1990) *Black Feminist Thought*, Boston: Unwin and Hyman.

Hitler, Adolf ([1925] 1992) *Mein Kampf*, translated by R. Mannheim, London: Pimlico.

Hoffman, Paul (1994) "The science of race," *Discover*, 15 (2): 4.

hooks, bell (1992) *Black Looks*, Boston: South End Press.

Hyam, Ronald (1990) *Empire and Sexuality: The British Experience*, Manchester: Manchester University Press.

Ifekwunigwe, Jayne O. (1997) "Diaspora's daughters, Africa's orphans? On lineage, authenticity and 'mixed race' identity," in H. Mirza (ed.) *Black British Feminism*, London: Routledge, pp. 127–52.

Jones, Lisa (1994) *Bulletproof Diva: Tales of Race, Sex and Hair*, New York: Doubleday.

Jordan, Glenn and Weedon, Chris (1995) *Cultural Politics*, Oxford: Blackwell.

Jordan, Winthrop (1974) *White Man's Burden*, Oxford: Oxford University Press.

Katz, William (1986) *Black Indians*, New York: Atheneum.

——— (1993) *Proudly Red and Black*, New York: Atheneum.

Kiernan, V. G. (1972) *The Lords of Human Kind: European Attitudes to the Outside World in the Imperial Age*, Harmondsworth, Middlesex: Penguin.

Kohn, Marek (1996) *The Race Gallery: The Return of Race Science*, London: Vintage.

Kuper, Leo (1974) *Race, Class and Power*, London: Duckworth.

Lawrence, Cecile Ann (1995) "Racelessness," in N. Zack (ed.) *American Mixed Race*, London: Rowman and Littlefield, pp. 25–38.

Linton, Ralph (1936) *The Study of Man*, New York: Appleton-Century.

Lionnet, Francoise (1989) *Anthropological Voices: Race, Gender and Self-Portraiture*, Ithaca, New York: Cornell University.

Lorde, Audre (1996) *The Audre Lorde Compendium*, London: Pandora.

Maja-Pearce, Adewale (1990) *How Many Miles to Babylon?*, London: Heinemann.

Malik, Kenan (1996) *The Meaning of Race*, London: MacMillan.

Mama, Amina (1995) *Beyond the Masks: Race, Gender and Subjectivity*, London: Routledge.

Marimba, Ani (1994) *Yurugu: An African-Centered Critique of European Cultural Thought and Behavior*, Trenton, New Jersey: Africa World Press.

Marquet, Marie-Madeleine (1983) *Le Métissage Dans La Poesie de Leopold Sedar Senghor*, Dakar: Nouvelle Edition Africaines.

Mercer, Kobena (1994) *Welcome to the Jungle: New Positions in Black Cultural Studies*, London: Routledge.

Miles, Robert (1989) *Racism*, London: Routledge.

Mills, Charles W. (1997) *The Racial Contract*, London: Cornell University.

Minh-ha, Trinh T. (1992) *The Framer Framed*, New York: Routledge.

Mirza, Heidi (ed.) (1997) *Black British Feminism*, London: Routledge.

Morton, Samuel (1850) "Additional observations on hybridity in animals and on some collateral subjects, being a reply to the objections of the Rev. John Bachman," *Charleston Medical Review*, 5: November.

Murray, Charles and Hernstein, Richard (1994) *The Bell Curve*, New York: Free Press.

Nettleford, Rex (1970) *Mirror, Mirror: Identity, Race and Protest in Jamaica*, Jamaica: William, Collins and Sangster.

Nott, Josiah and Gliddon, George (1854) *Types of Mankind*, Philadelphia: J. B. Lippincott.

Omi, Michael and Winant, Howard (1986) *Racial Formation in the United States*, New York: Routledge.

Opitz, May (ed.) (1986) *Showing Our Colors: Afro-German Women Speak Out*, Amherst: University of Massachusetts.

Owen, Charlie (1996) "'Mixed parentage' and the census," unpublished paper, presented at the conference, "Race into the Future," University of Warwick.

Papastergiadis, Nikos (1995) "Restless hybrids," *Third Text*, 32: 9–18.

Paredes, Anthony (1997) "Race is not something you can see," *Anthropology Newsletter*, 38 (9): 1–6.

Phoenix, Ann and Tizard, Barbara (1993) *Black, White or Mixed Race?* London: Routledge.

Phoenix, Ann and Owen, Charlie (1996) "From miscegenation to hybridity: mixed relationships and mixed parentage in profile," in B. Bernstein and J. Brannen (eds.) *Children, Research and Policy*, London: Taylor and Francis.

Provine, William (1973) "Geneticists and the biology of race crossing," *Science*, 182 (4114): 790–6.

Ramdin, Ron (1987) *The Making of the Black Working Class in Britain*, Aldershot: Wildwood House.

Rashidi, Runoko (1985) "Ancient and modern Britons," in I. Van Sertima (ed.) *African Presence in Early Europe*, London: Transaction Press, pp. 251–60.

Rattansi, Ali and Westwood, Sally (eds.) *Racism, Modernity and Identity*, Cambridge: Polity.

Rich, Paul (1986) *Race and Empire in British Politics*, Cambridge: Cambridge University Press.

Richmond, Anthony (1955) *The Color Problem*, Harmondsworth, Middlesex: Penguin.

Rodney, Walter (1981) *How Europe Underdeveloped Africa*, Washington: Howard University.

Rogers, J. A. (1944) *Sex and Race, Vol. III*, St. Petersburg, Florida: Helga Rogers.

—— (1952) *Nature Knows No Color Line*, St.Petersburg, Florida: Helga Rogers.

Root, Maria P. (ed.) (1992) *Racially Mixed People in America*, London: Sage.

—— (ed.) (1996) *The Multiracial Experience: Racial Borders as the New Frontier*, London: Sage.

Russell, Kathy, Wilson, Midge A. and Hall, Ronald (1992) *The Color Complex*, New York: Anchor.

Small, Stephen (1994) *Racialized Barriers*, London: Routledge.

Snowden, Frank (1983) *Before Color Prejudice: The Ancient View of Blacks*, Cambridge, Massachusetts: Harvard University.

Spencer, Jon Michael (1997) *The New Colored People: The Mixed Race Movement in America*, London: New York University Press.

Spickard, Paul (1989) *Mixed Blood: Intermarriage and Ethnic Identity in the Twentieth Century America*, London: University of Wisconsin.

Stanton, William (1960) *The Leopard's Spots: Scientific Attitudes Toward Race in America, 1815–1859*, Chicago: University of Chicago Press.

Stocking, George (1982) *Race, Culture and Evolution*, Chicago: University of Chicago.

Stolcke, Verena (1993) "Is sex to gender as race is to ethnicity?" in T. del Valle, *Gendered Anthropology*, London: Routledge, pp. 17–38.

Stonequist, Everett (1937) *Marginal Man*, New York: Russell and Russell.

Walvin, James (1973) *Black and White: The Negro and English Society*, London: Allen Lane.

Weekes, Debbie (1997) "Shades of Blackness: young female constructions of beauty," in H. Mirza (ed.) *Black British Feminism*, London: Routledge, pp. 113–26.

Welsing, Frances Cress (1991) *The Isis Papers*, Chicago: Third World Press.

Werbner, Pnina and Modood, Tariq (eds.) (1997) *Debating Cultural Hybridity*, London: Zed.

Williamson, Joel (1995) *New People: Miscegenation and Mulattoes in the United States*, London: Louisiana State University.

Wilson, Anne (1987) *Mixed Race Children*, London: Allen and Unwin.

Wolcott, Harry (1995) "Making a study 'more ethnographic'," in J. Van Maanen (ed.) *Representation in Ethnography*, London: Sage, pp. 79–111.

Young, Lola (1996) *Fear of the Dark: 'Race,' Gender and Sexuality in the Cinema*, London: Routledge.

Young, Robert (1995) *Colonial Desire: Hybridity in Theory, Culture and Race*, London: Routledge.

Zack, Naomi (1993) *Race and Mixed Race*, Philadelphia: Temple University Press.

—— (ed.) (1995) *American Mixed Race*, London: Rowman and Littlefield.

—— (ed.) (1997) *Race/Sex: Their Sameness, Difference and Interplay*, London: Routledge.

2 Returning(s): Relocating the critical feminist auto-ethnographer

Alibhai-Brown, Yasmin and Montague, Anne (1992) *The Color of Love*, London: Virago.

Anderson, Benedict (1991) *Imagined Communities*, London: Verso.

Ang-Lygate Magdalene (1997) "Charting the spaces of (un)location: on theorizing diaspora," in H. Mirza (ed.) *Black British Feminism*, London: Routledge, pp. 153–68.

Anthias, Floya and Yuval-Davis, Nira (1992) *Racialized Boundaries*, London: Routledge.

Anzaldua, Gloria (1987) *Borderlands/La Frontera: The New Mestiza*, San Francisco: aunt lute books.

Appiah, Anthony (1992) *In My Father's House: Africa in the Philosophy of Culture*, Oxford: Oxford University Press.

Back, Les (1996) *New Ethnicities and Urban Youth Cultures*, London: UCL Press.

Bainbridge, Beryl (1985) *English Journey,* London: Fontana.

Baldwin, James (1955) *Notes of a Native Son*, Boston: Beacon Press.

Banton, Michael (1967) *Race Relations*, London: Tavistock.

Barth, Frederik (ed.) (1969) *Ethnic Groups and Boundaries*, London: Allen and Unwin.

Benson, Sue (1981) *Ambiguous Ethnicity*, Cambridge: Cambridge University Press.

Bhaba, Homi (1994) *The Location of Culture*, London: Routledge.

Bourdieu, Pierre (1984) *Distinction: A Social Critique of the Judgement of Taste*, Cambridge, Massachusetts: Harvard University Press.

Boyce-Davies, Carole (1994) *Black Women, Writing and Identity*, London: Routledge.

Brah, Avtar (1996) *Cartographies of Diaspora*, London: Routledge.

Chrisman, Laura (1997) "Journey to death: Gilroy's *Black Atlantic*," *Race and Class*, 39 (2): 51–64.

Cliff, Michelle (1980) *Claiming an Identity They Taught Me to Despise*, Watertown, Massachusetts: Persephone Press.

Clifford, James (1986) "Partial truths," in J. Clifford and M. George (eds.) *Writing Culture*, Berkeley: University of California Press, pp. 1–26.

Cohen, Robin (1994) *Frontiers of Identity*, London: Longman.

—— (1997) *Global Diasporas*, London: UCL Press.

Center for Contemporary Cultural Studies (eds.) (1982) *The Empire Strikes Back: Race and Racism in 70's Britain*, London: Hutchinson.

Davidson, Basil (1992) *The Black Man's Burden*, New York: Random House.

Dennis, Ferdinand (1988) *Behind the Frontlines: Journey into AfroBritain*, London: Victor Gollancz.

Diop, Cheik Anta (1991) *Civilization or Barbarism: An Authentic Anthropology*, New York: Lawrence Hill.

Drachler, Jacob (ed.) (1975) *Black Homeland, Black Diaspora*, London: National University Publications.

Featherstone, Mike, Lash, Scott and Robe, Roland (eds.) (1995) *Global Modernities*, London: Sage.

Fryer, Peter (1984) *Staying Power: The History of Black People in Britain*, London: Pluto.

Gerzina, Gretchen (1995) *Black England: Life Before Emancipation*, London: John Murray.

Gilroy, Paul (1987) *There Ain't No Black in the Union Jack*, London: Hutchinson.

—— (1991) "It ain't where you're from it's where you're at," *Third Text*, 13: 3–16.

—— (1993) *The Black Atlantic*, London: Verso.

—— (1996) "Route work: the black Atlantic and the politics of exile," in I. Chambers and L. Curtis (eds.) *The Post-Colonial Question*, London: Routledge, pp. 17–29.

Hall, Stuart (1991) "Old and new identities, old and new ethnicities," in A. King (ed.) *Culture, Globalization and the World System*, London: MacMillan, pp. 41–68.

—— (1996) "The formation of a diasporic intellectual," in D. Morley and K.-H. Chen (eds.) *Stuart Hall: Critical Dialogues in Cultural Studies*, London: Routledge, pp. 484–503.

Herskovits, Melville (1958) *The Myth of the Negro Past*, Boston: Beacon Press.

Hesse, Barnor (1993) "Black to front and black again: racialization through contested times and spaces," in M. Keith and S. Pile (eds.) *Place and the Politics of Identity*, London: Routledge, pp. 162–82.

Hymes, Dell (1974) "The use of anthropology," in D. Hymes (ed.) *Reinventing Anthropology*, New York: Vintage Books, pp. 3–82.

Ifekwunigwe, Jayne O. (1997) "Diaspora's daughters, Africa's orphans? On lineage, authenticity and 'mixed race' identity," in H. Mirza (ed.) *Black British Feminism*, London: Routledge, pp. 127–52.

Jackson, Jean (1995) "Dejá entendu: the liminal qualities of anthropological fieldnotes," in J. Van Maanen (ed.) *Representation in Ethnography*, London: Sage, pp. 36–78.

Jordan, Glenn and Weedon, Chris (1995) *Cultural Politics*, Oxford: Blackwell.

Kiernan, V. G. (1972) *The Lords of Human Kind: European Attitudes to the Outside World in the Imperial Age*, Harmondsworth, Middlesex: Penguin.

Lavie, Smadar and Svedenburg, Ted (eds.) (1997) *Displacement, Diaspora, and Geographies of Identity*, London: Duke University Press.

Maja-Pearce, Adewale (1990) *How Many Miles to Babylon?* London: Heinemann.

Malik, Kenan (1996) *The Meaning of Race*, London: MacMillan.

Mama, Amina (1995) *Beyond the Masks: Race, Gender and Subjectivity*, London: Routledge.

Marcus, George and Fischer, Michael (1986) *Anthropology as Cultural Critique*, Chicago: University of Chicago.

Mercer, Kobena (1994) *Welcome to the Jungle: New Positions in Black Cultural Studies*, London: Routledge.

Miles, Robert (1989) *Racism*, London: Routledge.

Minh-ha, Trinh T. (1989) *Woman, Native, Other: Writing Postcoloniality and Feminism*, Bloomington, Indiana: Indiana University.

—— (1990) "Not you/like you: post-colonial women and the interlocking questions of identity and difference," in G. Anzaldua (ed.) *Making Face, Making Soul*, San Francisco: aunt lute Press, pp. 371–5.

Mirza, Heidi (ed.) (1997) *Black British Feminism*, London: Routledge.

Moore, Henrietta (1988) *Feminism and Anthropology*, Cambridge: Polity.

Mudimbe, V. Y. (1988) *The Invention of Africa*, Bloomington, Indiana: Indiana University.

Patterson, Sheila (1965) *Dark Strangers: A Study of West Indians in London*, Harmondsworth, Middlesex: Penguin.

Phillips, Caryl (1987) *The European Tribe*, New York: Farrar Straus Giroux.

Phoenix, Ann and Tizard, Barbara (1993) *Black, White or Mixed Race?* London: Routledge.

Pieterse, Jan (1990) *Empire and Emancipation*, London: Pluto Press.

Pile, Steve and Keith, Michael (eds.) (1993) *Place and the Politics of Identity*, London: Routledge.

Powdermaker, Hortense (1966) *Stranger and a Friend*, New York: W. W. Norton.

Priestley, J. B. (1987) *An English Journey*, Harmondsworth, Middlesex: Penguin.

Probyn, Elspeth (1990) "Travels in the postmodern: making sense of the local," in L. Nicholson (ed.) *Feminism and Postmodernism*, London: Routledge, pp. 176–89.

Pryce, Ken (1986) *Endless Pressure: West Indian Lifestyles in Bristol*, second edn., Bristol: Bristol Classical Press.

Ramdin, Ron (1987) *The Making of the Black Working Class in Britain*, Aldershot, Hants.: Wildwood House.

Rashidi, Runoko (1985) "Ancient and modern Britons," in I. Van Sertima (ed.) *African Presence in Early Europe*, London: Transaction Press, pp. 251–60.

Rashidi, Runoko (1992) *Introduction to the Study of African Classical Civilizations*, London: Karnak House.

Rattansi, Ali and Westwood, Sally (eds.) *Racism, Modernity and Identity*, Cambridge: Polity.

Rich, Paul (1986) *Race and Empire in British Politics*, Cambridge: Cambridge University Press.

Richmond, Anthony (1955) *The Color Problem*, Harmondsworth, Middlesex; Penguin.

—— (1973) *Migration and Race Relations in an English City*, Oxford: Oxford University Press.

Robinson, Derek (1973) *A Shocking History of Bristol*, Bristol: Abson Books.

Rodney, Walter (1981) *How Europe Underdeveloped Africa,* Washington: Howard University.

Schwarz, Bill (ed.) (1996) *The Expansion of England*, London: Routledge.

Segal, Ronald (1995) *The Black Diaspora*, London: Faber and Faber.

Sibley, David (1995) *Geographies of Exclusion*, London: Routledge.

Small, Stephen (1994) *Racialized Barriers*, London: Routledge.

Snowden, Frank (1983) *Before Color Prejudice: The Ancient View of Blacks*, Cambridge, Massachusetts: Harvard University.

Somers, Margaret and Gibson, Gloria (1994) "Reclaiming the epistemological 'Other': narrative and the social constitution of identity," in C. Calhoun (ed.) *Social Theory and the Politics of Identity*, Oxford: Blackwell, pp. 37–99.

Thompson, Robert Farris (1984) *Flash of the Spirit: African and Afro-American Art and Philosophy*, New York: Vintage.

Trudgill, Peter (1974) *Sociolinguistics*, Harmondsworth, Middlesex: Penguin.

Turner, Terence (1994) "Anthropology and multiculturalism: what is anthropology that multiculturalists should be mindful of it?" in D. Goldberg (ed.) *Critical Multiculturalism*, Oxford: Blackwell, pp. 406–25.

Van Maanen, John (ed.) (1995) *Representation in Ethnography*, London: Sage.

Van Sertima, Ivan (1976) *They Came Before Columbus*, New York: Random House.

—— (ed.) (1985) *African Presence in Early Europe*, London: Transaction Publishers.

—— (ed.) (1988) *Black Women in Antiquity*, London: Transaction Publishers.

Walvin, James (1973) *Black and White: The Negro and English Society*, London: Allen Lane.

—— (1996) *Questioning Slavery*, London: Routledge.

Williams, Chancellor (1987) *The Destruction of Black Civilization*, Chicago: Third World Press.

Willis, Susan (1985) "Black women writers take a critical perspective," in G. Greene and C. Khan (eds.) *Making a Difference: Feminist Literary Criticism*, New York: Methuen, pp. 211–37.

Windsor, Rudolph (1982) *From Babylon to Timbuktu: A History of Ancient Black Races Including the Black Hebrews*, Atlanta: Windsor's Golden Series.

Wolcott, Harry (1995) "Making a study 'more ethnographic'," in J. Van Maanen (ed.) *Representation in Ethnography*, London: Sage, pp. 79–111.

Wolf, Margery (1992) *A Thrice Told Tale: Feminism, Postmodernism and Ethnographic Responsibility*, Stanford: Stanford University.

Young, Lola (1996) *Fear of the Dark: "Race," Gender and Sexuality in the Cinema*, London: Routledge.

Young, Robert (1995) *Colonial Desire: Hybridity in Theory, Culture and Race*, London: Routledge.

3 Setting the stage: invoking the *griot(te)* traditions as textual strategies

Aptheker, Bettina (1989) *Tapestries of Life: Women's Work, Women's Consciousness and the Meaning of Daily Experience*, Amherst: University of Massachusetts.

Ashcroft, Bill, Griffiths, Gareth and Tiffin, Helen (1989) *The Empire Writes Back: Theory and Practice in Postcolonial Literature*, London: Routledge.

Bakhtin, Mikhail (1953/1981) "Discourse in the novel," in M. Holquist (ed.) *The Dialogic Imagination*, Austin: University of Texas, pp. 259–442.

Barkley Brown, Elsa (1989) "African American women's quilting: a framework for conceptualizing and teaching African American women's history," *Signs*, 14 (4): 921–9.

Bloom, Harold (ed.) (1996) *Black American Women Poets and Dramatists*, New York: Chelsea House.

Boyce-Davies (1994) *Black Women, Writing and Identity*, London: Routledge.

Braxton, Joanne and McLaughlin, Andrée Nicola (1990) (eds.) *Wild Women in the Whirlwind: Afra-American Culture and the Contemporary Literary Renaissance*, New Brunswick, New Jersey: Rutgers.

Brodski, Bella and Schenck, Celeste (eds.) (1988) *Life/Lines: Theorizing Women's Autobiography*, Ithaca, New York: Cornell University.

Broe, Mary Lynn and Ingram, Angela (eds.) (1989) *Women's Writing in Exile*, Chapel Hill, North Carolina: University of North Carolina.

Busby, Margaret (ed.) (1992) *Daughters of Africa*, New York: Ballantine Books.

Chester, Galina and Jegede, Tunde (1987) *The Silenced Voice: The Hidden Music of the Kora*, London: Diabaté Arts.

Clifford, James (1988) *The Predicament of Culture*, Cambridge: Harvard University.

Cobham, Rhonda and Collins, Merle (eds.) *Watchers and Seekers: Creative Writing by Black Women*, New York: Peter Bedrick.

Denis-Consant, Martin (1995) "The choices of identity," *Social Identities*, 1 (1): 5–20.

Diop, Samba (1995) *The Oral History and Literature of the Wolof People of Waalo, Northern Senegal: The Master of the Word (Griot) in the Wolof Tradition*, Lampeter, Wales: Edwin Mellen.

Ellison, Ralph (1953) *Shadow and Act*, New York: Vintage.

Fabian, Johannes (1991) *Time and the Work of Anthropology*, London: Harwood.

Fanon, Frantz (1967) *Black Skin, White Masks*, New York: Grove Press.

Farrar, Roy (1995) "Praise song: challenge," in L. Goss and C. Goss (eds.) *Jump Up and Say*, New York: Touchstone, p. 23.

Fine, Gary and Martin, Daniel (1995) "Humor in ethnographic writing: sarcasm, satire and irony as voices in Erving Goffman's asylums," in J. Van Maanen (ed.) *Representation in Ethnography*, London: Sage, pp. 165–97.

Finnegan, Ruth (1992) *Oral Traditions and the Verbal Arts*, London: Routledge.

Geertz, Clifford (1973) *The Interpretation of Cultures*, New York: Basic Books.

Gersie, Alida and King, Nancy (1990) *Storymaking in Education and Therapy*, London: Jessica Kingsley.

Gilroy, Paul (1993a) *Small Acts: Thoughts on the Politics of Black Culture*, London: Serpent's Tail.

—— (1993b) *The Black Atlantic*, London: Verso.

Goffman, Erving (1959) *Presentation of Self in Everyday Life*, New York: Anchor Books.

Golden, Marita and Richards Shreve, Susan (eds.) (1995) *Skin Deep: Black Women and White Women Write About Race*, New York: Nan A. Talese.

Hall, Becky (1996) "Heroines: black skin, blue eyes and muslin," *Soundings*, 3: 161–4.

Hall, Stuart (1990) "Cultural identity and diaspora," in J. Rutherford (ed.) *Identity: Community, Culture, Difference*, London: Lawrence and Wishart, pp. 222–37.

Heilbrun, Carol (1989) *Writing a Woman's Life*, London: Women's Press.

Jegede, Tunde (1994) *African Classical Music and the Griot Tradition*, London: Diabaté Arts.

Jones, Joy (1994) *Between Black Women: Listening with the Third Ear*, Chicago: African American Images.

Landman, Christina (ed.) *Digging Up Our Foremothers: Stories of Women in Africa*, Pretoria: University of South Africa.

Langness, L. L. and Frank, Gelya (1981) *Lives: An Anthropological Approach to Biography*, Novato, California: Chandler and Sharp.

Lavie, Smadar (1990) *The Poetics of Military Occupation: Mzeina Allegories of Bedouin Identity Under Israeli and Egyptian Rule*, Berkeley: University of California.

MacDougall, David (1993) "The subjective voice in ethnographic film," paper presented at the University of California, Berkeley.

Maja-Pearce, Adewale (1990) *How Many Miles to Babylon?* London: Heinemann.

Mama, Amina (1995) *Beyond the Masks: Race, Gender and Subjectivity*, London: Routledge.

Minh-ha, Trinh T. (1989) *Woman, Native, Other: Writing Postcoloniality and Feminism*, Bloomington, Indiana: Indiana University.

—— (1991) *When the Moon Waxes Red: Representation, Gender and Politics*, London: Routledge.

Nasta, Shusheila (1991) *Motherlands: Black Women's Writing From Africa, the Caribbean and South Asia*, London: Women's Press.

Oguibe, Olu (1994) *Sojourners*, London: African Refugee Publishing Collective.

Owen, Charlie (1997) " 'Mixed race' in official statistics, rethinking 'mixed race'," conference paper, London, National Institute for Social Work.

Owusu, Kwesi (ed.) *Storms of the Heart: An Anthology of Black Arts and Culture*, London: Camden Press.

Price, Richard (1983) *First Time: The Historical Vision of an Afro-American People*, Baltimore: Johns Hopkins University.

Probyn, Elspeth (1990) "Travels in the postmodern: making sense of the local," in L. Nicholson (ed.) *Feminism and Postmodernism*, London: Routledge, pp. 176–89.

Rabinow, Paul and Sullivan, William (eds.) (1979) *Interpretive Social Science*, Berkeley: University of California.

Rosaldo, Renato (1989) *Culture and Truth: The Remaking of Social Analysis*, Boston: Beacon Press.

Scott, Patricia (ed.) (1994) *Life Notes: Personal Writings by Contemporary Black Women*, New York: W. W. Norton.

Soyinka, Wole (1978) *Myth, Literature and the African World*, Cambridge: Cambridge University.

Tedlock, Dennis and Mannheim, Bruce (eds.) (1995) *The Dialogic Emergence of Culture*, Chicago: University of Illinois.

Tiffen, Chris and Lawson, Alan (eds.) (1994) *De-Scribing Empire: Postcolonialism and Textuality*, London: Routledge.

Vansina, Jan (1985) *Oral Tradition as History*, Madison, Wisconsin: University of Wisconsin.

Wolcott, Harry (1995) "Making a study 'more ethnographic'," in J. Van Maanen (ed.) *Representation in Ethnography*, London: Sage, pp. 79–111.

Wolf, Margery (1992) *A Thrice Told Tale: Feminism, Postmodernism and Ethnographic Responsibility*, Stanford: Stanford University.

Preamble Could I be a part of your family?
Preliminary/contextualizing thoughts on psychocultural politics of transracial placements and adoption

Ahmed, Shama, Cheetham, Juliet and Small, John (eds.) (1986) *Social Work with Black Children and Their Families*, London: B. T. Batsford.

Anthias, Floya and Yuval-Davis, Nira (1992) *Racialized Boundaries*, London: Routledge.

Barn, Ravinder (1998) "White mothers of 'mixed parentage' children: policy implications," seminar paper, "Racism and 'mixed race' families," London: Local Government Association.

Bartholet, Elizabeth (1994) "Race matching in adoption: an American experience," in I. Gaber and J. Aldridge (eds.) (1994) *In The Best Interests of the Child*, London: Free Association Books, pp. 151–87.

Boushel, Margaret (1996) "Vulnerable multiracial families and early year services," *Children and Society*, 10: 1–20.

Braithwaite, E. R. (1962) *Paid Civil Servant*, London: Bodley Head.

Cohen, Phil (1994) "Yesterday's words, tomorrow's world: from the racialization of adoption to the politics of difference," in I. Gaber and J. Aldridge (eds.) *In The Best Interests of the Child*, London: Free Association Books, pp. 43–76.

—— (1995) "Frameworks for the study of adoptive identities," working paper one, Dagenham, Essex: Centre for Adoption and Identity Studies, University of East London.

Craven-Griffiths, Jennifer (1994) "The law and transracial families," in I. Gaber and J. Aldridge (eds.) *In The Best Interests of the Child*, London: Free Association Books, pp. 116–35,

Fryer, Peter (1984) *Staying Power: The History of Black People in Britain*, London: Pluto.

Gaber, Ivor and Aldridge, Jane (eds.) (1994) *In the Best Interests of the Child: Culture, Identity and Transracial Adoption*, London: Free Association Books.

Gerzina, Gretchen (1995) *Black England: Life Before Emancipation*, London: John Murray.

Gilroy, Paul (1987) *There Ain't No Black in the Union Jack*, London: Hutchinson.

Goffman, Erving (1961) *Asylums: Essays on the Social Situations of Mental Patients and Other Inmates*, Garden City, New York: Anchor Books.

Kannan, C. T. (1972) *Inter-Racial Marriages in London*, London: Kannan.

Kareh, Diane (1970) *Adoption and the Colored Child*, London: Cox and Wyman.

Kay, Jackie (1991) *The Adoption Papers*, Newcastle-upon-Tyne: Bloodface Books.

Kirton, Derek (1995) "'Race,' identity and the politics of adoption," paper two, Dagenham, Essex: Centre for Adoption and Identity Studies, University of East London.

McKenzie-Mavinga, Isha and Perkins, Thelma (1991) *In Search of Mr. McKenzie*, London: Women's Press.

Miles, Robert (1989) *Racism*, London: Routledge.

Olumide, Jill (1998) "Discussion comments," seminar, "Racism and 'Mixed Race' Families," London: Local Government Association.

Omi, Michael and Winant, Howard (1986) *Racial Formation in the United States*, New York: Routledge.

Ramdin, Ron (1987) *The Making of the Black Working Class in Britain*, Aldershot, Hants: Wildwood House.

Richards, Barry (1994) "What is Identity?" in I. Gaber and J. Aldridge (eds.) *In The Best Interests of the Child*, London: Free Association Books, pp. 77–88.

Scheper-Hughes, Nancy and Lovell, Anne (eds.) (1987) *Psychiatry Inside Out: Selected Writings of Franco Basaglia*, New York: Columbia University.

—— (1992) *Death Without Weeping: The Violence of Everyday Life in Brazil*, Berkeley: University of California.

Simon, Rita (1994) "Transracial adoption: the American experience," in I. Gaber and J. Aldridge (eds.) *In The Best Interests of the Child*, London: Free Association Books, pp. 136–50.

Small, Stephen (1994) *Racialized Barriers*, London: Routledge.

Thoburn, June (1988) *Child Placement: Principles and Practice*, Aldershot, Hants.: Wildwood House.

Tizard, Barbara and Phoenix, Ann (1994) "Black identity and transracial adoption," in I. Gaber and J. Aldridge (eds.) *In The Best Interests of the Child, London*: Free Association Books, pp. 89–102.

Wallman, Sandra (1984) *Eight London Households*, London: Tavistock.

Wilson, Anne (1987) *Mixed Race Children*, London: Allen and Unwin.

10 Let Blackness and Whiteness wash through: competing discourses on bi-racialization and the compulsion of genealogical erasures

Ahmed, Sara (1997) " 'It's a sun tan isn't it?' Autobiography as an identificatory practice," in H. Mirza (ed.) *Black British Feminism*, London: Routledge.

Alexander, Claire (1996) *The Art of Being Black*, Oxford: Oxford University Press.

Alibhai-Brown, Yasmin and Montague, Anne (1992) *The Color of Love*, London: Virago.

Allen, Theodore (1994) *The Invention of the White Race*, London: Verso.

Amadiume, Ifi (1987) *Male Daughters, Female Husbands*, London: Zed.

Amit-Talai, Verity and Knowles, Caroline (eds.) *Resituating Identities*, Peterborough, Ontario: Broadview Press.

Anthias, Floya and Yuval-Davis, Nira (1992) *Racialized Boundaries*, London: Routledge.

Appiah, Anthony (1992) *In My Father's House: Africa in the Philosophy of Culture*, New York: Oxford University Press.

Appiah, Kwame Anthony and Gates, Henry Louis (eds.) (1995) *Identities*, Chicago: University of Chicago.

Aspinall, Peter (1995) "Department of Health's requirement for mandatory collection of data on ethnic group of inpatients," *British Medical Journal*, 311: 1006–9.

—— (1997) "The conceptual basis of ethnic group terminology and classifications," *Social Science and Medicine*, 45 (5): 689–98.

Back, Les (1996) *New Ethnicities and Urban Youth Cultures*, London: UCL Press.

Baldwin, James (1955) *Notes of a Native Son*, Boston: Beacon Press.

Banton, Michael (1967) *Race Relations*, London: Tavistock.

Barth, Frederik (ed.) (1969) *Ethnic Groups and Boundaries*, London: Allen and Unwin.

Benson, Sue (1981) *Ambiguous Ethnicity*, Cambridge: Cambridge University Press.

Bhaba, Homi (1994) *The Location of Culture*, London: Routledge.

Bonnett, Alastair (1997) "Constructions of whiteness in European and American anti-racism," in P. Werbner and T. Modood (eds.) *Debating Cultural Hybridity*, London: Zed, pp. 173–92.

Boushel, Margaret (1996) "Vulnerable multiracial families and early year services," *Children and Society*, 10: 1–20.

Boyce-Davies (1994) *Black Women, Writing and Identity*, London: Routledge.

Brah, Avtar (1996) *Cartographies of Diaspora*, London: Routledge.

Butler, Judith and Scott, Joan (eds.) (1992) *Feminists Theorize the Political*, London: Routledge.

Camper, Carol (ed.) (1994) *Miscegenation Blues: Voices of Mixed Race Women*, Toronto: Sister Vision Press.

Canaan, Andrea (1981) "Brownness," in C. Moraga and G. Anzaldua (eds.) *This Bridge Called My Back*, New York: Kitchen Table Press, pp. 232–7.

Chapkis, Wendy (1986) *Beauty Secrets: Women and the Politics of Appearance*, Boston: South End Press.

Charles, Helen (1996) "White skins, straight masks," in D. Jarret-MacAuley (ed.) *Reconstructing Womanhood, Reconstructing Feminism*, London: Routledge, pp. 136–55.

Chodorow, Nancy (1978) *The Reproduction of Mothering: Psychoanalysis and the Sociology of Gender*, Berkeley: University of California.

Cliff, Michelle (1980) *Claiming an Identity They Taught Me to Despise*, Watertown, Massachusetts: Persephone Press.

Collins, Patricia Hill (1990) *Black Feminist Thought*, Boston: Unwin Hyman.

—— (1994) "Shifting the center: race, class, and feminist theorizing about motherhood," in Nakano Glenn, E., Chang, G. and Rennie Forcey, L. (eds.) *Mothering, Ideology, Experience and Agency* London: Routledge, pp. 45–66.

Centre for Contemporary Cultural Studies (eds.) (1982) *The Empire Strikes Back: Race and Racism in 70's Britain*, London: Hutchinson.

Dent, Gina (ed.) (1992) *Black Popular Culture*, Seattle, Washington: Bay Press.

Dixie, John (1997) "Developing the question on ethnicity for the 2001 Census," conference paper, "Rethinking 'Mixed Race'," National Institute for Social Work: London.

DuBois, W. E. B. (1969) *The Souls of Black Folk*, New York: New American Library.

Dyer, Richard (1997) *White: Essays on Race and Culture*, London: Routledge.

Essed, Philomena (1991) *Understanding Everyday Racism*, London: Sage.

Evaristo, Bernadine (1997) *Lara*, Tunbridge Wells, Kent: Angela Royal Publishing.

Ewart, Cossar (1900) *Guide to the Zebra Hybrids, etc.*, Edinburgh: T&A Constable.

Fanon, Frantz (1967) *Black Skin, White Masks*, New York: Grove Press.

Fernandez, Carlos (1996) "Government classification of multiracial/multiethnic people," in M. Root (ed.) *The Multiracial Experience*, London: Sage, pp. 15–36.

Fine, Michelle, Weis, L., Powell, L. and Mun Wong, L. (eds.) (1997) *Off White: Readings on Race, Power and Society*, London: Routledge.

Frankenberg, Ruth (1993) *White Women, Race Matters: The Social Construction of Whiteness*, London: Routledge.

—— (ed.) (1997) *Displacing Whiteness: Essays in Social and Cultural Criticism*, London: Duke University.

Fryer, Peter (1984) *Staying Power: The History of Black People in Britain*, London: Pluto.

Gaber, Ivor and Jane Aldridge (eds.) (1994) *In the Best Interests of the Child*, London: Free Association Books.

Gerzina, Gretchen (1995) *Black England: Life Before Emancipation*, London: John Murray.

Gilroy, Paul (1987) *There Ain't No Black in the Union Jack*, London: Hutchinson.

—— (1991) " 'It ain't where you're from it's where you're at',"*Third Text*, 13: 3–16.

—— (1993) *The Black Atlantic*, London: Verso.

Goldberg, David Theo (ed.) (1994) *Critical Multiculturalism,* Oxford: Blackwell,

—— (1995) "Made in the USA," in N. Zack (ed.) *American Mixed Race*, London: Rowman and Littlefield, pp. 237–56.

Griffin, Achille (1913) *Le Zebre: Studio Zoologico Popolare*, Milan: Ulrico Hoepli.

Hall, Catherine (1992) *White, Male and Middle Class*, Cambridge: Polity.

Hall, Stuart (1991) "Old and new identities, old and new ethnicities," in A. King (ed.) *Culture, Globalization and the World System*, London: MacMillan, pp. 41–68.

Haizlip, Shirlee (1994) *The Sweeter the Juice: A Family Memoir in Black and White*, New York: Simon and Schuster.

Head, Bessie (1974) *A Woman Alone*, London: Heinemann.

—— (1990) *A Question of Power*, London: Heinemann.

Hernandez-Ramdwar, Camille (1994) "Ms. Edge innate," in C. Camper (ed.) *Miscegenation Blues*, Toronto: Sister Vision Press, pp. 2–7.

Herskovits, Melville (1958) *The Myth of the Negro Past*, Boston: Beacon Press.

Hesse, Barnor (1993) "Black to front and black Again: racialization through contested times and spaces," in M. Keith and S. Pile (eds.) *Place and the Politics of Identity*, London: Routledge, pp. 162–82.

Hewitt, Roger (1986) *White Talk, Black Talk*, Cambridge: Cambridge University Press.

hooks, bell (1992a) "Representing whiteness in the black imagination," in L. Grossberg, C. Nelson, P. Treichler and L. Baughman (eds.) *Cultural Studies*, London: Routledge, pp. 338–46.

—— (1992b) *Black Looks*, Boston: South End Press.

Hurtado, Aida and Stewart, Abigail (1997) "Through the looking glass: implications of studying whiteness for feminist methods," in M. Fine, L. Weiss, L. Powell and L. Mun Wong (eds.) *Off White*, London: Routledge, pp. 297–311.

Ifekwunigwe, Jayne O. (1997) "Diaspora's daughters, Africa's orphans? On lineage, authenticity and 'mixed race' identity," in H. Mirza (ed.) *Black British Feminism*, London: Routledge, pp. 127–52.

Jones, Lisa (1994) *Bulletproof Diva: Tales of Race, Sex and Hair*, Doubleday: New York.

Jones, Simon (1988) *Black Culture, White Youth*, London: MacMillan.

Jordan, Glenn and Weedon, Chris (1995) *Cultural Politics*, Oxford: Blackwell.

Katz, William (1986) *Black Indians*, New York: Atheneum.

—— (1993) *Proudly Red and Black*, New York: Atheneum

Killingray, David (ed.) (1994) *Africans in Britain*, Ilford, Essex: Frank Cass.

Kinsley, Claire Huang (1994) "Questions people have asked me. Questions I have asked myself," in C. Camper (ed.) *Miscegenation Blues*, Toronto: Sister Vision Press, pp. 113–32.

Kuper, Leo (1974) *Race, Class, and Power*, London: Duckworth.

Levins, Morales Aurora (1981) "…And even Fidel can't change that," in C. Moraga and G. Anzaldua (eds.) *This Bridge Called My Back: Writings by Radical Women of Color*, New York: Kitchen Table Press, pp. 53–6.

Mclaren, Peter (1994) "White terror and oppositional agency: towards a critical multiculturalism," in D. Goldberg (ed.) *Critical Multiculturalism*, Oxford: Blackwell, pp. 45–74.

McLaughlin, Andrée Nicola (1990) "Black women, identity and the quest for humanhood and wholeness: wild women in the whirlwind," in J. Braxton and A. McLaughlin (eds.) *Wild Women in the Whirlwind*, New Brunswick, New Jersey: Rutgers, pp. 70–88.

Majaj, Lisa Suhair (1994) "Boundaries, borders, horizons," in C. Camper (ed.) *Miscegenation Blues*, Toronto: Sister Vision Press, pp. 56–95.

Maja-Pearce, Adewale (1990) *How Many Miles to Babylon?* London: Heinemann.

Malik, Kenan (1996) *The Meaning of Race*, London: MacMillan.

Mama, Amina (1995) *Beyond the Masks: Race, Gender and Subjectivity*, London: Routledge.

Marable, Manning (1995) *Beyond Black and White*, London: Verso.

Mercer, Kobena (1994) *Welcome to the Jungle: New Positions in Black Cultural Studies*, London: Routledge.

Miles, Robert (1989) *Racism*, London: Routledge.

Minh-ha, Trinh T. (1989) *Woman, Native, Other: Writing Postcoloniality and Feminism*, Bloomington, Indiana: Indiana University.

Mirza, Heidi (ed.) (1997) *Black British Feminism*, London: Routledge.

Modood, Tariq (1988) "Black racial equality and Asian identity," *New Community*, 14 (3): 397–404.

Modood, Tariq, Berthoud, Richard, Lakey, Jane, Nazroo, James *et al.* (1997) *Ethnic Minorities in Britain*, London: Policy Studies Institute.

Mohantey, S. P. (1989) "Kipling's children and the color line," *Race and Class*, 31 (1): 21–40.

Morrison, Toni (1993) *Playing in the Dark: Whiteness and the Literary Imagination*, London: Picador.

Nakano Glenn, Evelyn, Chang, Grace and Rennie Forcey, Linda (eds.) (1994) *Mothering: Ideology, Experience and Agency*, London: Routledge.

Nakashima, Cynthia (1996) "Voices from the movement: approaches to multiraciality," in M. Root (ed.) *The Multiracial Experience*, London: Sage, pp. 79–97.

Okamura, John (1981) "Situational ethnicity," *Ethnic and Racial Studies*, 4 (4): 452–65.

Omi, Michael and Winant, Howard (1986) *Racial Formation in the United States*, New York: Routledge.

Owen, Charlie (1998) "'Mixed race' and the census," seminar paper, "Racism and 'Mixed Race' Families," London: Local Government Association.

Paulse, Michele (1994) "Commingled," in C. Camper (ed.) *Miscegenation Blues*, Toronto: Sister Vision Press, pp. 43–51.

Phoenix, Ann and Owen, Charlie (1996) "From miscegenation to hybridity: mixed relationships and mixed parentage in profile," in B. Bernstein and J. Brannen (eds.) *Children, Research and Policy*, London: Taylor and Francis.

Phoenix, Ann and Tizard, Barbara (1993) *Black, White or Mixed Race?* London: Routledge.

Phoenix, Ann and Bhavnani, Kum Kum (eds.) (1994) *Shifting Identities, Shifting Racisms*, London: Sage.

Rattansi, Ali and Westwood, Sally (eds.) *Racism, Modernity and Identity*, Cambridge: Polity.

Rich, Adrienne (1977) *Of Woman Born: Motherhood as Experience and Institution*, London: Virago.

—— (1986) *Blood, Bread and Poetry*, London: Virago.

Rich, Paul (1986) *Race and Empire in British Politics*, Cambridge: Cambridge University Press.

Roediger, David (1991) *The Wages of Whiteness*, London: Verso.

—— (1994) *Towards the Abolition of Whiteness*, London: Verso.

Root, Maria P. (ed.) (1992) *Racially Mixed People in America*, London: Sage.

—— (ed.) (1996) *The Multiracial Experience: Racial Borders as the New Frontier*, London: Sage.

Russell, Kathy, Wilson, Midge and Hall, Ronald (1992) *The Color Complex: The Politics of Skin Color Among African Americans*, New York: Doubleday.

S. R. W. (1994) "Untitled," in C. Camper (ed.) *Miscegenation Blues*, Toronto: Sister Vision Press, pp. 255–6.

Scales-Trent, Judy (1995) *Notes of a White Black Woman*, University Park, Pennsylvania: Pennsylvania State University.

Small, Stephen (1994) *Racialized Barriers*, London: Routledge.

Snowden, Frank (1983) *Before Color Prejudice: The Ancient View of Blacks*, Cambridge, Massachusetts: Harvard University.

Stack, Carol (1976) *All Our Kin*, New York: Harper and Row.

Stack, Carol and Burton, Linda (1994) "Kinscripts: reflections on family, generation and culture," in E. Nakano Glenn, G. Chang and L. Rennie Forcey (eds.) *Mothering*, London: Routledge, pp. 33–44.

Tegetmeier, W. B. and Sutherland, C. L. (1895) *Horses, Asses, Zebras, Mules and Mule Breeding*, London: Horace Cox.

Ware, Vron (1992) *Beyond the Pale: White Women, Racism and History*, London: Verso.

Weekes, Debbie (1997) "Shades of Blackness," in H. Mirza (ed.) *Black British Feminism*, London: Routledge, pp. 113–26.

Wellman, David (1977) *Portraits of White Racism*, Cambridge: Cambridge University Press.

Williams, Chancellor (1987) *The Destruction of Black Civilization*, Chicago: Third World Press.

Williams, Patricia J. (1997) *Seeing a Color Blind Future*, London: Virago.

Wilson, Anne (1987) *Mixed Race Children*, London: Allen and Unwin.

Windsor, Rudolph (1982) *From Babylon to Timbuktu: A History of Ancient Black Races Including the Black Hebrews*, Atlanta: Windsor's Golden Series.

Young, Lola (1996) *Fear of the Dark: "Race," Gender and Sexuality in the Cinema*, London: Routledge.

Young, Robert (1993) *White Mythologies: Writing History and the West*, London: Routledge.

—— (1995) *Colonial Desire: Hybridity in Theory, Culture and Race*, London: Routledge.

Zack, Naomi (1993) *Race and Mixed Race*, Philadelphia: Temple University Press.

—— (ed.) (1995) *American Mixed Race*, London: Rowman and Littlefield.

Zhana (ed.) (1988) *Sojourn,* London: Methuen.

INDEX

Achebe, Ike 61n1
acknowledgements, Ben-Ari xv
Adams, Jo 69n2
Additive Blackness 91n5, 143–4n9,
    167n15, 183, 186
adoption 63–4, 67
African Caribbean communities 157n5,
    179
African Liberation Day 107
Africanness 167–8n16, 190
Afro-Germans 7, 112n9
Ageyman, Opoku 21
Ahmad, Aijaz 22
Ahmed, Sara 191
Akomfrah, John 39
Akousa: Black identity 8, 112–13;
    Black sisterhood 111, 112; childhood
    52, 55, 103–4; church 104; dancing
    110; father from Barbados 103–4;
    fictive kin 104, 175; home 104,
    104n2; mother from Ireland 103,
    105, 108–9, 114–15; partner choice
    82n15; physical appearance 103,
    106–7, 191; Rastafarian 102; school
    109–11; sister Sarah 102, 107, 108;
    smile 102, 107; surrogate family
    104, 105–6, 115; White Englishness
    acknowledged 109, 109n6
alcohol/substance abuse 74n6
Aldridge, Jane 66, 185
Alger, Horatio 35
Alibhai-Brown, Yasmin 182, 183
Amadiume, Ifi 176
American Anthropological Association
    22n1
ancestors, honored 170
Andrew 52

Aneya 16
Ang-Lygate, Magdalene 43
Anthias, Floya 12, 13
anthropology, culture 1
Anzaldua, Gloria 21, 46
apartheid 8
Ashcroft, Bill 60
Asian children 76, 77
Aspinall, Peter 178, 179
assimilation, speech patterns 34
Association of Black Social Workers and
    Allied Professionals 67
auto-ethnography 29, 30–40, 55

Bachman, John 3–4
Bakhtin, Mikhail 55–6
Baldwin, James 40, 105–6, 183
Bambi 52, 82n15
Banton, Michael 8
Barkley Brown, Elsa 57
Barn, Ravinder 63, 66
Barth, Frederik 2
Basinger, Kim xv
Bassaglia, Franco 64
Behar, Ruth 195, 196n3
belonging xiii, 53, 95n12; see also not
    belonging
Ben-Ari, Eyal xv
Benedict, Ruth 11
Bhaba, Homi 21
bi-racialization 12–13, 65; attitudes
    185; Blackness 94n10;
    discriminatory practices 194; gender
    politics 69n2; home 41–2;
    institutions of violence 64–5;
    labeling 107n4; life events 191; and
    patriarchy 63; sexual liaisons 15;

215

Similola 64, 65, 181–2; stigma 112n9; and Whiteness 188; zebra metaphor 181–2; *see also métis(se)* children 20
Biafran War 33, 35, 48n3, n6
bicultural preservation 140n4
biology, race 10–11, 13
birth fathers 50, 51; *see also* fathering
birth mothers 50–1, 55, 171–4; *see also* mothers
Bisi: art influences 142–3; Black consciousness 147; childbearing 146–7; childhood 52, 55, 133; class 149; coping mechanisms 143; death of father's step-mother 138–9; father 133, 137; food 30; husband 132, 134–6, 137–8, 147n15; mother 133, 134, 148, 146–7, 172; nationality 145, 145n11; Newcastle family 138, 140–1; Nigeria 133, 139–40; race of children 14, 149–50; racial identity 143, 144; school 142; self-portrait 136–7n2; sister Yemi 153, 162, 166; White English culture 133n1, 148n16, n18, 172; Whiteness/Blackness 143n8, 148n18
Black consciousness 147, 167–8, 186
Black daughters, White English mothers 50–1, 55, 171–4
Black feminism 173
Black identity: Akousa 8, 112–13; compensatory 187; denied 72, 90; essentialized 5, 60; fostering 67; imperialism 56; Sarah 130–1; Similola 97–9
Black masculinities 51
Black mother, White children 82–3n17
Black Power Movement 55, 108, 130–1, 167n15
Black-washing 185
Blackness: Additive 91n5, 143–4n9, 167n15, 183, 186; authentic 73n5, 94n10, 107n4, 174, 184; awareness 147, 167–8, 186; bi-racialization 94n10; and Britishness 85; compulsory 184; economic/social 170; *métis(se)* children 90, 91; negative constructions 89n1; prayed for 108, 113; pride in 80; statuses (Davis) 15–16; supremacy 9; totalizing 177
Bloom, Harold 59

The Body Beautiful film 173
Bond, Peter 187
bongo foot 119–20n2
Bonnett, Alastair 188
Bourdieu, Pierre 36
Boushel, Margaret 63, 67, 179, 185
Boyce-Davies, Carole 42, 53
Brah, Avtar 177, 190
Braithwaite, E. R. 62
Brand, Christopher 8
Bristol 36, 186–7; *see also* Thatchapee
Britain: Caribbean men/White women 15; Child Welfare State 63, 65–6; Children's Act (1989) 65, 66, 67, 94n9; demographic changes in ethnicity 179; monocultural xii
British Agency for Adoption and Fostering 64
Britishness, Blackness 85
Broca, Paul 4
Burton, Linda 175

Campbell, Horace 196n1
Camper, Carol 185–6
Canaan, Andrea 184
cannabis psychosis 157n5
Cardiff's Tiger Bay 91–2n6
caste system, double 170
Census (2001) 194
Census classification 17, 177–9, 180
Charles 52
childbearing 146–7
children, death of 65
Children's Act (1989) 65, 66, 67, 94n9
children's homes 68–9, 71–7, 89; *see also* local authority care
Chodorow, Nancy 171
class system 35–6, 149
Claudia 51, 186
Cliff, Michelle 47
Clifford, James 45, 46
Clive 52
clothes, presentation 99–101
code-switching 34, 35
commerce, sexual 5
commodification, *métis(se)* children 63–4
community: destroyed 124, 124n5; for *métis(se)* children 81–2n15, 92n6
computerized hybridity 39–40
consciousness: Black 147, 167–8, 186; double 54

cultural capital 36
cultural identity 50
cultural surrogates 68, 111n7, 112, 175–6
culture: anthropology 1; biculture 140n4; hybridity 9–10; Igbo 30, 32, 35; mixed race 18–19; popular 45; race xii, 13, 85–6; Yoruba 160–1, 166, 176
cyborg 23n8
Cyrus 52

Darwin, Charles 3, 6, 11
daughter, male 176
Davis, James F. 15–16
Delany, Martin 23n7
Delia 52
Denis-Constant, Martin 58–9
difference: métis(se) children 92n7, 93n8; solidarity 127–8
Diop, Cheik Anta 13, 41
Diop, Samba 18, 61n2, 140n4
discrimination 194
Dixie, John 178
Duster, Troy 181
Dworkin, Anthony 9, 11
Dyer, Richard 2

Elise 52
Ellison, Ralph 56
empowerment 40, 150n21
England 35, 36, 141n6, 142; see also Britain
English–African Diaspora 40–5, 53–4, 66, 182–3, 184, 195
Englishness xiii; métis(se) children, White birth mothers 50, 51, 55; and Whiteness 39, 42–3, 49n10
Essed, Philomena 172
ethnography 46, 55–7, 60, 61; see also auto-ethnography
Eugenics 6, 8
Evaristo, Bernadine 170, 190
exclusion 189

family 62, 69n1
family surrogates 104, 105–6, 115, 118–21, 123; see also fictive kin
Fanon, Frantz 29, 56, 143n7, 170
Farrar, Roy 58

fathering, and birth fathers 50, 51, 72n1
feminism 40–7, 48n1, 173
Fenton, Steve 39
Fernandez, Carlos 180
fictive kin 104, 175; see also family surrogates
Fine, Gary 59
Finnegan, Ruth 61
Fischer, Michael 45
folk concept of race 6, 11–12
fostering: métis(se) children 66, 67; transracial 94n9
Frank, Gelya 61
Frankenburg, Ruth 189
Freeman, Jane Plate 2 25
Freeman, Lionel Plate 1 vii
Freeman, Mary Plate 1 vii
Friedman, Jonathan xii

Gaber, Ivor 66, 185
Gabriel, Stephanie 157n5
Galton, Francis 6–7
gender politics 69n2, 126n6
genetics, Mendelian 6, 11–12
genotypic traits 15, 37, 94–5n10, 184
geopolitics 145n11, 192n2
Gersie, Alida 55
Gibson, Gloria 42
Gilroy, Paul 42, 54, 69n1
Gist, Noel 9, 11
Gliddon, George 4
Goffman, Erving 56, 64
Gossett, Thomas 3, 6
grandmothers (White), Black grand-daughters 75n8, 76, 76n9, 78–9, 172–3
griot 1, 23n4, 57–61
griotte 58, 59–60
Guardian 179
Guyana 36, 38

hair, and politics 37
Haiti, Whiteness 188
Hall, Becky 56
Hall, Stuart 42, 50
Haraway, Donna 23n8
Harmony 52
Heilbrun, Carol 59
Hernandez-Ramdwar, Camille 174
Hernton, Calvin 4

Herrnstein, Richard 8
heterosexuality, compulsory 183–4
hierarchies, race 2–3, 194
Hitler, Adolf 7
Hoffman, Paul 12
home: bi-racialized 41–2; Caribbean
    104n2, 115; for Yemi 153n1
Homo sapiens 11
hooks, bell 13, 92n7, 189
house ownership 123–4, 123n4
hybrid identity xii–xiii
hybrid spaces 20–1
hybridity 3, 4, 9–10, 23n8, 39–40
Hymes, Dell 47

identity: Black 8, 56, 60, 67, 97–9,
    112–13, 130–1, 187; Black (denied)
    72, 90; constructed 56, 77n10, 178,
    181; cultural 50; empowerment 40;
    family 62; hybrid xii–xiii; narratives
    58–9; physical appearance 46; race
    xii–xiii, 143, 144
identity politics 37, 42, 181
Ifekwunigwe, Chief Aaron Nsiegbuna
    Plate 4 27
Ifekwunigwe, Florence *Plate 4* 27
Ifekwunigwe, Jayne O. *Plate 3* 26, 178;
    auto-ethnography 29, 30–40;
    English Geordie ancestors 38; as
    feminist 43–5, 48n1; Guyanese
    ancestors 36, 38; as *métisse* 46–7;
    Nigerian ancestors 38; as poet v, 116;
    siblings 37
Igbo art form 148n17
Igbo culture 30, 32, 35
Igbo language 36
Igbo naming tradition 30, 32
Igbo proverbs 50, 62
institutions of violence 64–5
intelligence, and race 7
interbreeding 2, 3, 9
intermarriages 6–7, 9
interplay of voices 55
Irie 1, 157n6

Jackson, Michael 97n15
Jacobs, Dan 48n3
Janice 51
Jegede, Tunde 61
Jensen, Arthur 8
Jones, Lisa 180

Kareh, Diane 66
Keith, Michael 43
kin: fictive 104, 175; one drop rule 183
King, Nancy 55
Kinsley, Claire Huan 174

Langness, L. L. 61
Lavie, Smadar 23n8, 58
Lawrence, Cecile Ann 13
Lena 52
Leo 53
lesbianism 183–4
life events, bi-racialization 191
Linnaeus, Carolus 3
literacy 58
Liverpool: Black house ownership
    123–4, 123n4; *métissage* 105–6;
    racism 128–9
local authority care 62–3, 179; *see also*
    children's homes
Lorde, Audre 9, 29, 184
Los Angeles 33, 34
Louie 53
Lovell, Anne 64, 65

MacDougall, David 55
McKenzie-Mavinga, Isha 68, 71
madness 157, 157n6
Maja-Pearce, Adewale 41–2, 184
Majaj, Lisa Suhair 186
Mama, Amina 56, 182, 185, 186
Marcus, George 45
marginality 46, 60, 73n5
marijuana psychosis 157, 157n5
Marley, Bob 196n1
Martin, Daniel 59
masculinities, Black 51, 96, 96n13
Mbari art form 148, 148n17
Mead, Margaret 105–6
Mendel, Gregor 11
Mendelian genetics 6, 11–12
Mercer, Kobena 9–10
métis(se) children 17, 19–22; adoption
    63–4, 67; bicultural preservation
    140n4; and Blackness 90, 91; in care
    62–3, 179; commodified 63–4;
    community 81–2n15, 92n6; as
    different 92n7, 93n8; disoriented
    94n9; family life 155–6n4; fostered
    66, 67; girls'/boys' experiences 51,
    123n3; identity construction 77n10,

178, 181; multiracialized 20; not belonging 150n21; parenting needs 129n11; praying to be Black 108, 113; praying to be White 73, 90; public/private realities 182; race of mother/father 50, 51, 55, 140n4; testimonies 60; Whiteness 90, 142–3, 143n7, 190
métissage 18, 19–22, 42, 81–2n15, 105–6
Minh-ha, Trinh T. 9, 17, 19, 44, 53, 60
mirrors 185–6
Mirza, Heidi 177
missions 68–9
mixed ethnic category 179, 180
mixed race 14–15; culture 18–19; diversity 17–18; slavery 5; stereotypes 16; terminology 16–22, 24n13; *see also métis(se)* children
mixed race theorizing xiii, 196n2, n4
Modood, Tariq 10, 177, 179, 193n3
Mohantey, S. P. 189
Montague, Anne 182, 183
Moore, Henrietta 44
Morales, Levins 171
Morton, Samuel 3
mother love, child death 65
mother surrogates 55, 68, 73n3, 175
mothers: cultural influence 78, 172; race 50–1, 55, 82–3n17
mulattoes 3, 15, 21
Murray, Charles 8

name-calling 90, 129
naming traditions 30, 32, 166
Nando afterschool project 16
narratives: belonging 53; identity 58–9; redemption 76n9, 79n12
National Front 8
Nazism 7, 8, 112n9
negriscence 186
Nelson, Lancashire 33
Nigeria: ancestral background 38; Biafran War 33, 35; Igbo culture 30, 32, 35; masculinity 96, 96n13; skin color 166–7n13
not belonging 150n21
Nott, Josiah 4

Okamura, John 178
Okri, Ben 155n3

Oliver 53
Olumide, Jill 66
one drop rule 23n9; kinship 183; mothers/daughters 51, 55, 171, 174; skin color awareness 37; slavery 5; status 13, 15, 181
Onwurah, Ngozi 173
Opitz, May 7
The Oprah Winfrey Show 16
orality 58, 59–60
Ossie 52
Otherness 44; *see also* difference
Owen, Charlie 178
oyingbo complexion 38, 48n7

paternal origins 72n1
patriarchy 15, 63
Paulse, Michele 173, 185
performance, presentation 56
Perkins, Thelma 68, 71
phenotypic traits 11, 13–14, 15, 37, 94–5n10, 184
Phoenix, Ann 178
physical appearance 37, 46, 64, 171, 182; *see also* skin color
Pile, Steve 43
Policy Studies Institute 179, 192n3
politics: adoption 63–4; gender 69n2, 126n6; identity 37, 42, 181; race 80; spatiality 43
popular culture 45
poverty xii–xiii, 65
Powell, Enoch 8
presentation 56, 99–101
Price, Richard 61
Probyn, Elspeth 47
Provine, William 7

race: biology 10–11, 13; constructions xii, 1–3, 82–3n17; culture xii, 13, 85–6; folk concept 6, 11–12; identity xii–xiii, 143, 144; and intelligence 7; physical traits 37; politics 80; self-determined 17; and sex 4, 95–6, 96–7n14; social hierarchies 2–3, 194
racial awareness 74, 75n7, 80, 122
racial epithets 129n11
racial hygiene 8
racial supremacy 7, 9
racism 12; Liverpool 128–9; in school

77–8, 83–4, 92–3, 109, 110, 130;
  violence 192–3n3; *see also* bi-
  racialization
rage 74n6, 162–3
Ranger, Chris 157n5
rap music 45
Rashidi, Runoko 41
Rastafarianism 23n6, 102, 102n1,
  126n6
Red 52
red ibo 120n2
redemption: narrative 76n9, 79n12;
  testimonies of 47, 195
revisionist scholars 41
Rich, Adrienne 171, 183
Rich, Paul 8
Rogers, J. A. 7
Root, Maria 17
Rosaldo, Renato 59
Ruby: bi-racialized violence 64, 65;
  Black pride 80; as British Black 85;
  children 82–4, 86; children's home
  51, 55, 71–7; children's race 13–14;
  father 69, 79–80, 79n13, 176–7;
  father-in-law 86; grandmother 75n8,
  76, 76n9, 78–9, 172–3; husband 79,
  80, 84–5; mother 78; mother-in-law
  86–7; Nigerian family 80; racial
  awareness 74, 75n7, 80; as scapegoat
  75; schooling 77–8, 78n11;
  upbringing 51, 55, 62–3, 66, 67–8
Russell, Kathy 182

Sandra 16
Sarah: Black identity 130–1; brother
  123, 124–5; childhood 52, 55,
  126–7, 126n8; difference 127–8;
  father 122–3; father of son 82n15;
  fictive kin 175; friends 127; houses
  from childhood 118n1; injured foot
  119–20; as librarian 116; mother
  117–18, 125, 126–7; name-calling
  129; as poet 116–17; pregnancy
  125–6; racial awareness 122; school
  128, 129–31; self-reflection 126n7;
  sexual abuse 121; surrogate family
  118–21, 123
Scales-Trent, Judy 177, 191
Scheper-Hughes, Nancy 64, 65
school, racism 77–8, 83–4, 92–3, 130
self-destruction 74n6
self-esteem 91

self-portrait, Bisi 136–7n2
self-reflection 126n7, 185–6
sexual abuse 121
sexuality: commerce 5; and race 4,
  95–6, 96–7n14
Sharon 51, 112n8, 186
Shephard, Sam 170
Similola: adolescence 91; bi-racialization
  64, 65, 181–2; Black identity 97–9;
  childhood 89–90; children's home
  89; college in Bristol 97; double
  identities 97–101, 171; father 69,
  176; first sexual encounter 95–6;
  name-calling 90; parents 88; school
  92–3; upbringing 62–3, 66, 67–8;
  White English culture 172
skin color: Akousa 103, 107; awareness
  37, 166–7n13, 182; Guyanese family
  38; as handicap 62; Nigeria
  166–7n13; *oyingbo* 38, 49n7; shame
  79n12
skinwalking 191
slavery 15, 64
Small, Stephen 179
Smith, Barbara 48n1
social hierarchies 2–3, 45
social services 76–7
Somers, Margaret 42
South Africa, apartheid 8
Soyinka, Wole 56
spatiality 43
species, diversity 3
speech patterns, assimilation 34
Stack, Carol 153n1, 175
sterilization, forced 7–8, 112n9
Stocking, George 6
Stonequist, Everett 14, 15, 19
strawberries 141n6
subjectivity, complex 29, 191
suicide attempts 74n6, 152, 158–60,
  171, 175
surrogates: cultural 68, 111n7, 112,
  175–6; family 104, 105–6, 115,
  118–21, 123; mother 55, 68–9,
  73n3, 175
Swedenburg, Ted 23n8

terminology of mixed race 16–22,
  24n13
testimonies 54–5, 59–60, 195
Thatchapee 1, 22n2, 45, 116
theater, ritual 56

Time 39, 40
Tizard, Barbara 178

US xii, 33, 34, 35–6

Van Maanen, John 44
Van Sertima, Ivan 41
Vansina, Jan 60
violence 64–5, 192–3n3
The Voice 64

Wah, Fred xii
Wales 91–2n6
Walker, Alice 111
Weekes, Debbie 185
Welsing, Francis Cress 9
Werbner, Pnina 10
White-washing, Black children 74n6
Whiteness xiii; in Africa 191; bi-
    racialization 188; birth mothers
    50–1, 55, 171–4; and Englishness
    39, 42–3, 49n10; exclusion 189;
    métis(se) children 90, 142–3, 143n7,
    190; as norm 90n4, 178, 188; prayed
    for 73, 90; privileged 143n8, 144n9,
    148n19, 150
Williams, Patricia J. 188
Williamson, Joel 5, 10
Willis, Paul 39

Willis, Susan 29
Wilson, Anne 92n6, 178
Wolcott, Harry 17, 46
Wolf, Margery 47, 60
Woods, Tiger 16–17

Yemi: attempted suicide 152, 158–60,
    171, 175; Black consciousness
    167–8; breast size 168–9, 169n17;
    childhood 52, 55, 155–6;
    English/Nigerian life 152, 154–5,
    160–1, 176; father 152, 153, 160–1,
    176; as father's son 165–6;
    grandfather 165; grandmother
    163–4; home 153n1; husband
    82n15, 132, 165–6; mother 153–4,
    157, 158–9, 166, 172; Newcastle
    family 163–4; rage 162–3; school
    154, 156–7; sister Bisi 153, 162,
    166; sister Kemi 161, 163, 164–5;
    stigmatized 112n9; as White 143n7
Yoruba culture 160–1, 166, 176
Young, Robert 5, 10
Younge, Gary 179
Yuval-Davis, Nira 12, 13

Zack, Naomi 10, 11, 22n1, 179, 190
Zaynab 51
zebra metaphor 181–2
Zhana 192